Sara Miller Kirby

Kindergarten Papers

Sara Miller Kirby

Kindergarten Papers

ISBN/EAN: 9783337132477

Printed in Europe, USA, Canada, Australia, Japan

Cover: Foto ©ninafisch / pixelio.de

More available books at **www.hansebooks.com**

KINDERGARTEN PAPERS.

COPYRIGHT, 1896,
BY
THE BUTTERICK PUBLISHING COMPANY (LIMITED).

METROPOLITAN CULTURE SERIES.

KINDERGARTEN PAPERS

BY

SARA MILLER KIRBY.

BIRTHPLACE OF FROEBEL.

CONTENTS.

FIRST PAPER.
FROEBEL AND HIS PRINCIPLES.

Biographical—Dawn of the Kindergarten Idea—Based upon Play and Treating it in a Systematic Manner—The Three-fold Education. . . 15

SECOND PAPER.
THE GIFTS EXPLAINED.

Origin of the Name—Ten in Number—What they Are—Uses of the First Gift—Musical Selections to Accompany it. 22

THIRD PAPER.
THE SECOND GIFT.

Ball, Cube and Cylinder—The Law of Unity—Symbolism—Practical Uses—In Connection with Sewing. 33

FOURTH PAPER.
THE THIRD GIFT.

Review of Principles—First of the Building Gifts—Forms of Knowledge—Life Sequences—Forms of Beauty—Mrs. Hubbard's Formulæ. . 42

CONTENTS.

FIFTH PAPER.

THE FOURTH GIFT.

                                                              PAGE

A Two-Inch Wooden Cube Divided—Relationship to the Third—Various Sequences—The "Baker" Song—Sequence in Third and Fourth Gifts Combined.   53

SIXTH PAPER.

THE FIFTH GIFT.

A Three-Inch Wooden Cube Divided—Compared with Previous Gifts—The new Fraction—Uses—Sequences.   67

SEVENTH PAPER.

THE SIXTH GIFT.

A Three-Inch Wooden Cube Divided—Forms of Knowledge—Forms of Comparison, of Beauty and of Life—Sequence. "Grasshopper Green."   -   76

EIGHTH PAPER.

THE SEVENTH GIFT.

Circle—Square—Right-angled Isosceles Triangle—Equilateral Triangle—Right-angled Scalene Triangle—Obtuse-angled Triangle—Uses of this Gift Manifold.   82

NINTH PAPER.

THE EIGHTH, NINTH AND TENTH GIFTS.

Wire Rings, Sticks, Seeds—Summary and Analysis of all the Gifts—"The Four Apple Trees."   91

TENTH PAPER.

THE OCCUPATIONS.

Advantages of Early Manual Training—Sewing—Weaving—Paper Folding—Paper Cutting and Pasting—Peas Work—Clay Modelling—Parquetry—Drawing—Pricking—The Peg Board.   -   .   .   .   101

CONTENTS.

ELEVENTH PAPER.

CHRISTMAS WORK.

Its Moral Significance—Articles that may be made as Gifts by the Children—Needle Case—Calendar—Sachet Holders—Handkerchief Case—Shaving Papers—Match Holders. 109

TWELFTH PAPER.

THE GAMES.

Play Universal—A Glimpse of Froebel—Play the Business of Childhood—Physical and Ethical—Management of the Games—Mrs. Walter Ward's Suggestions—"The Blacksmith." 117

THIRTEENTH PAPER.

DIE MUTTER UND KOSELIEDER.

Adverse Criticism—Miss Brooks' Classification—First Group—Play of the Limbs—The Falling Game—The Weather Vane—"All's Gone "—"Tick-Tack"—Second Group—Thumbs and Fingers—Flower Basket—Coo-Coo—Third Group—Beckon to Chickens—Pigeon House—Fishes—Fourth Group—The Labor Plays—Fifth Group—Direct Moral Training—Sixth Group—The Inner-uniting Life—Conclusion. . . . 123

FOURTEENTH PAPER.

A DAY IN THE KINDERGARTEN.

The School Room—Pictures—Hours—Beginning the Day—"Good-Morning" Songs—The Morning Talk—Subjects—Lessons in Discipline—Games—The Occupation—A Week of Kindergarten Work. . . 145

FIFTEENTH PAPER.

THE HOME KINDERGARTEN.

Frau Schrader's Work—Mothers' Clubs—Household Work—Books for Mothers—Materials. 154

CONTENTS.

SIXTEENTH PAPER.

TRAINING AND TRAINING SCHOOLS.

PAGE

Natural Qualifications for the Work—Love for Children—Music—General Preparation—Private, Public and Mission Schools—The Training Teacher —Salaries—Prominent Training Schools and their Requirements. - 161

SEVENTEENTH PAPER.

TOPICS OUTLINED.

Laying out the Year's Work in the Kindergarten—For Autumn, Winter, Spring, Summer—Plant Lessons—Easter—Grass Mowing—The Carpenter. - 168

ADDENDUM.

THE NEW CENTURY BUSY WORK.

A Connecting Link between the Kindergarten and the Common School.—The Educational Value of Reproductions from Famous Works of Art—"Fairy Tale and Fable." - 174

COME, LET US LIVE WITH OUR CHILDREN.
FROEBEL.

INTRODUCTION.

This book has been written with a very definite purpose. The Editor of THE DELINEATOR, a popular magazine for the home, read very extensively throughout the entire country, received frequent inquiries regarding the Kindergarten, and proposed to meet the needs of his subscribers by publishing a series of articles which should contain a clear and simple statement of the underlying principles of the Kindergarten system, and which should give illustrations of the methods employed in carrying out those principles.

Mrs. Sara Miller Kirby, a graduate of Teachers' College, New York City, was asked to undertake the work. How well she has performed her task is shown by numerous and cordial responses from every part of this country and of the British provinces.

That these papers may be more available for use, and so may the better serve the great constituency of mothers for whom they were prepared, they have been put into book form.

The demand for such a book is one of the notable signs of the times. A great movement is now going forward which, in general terms, is spoken of as *The New Education*. At the foundation of this New Education is the Kindergarten system, whose development will be an upward and onward movement of humanity. It is an inclusive movement; the home, the church, the school and the university feel its energy, and the philanthropist and the reformer recognize the fact that in its demand for a true, all-sided education for all children, from earliest childhood onward, the Kindergarten has struck at the central difficulty of all our present social ills.

It is the home that chiefly makes the child. That mothers are so generally looking for more light regarding the best means of early child-culture is evidence that a new day has dawned, a day of spiritual uplifting and of the development of the higher possibilities of humanity.

This little book goes forth to do its share towards the promotion of this higher life of the people.

ANGELINE BROOKS.

Teachers' College, New York City,
    March 10, 1896.

AUTHOR'S PREFACE.

It has been my purpose in writing these "Papers," which first appeared in THE DELINEATOR, to bring the Kindergarten plainly before the people. For this reason, while I have not ignored the psychological principles underlying the subject, I have divested it of the excess of technicality sometimes associated with its exposition and have endeavored rather to present a readable or "popular" explanation of "the new education."

Many of the Kindergarten books now upon the market, while interesting to those trained in this work, do not attract the uninitiated. Besides, the subject of the Kindergarten, embracing, as it does, the beginnings of everything, is necessarily so broad a field that most books are devoted to only one phase of the work. In writing generally upon the subject, it has not been possible to do more than scatter seeds, as it were, of the Kindergarten tree. But a seed of Kindergarten thought planted in any reasonably fertile soil is bound, by its very nature, to take root and grow. America, with its free, progressive people, Froebel considered the "land of promise" for the Kindergarten cause.

As these "Papers" have successively appeared, assurances have come to me, both from the home and the educational field, that my effort has not been in vain, and so I feel encouraged to send this book out upon the world, hoping that it may be the means of awakening an interest in child-life which will lead to further studies and thus widen the circle of influence until its effect is felt, not only in the home, but by all who have to do with the lives and education of little children.

SARA MILLER KIRBY.

Poughkeepsie, N. Y.,
February, 1896.

For permission to use quotations, selections, songs, music, etc., the publishers are indebted to the courtesy of Miss Angeline Brooks, Miss Emilie Poulsson, the Milton Bradley Co., the Lothrop Publishing Co. and the Oliver Ditson Co.

FREDERICK FROEBEL.

KINDERGARTEN PAPERS.

FIRST PAPER.

FROEBEL AND HIS PRINCIPLES.

To meet the manner and tendencies of this growing age a new system of education has been demanded, a system in which the loving heart shall be deemed of equal importance with the thinking head and the trained hand. "Out of the heart are the issues of life," and "From the abundance of the heart the mouth speaketh." Phillips Brooks, when dying, said that he had wished to see the attainments of the next twenty years, but these attainments will be sadly marred unless the loving heart is more fully cultivated. The intelligent observer of the times sees this lack at the root of many of our troubles. Intellectual giants accomplish much, and so do men of brawn, but these are not so much needed as are sensible, capable men and women who are loyal to country and faithful to the home life and its relations and who recognize a brother in the fellow-man.

Frederick Froebel, the founder of the Kindergarten, whose lonely childhood and thoughtful mind led him to look deeply into these matters, felt that the want of a proper development of the human being was due to a *lack of unity in training* and a *non-conformity to the laws of nature*. The time to begin this right education, which Froebel defines as "emancipation—the setting free of the bound-up forces of the body and soul," is when the child is in its mother's arms. And in this connection Froebel says of the mother, "With the knowledge that a divine spark slumbers in the little being on her lap, there must kindle in her a holy zeal and desire to fan this spark into a flame, and to educate for humanity a worthy citizen." Before giving a further outline of Froebel's principles, it will be necessary to know something of the life and work of the man who devised this wonderful system and successfully built up its practice.

Frederick Froebel was born at Oberweissbach, a village of Schwarzburg, in Thuringian Forest, Germany, on April 21, 1782. His mother died when he was nine months old, and his father, the hard-working pastor of a congregation of some five thousand people, left him entirely to the care of servants and older brothers and sisters. Froebel tells us, "I had no more a father than a mother, for, owing to my father's preoccupation during my infancy, I always remained a stranger to him." When the boy was four years old, his father married again. The new mother at first responded to and encouraged the love of the lonely child, but on the birth of her own son, she repelled and estranged him. She attributed disturbances in the family life to his influence, and so represented matters to the father that he, being too busy to investigate, early accepted his son as a bad boy. The latter became more and more widely separated from his parents in thought and feeling; and, thus thrown upon himself, with his soul filled with grief at his isolation, he began to contemplate his own inner life. Of this he speaks thus in after years: "Fate decided upon me and chose me for its bearer without having consulted me beforehand. It showed me the importance of an education conformable to nature by giving me bitter experiences and deprivations, while the early loss of my mother threw me upon self-education. What one has been obliged to contend with bitterly, he wishes to soften to his fellow-men. Thus the necessity for self-education led me to the education of my fellow-men."

At an early age, he was placed in the girls' class of the village school. Here he was much influenced by the neatness and order of the place, by the Scriptural verses learned by the children from the Sunday services and repeated during the week, and by the songs that were sung. Of the songs, he speaks of two, "Soar above, my heart and soul," and "It costeth much to be a Christ," as impressing him deeply, and says that in after years, when he was a struggling, striving man, they became a source of great encouragement and joy. The boy was often a silent listener while his father taught and conversed with his flock, and he very early became much disturbed by what seemed to him discordancy in life, and especially in matrimonial and family life; he could not understand how it was that man alone should be so created that it was hard for him to do right. Speaking of this to an older brother when showing him his delight in the beautiful harmony of some hazel blossoms, the brother pointed out to him the sexual difference in those flowers, and told him that this arrangement existed throughout all nature, even the flower world not being exempt. Froebel says: "Henceforth, human and natural life, soul and flower existence, were inseparable in my eyes, and my hazel blossoms I see still, like angels that open to me the great temple of Nature. It seemed as if I had the clue of Ariadne, which would lead me through all the wrong and devious ways of life, an emblem of man's life in its highest spiritual relations, and many things were thus solved for me."

He gives the above as one crisis in his inner life, and says two others occurred before his tenth year. The first of these sprang from discussions between his father and brother, to neither side of which could he strictly adhere. He came to this conclusion: "In every foolish idea a true side is to be found. When two contend for truth, it may be learned from both." second arose from his father's religious teachings. It seemed necessar him to put on Christ, but the fulfillment appeared impossible till the thought came that "Human nature, in itself, does not make it impossible for man to live and represent again the life of Jesus in its purity; man *can* attain to the purity of the life of Jesus if he only finds the right way to it."

When Froebel was about eleven years of age, his mother's uncle, Superintendent Hoffman, of Stadt-Ilm, a gentle, benevolent man, came to visit the family. Froebel became greatly attached to him, and he, seeing the unhappy situation of the boy, persuaded the father to give young Frederick into his charge. This was willingly done, and he passed five happy years in his uncle's house, enjoying the companionship of boys of his own age, hitherto denied him. In this life of freedom and confidence he grew in mind and body. His studies there impressed him favorably, except Latin, which he complains of as being miserably taught, and geography, which distressed him as having "no connection with life."

Now the necessity of choosing a calling arose. The step-mother would not allow of a studious life being taken up, as by two of his brothers, for fear the father's property would be diminished by the expense incurred; therefore, in 1797 he was apprenticed for two years to a forester. This man had an excellent reputation, but could not impart his knowledge. Froebel's two years passed without much benefit, and, leaving the forester, he went in 1799 to Jena as a student. Only in botany, of all his studies, could he see "the inner connection of things. It was all arbitrary, and no sequence of instruction." But his teacher of botany, who was also instructor in natural history, satisfied his desire to know the interdependence of nature. He says he especially laid hold of "the thought of the relation of animals, branching out on all sides; and that the bone or framework of fish, birds and man is one and the same; that of man is to be considered perfected as the ground type of all the rest which Nature strives to represent in their subordinate frames."

Two years later he left Jena, having become involved in debt through his generosity to his brother, and returned to his father's house. A position was then obtained for him on an estate at Hildburg. The father died in 1802, and then Froebel served as actuary of the forest court near Bamberg. In 1805, having received a legacy from an uncle, he yielded to his desire to study architecture, and went to Frankfort for that purpose. To insure his support, he took private pupils, and shortly afterward was introduced to Dr. Gruner, principal of the Model School just established in Frankfort. Gruner was so pleased with the young man that he immediately offered him a place in his school, urging him to give up architecture and become a teacher. Froebel finally accepted a position in the Model School; and of his work he writes to his brother: "It seemed to me as if I had found something not known and yet long desired, long missed; as if I had finally found my native element. I was like a fish in water or a bird in air."

Wishing for better methods of teaching, he turned for inspiration to Pestalozzi, whose name was then the educational watchword, and spent two weeks with him in his school at Yverdun, determining at the close of his visit to give greater study to Pestalozzi's methods when the opportunity should offer. This came in 1808, when he obtained the privilege of taking three private pupils with him into Pestalozzi's institute. Here he remained two years, teaching and studying; but still he was not satisfied; something was wanting. So, in 1810 he left Switzerland and entered the University of Göttingen as a student of languages and natural history. The latter study led him to desire a greater knowledge of mineralogy and crystallography, and for these branches he entered the Lectures at the Royal Museum, Berlin, in October, 1812. "It was there," says Lange, "that the persuasion ripened in his mind that all development is founded upon one law, and that this unity must be at the basis of all principles of development, their beginning and end. This conclusion was the fruit of a profound study of nature in its law of development, and the most careful contemplation of the child."

In 1813 came the call to arms for protection against Napoleon. Froebel joined the infantry division of the corps of Lutzow at Leipsic. In this connection he says: "Every one was called to arms to protect the Fatherland. I had indeed a home, a native land, I might say a motherland, but no fatherland. My native country did not call me. I was not Prussian, and so it happened, owing to my retired life, the call to arms inspired me little. It was something different that called me, not with enthusiasm but with a firm resolution, to enter the ranks of the German soldiers. It was the feeling and consciousness of the ideal Germany, that I respected as something high and holy in my spirit, and which I wished to be everywhere unfettered and free to act. Further, the firmness with which I held to my educational career decided me. Although I could not really say that I had a fatherland, yet it must happen that every boy, that every child who should later be educated by me, would have a fatherland, and that that fatherland now demanded protection, when the child himself could not defend it. I could not possibly think how a young man capable of bearing arms could become the teacher of children whose country he had not defended with his life-blood. This was the second thing that influenced me to my decision. Thirdly, the summons to war appeared to me a sign of the common need of man, of the country, of the time in which I lived, and I felt that it would be unworthy and unmanly not to struggle for the common necessity of the people among whom one lives, not to bear my part towards repelling a common danger. Every consideration was secondary to these convictions, even that which grew out of my bodily constitution, too feeble for such a life."

Shortly after leaving Dresden with the troops, Froebel met Langethal, a Thuringian like himself, and he in turn introduced his friend Middendorff, a young theological student from Berlin. A third acquaintance, with a young man by the name of Bauer, was also formed. These three were destined to play an important part in Froebel's life. In July, 1813, those who did not wish to serve longer were allowed to return home. Froebel, receiving the appointment of assistant to Prof. Weiss in the Mineralogical Museum at Berlin, went immediately to that position, and two years after he again met and became more closely united with his friends Middendorff and Langethal, who were then pursuing their theological studies in Berlin. While studying minerals in the Berlin Museum, he became more and more firmly impressed with the necessity of an education conformable to nature, and he resolved to give the remainder of his life to the education of humanity.

On this subject, he had many talks with his friends Middendorff and Langethal. As a starting-point he undertook the care and education of his sister's five children at Greisheim, and then and there began his great undertaking. Middendorff soon joined him. A year later the little school was removed to Kielhau, a village near Rudolstadt, where a small property had been purchased by his sister-in-law; and the next year Langethal joined his friends. A new school building was erected. Froebel about this time married Wilhelmine Hofmeister, daughter of a Prussian Counsellor of Berlin, a woman full of power and enthusiasm for his idea, and willing to make many sacrifices for the furthering of the work. Some years later he founded an institute in the Canton of Lucerne, Switzerland, and also one for girls at Willisau. In all of these enterprises, Middendorff, his nephew Barop, and Langethal worked zealously. In 1836, Frau Froebel's health being broken by her arduous labors and the loss of her mother, her husband and herself returned for a time to Berlin, and here it was that the idea of the Kindergarten dawned upon him.

Lange in his *Reminiscences* says: "It was now clear to him that for the elevation of all education, that of the earliest childhood, as the most important time for human development, was indispensable, and that in its behalf, *play*, as the first activity of the child, must be spiritualized and systematically treated." The first Kindergarten institution was founded at Blankenburg in 1837. In 1839, while presenting his idea of the Kindergarten in Dresden, his faithful wife died; but Froebel worked on and finally succeeded in establishing Kindergartens in Hamburg and Dresden. At the Guttenberg festival in 1840 the Kindergarten was made a national institution, and thus Germany placed herself in advance of all other countries in the matter of education. Nine years afterward the Baroness Von Marenholtz-Bülow, a woman of wealth and distinction, met Froebel and, learning the idea of the work, added her influence to the cause. She introduced Froebel to the Duke of Meiningen, who gave him one of his castles as a training-school for Kindergartners; to Diesterweg, a director of the Royal Seminary for teachers at Berlin; to the Minister of Education of Saxe-Weimar, and to many others in authority. She also brought Froebel and Middendorff to the courts of Meiningen and Weimar, besides interesting the Grand Duchess of Russia and the Countess of Hesse; and she has labored without interruption for the founding of Kindergartens throughout the principal European countries.

In 1851 the Prussian Minister of Education interdicted the Kindergarten because of some socialistic pamphlets published by Froebel's nephew but also supposed to have been written by Froebel himself. This proved a greatest to the educator, who had felt assured of quietness and success for his blow years. In June of the following year he died; but since his death his ideas have been steadily gaining ground in all civilized countries.

The Kindergarten, or child-garden, as the word means, begins with a child's first manifestations, and is designed to develop the little one for the purposes of life, as a plant in a garden is cultivated for its "fruits in due season." In the care of a plant the object to be attained is perfected growth, with flowers and fruit. In the development of a child the true object to be sought is the ripened fruit of character. To attain this object we must give the child a threefold education—physical, spiritual and moral; he must be educated in his relations to Nature, to God and to his fellow-man. First, there is physical education. The purpose of the body is to serve the uses of the soul, as the husk covers the grain of wheat; and as we give to the wheat plant good physical conditions that it may form the best grain, so we should consider the body physically that the soul may not be impeded in its attainments. Sunshine is one of the chief necessities for good growth in a plant, and the sunshine of love in a child's life gives coloring and direction to his whole being. He must possess a healthy body, that he may have free use of all his powers; and his mind, through the activity of his limbs and senses, will gain knowledge and attain fullest growth. Mrs. Peabody says: "The body is the garden in which God plants the human soul, to dress and to keep it. The loving mother is the first gardener of the human flower. Good nursing is the first word of Froebel's gospel of child nature."

A truly spiritual life is only entered into from the individual having grown into it. This growth commences in extreme youth. The child has an instinctive desire for God, an unconscious yearning which must be aroused and made conscious by stimulus from without. The design of life should be recognized from the very beginning, but as we do not know when religious development commences, we should exercise the greatest care that we be neither premature nor too late with the unfolding. "Children can no more become religious by their own unaided power than they can become anything else that is desired for them." Such tendencies should be given as will develop into religious character. Cultivate their right feelings; make them happy in their daily lives; unfold a love of Nature, and back of this a reverence for the Heavenly Father as the Giver of all good and perfect things. In telling what the farmer does, go back to the growth of the grain, and to God who gave the rain and sunshine for its perfecting. The material world is a symbol of the spiritual. Viewed in this light, the "book of nature" becomes sacred as an expression of God, and to teach the child about Nature becomes a duty. Child-life should be active, joyous, full of kindly deeds to others. By loving service to those about us we are led to a loving surrender to God.

The third relationship Froebel would have us consider for the child, is that with his fellow-man, involving social training. All the child's relationships start with the mother. Hers should, therefore, be the first and the closest of ties, and for this reason too many strangers must not be allowed to handle a little child, or his affections will become weak and unstable. On the other hand, however, too much seclusion leads to timidity, fear of strangers and selfishness. It is very important that a child should have intercourse with other children, and the benefits derived from the social relations of the Kindergarten are many. It affords the best connection with the home life. "Every new relationship of the child should be connected with what has gone before." He meets here a little community, an epitome of the race. The games and plays teach love of nature, care of animals, respect for all callings, cheerfulness in every condition of life, and belief that any good calling well followed is honorable. The child is thus early led to see the interdependence of all people.

Another important lesson is that the greatest freedom, both on the material and the spiritual plane, lies in obedience to law. The child discovers this when he is excluded from the games or work because he disturbs the unity. He learns to submit his will to that of others, and to do so not from fear of punishment but from love of right. "Whether a human being become a moral freedman, within the given limits, or a slave to his own or others' caprice, depends to a great extent on the foundation laid in the earliest days of his development." The child enters upon life a mere bundle of possibilities. He has to learn to observe, to compare, to reason and to show choice, likes and dislikes. He begins almost immediately to expand, and the feelings and will grow as much as the intellect. There is an unchangeable standard of right and wrong, and every being is able to form conceptions of both. Therefore, the child must be trained not only to know the truth but to gladly live up to it.

In thus considering the child's physical, spiritual and social training, we cannot fail to recognize the importance of infancy, when the child is, as Froebel calls him, "an all-absorbing eye," taking in everything. We should, therefore, be careful to surround him with nothing but what is pure and clean, for these early impressions affect the whole after life; and the training must be perfected through natural means, through symbols and through play. Froebel attaches great importance to the child's play. The first infantile manifestation is that of motion, and then the child endeavors to become acquainted with his own body. As he grows older, he seems constantly in motion. Having learned to walk, he runs back and forth, wants to touch and handle everything, climbs and jumps. He thus gains a knowledge of things, and acquires strength and skill. In all of this the child is not conscious that he is developing himself; he is merely gratifying a natural impulse. Having a dim presentiment of the future, he builds houses, digs in the dirt and performs in miniature other occupations of man. Later, when mingling with other children, his play gives moral cultivation as well as physical and mental. He is exercised in self-control and self-sacrifice, and learns to bear pain, to obey rules, to be alert and active. The child who plays perseveringly until physically tired, will grow up an earnest, steadfast man, well prepared to fight the battle of life.

"Labor performs the prescribed task, but play prescribes for itself."

"Come, let us live with our children;
   Earnestly, holily live,
   Learning ourselves the sweet lesson
   That to the children we give."

For further reading see :—

Kindergarten and Child-culture Papers, by Henry Barnard, LL. D.
The Kindergarten and School, by Four Active Workers.
Froebel and Education by Self-activity, by H. Courthope Bowen.

SECOND PAPER.

THE GIFTS EXPLAINED.

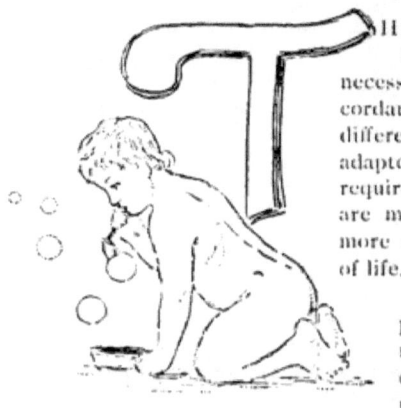

THE Kindergarten system includes all the external details and appliances that are necessary to educate the whole child in accordance with the laws of Nature, while the different divisions of the work are so perfectly adapted to his limited strength that all the requirements of mental and physical training are met, and the foundation is laid for the more difficult after-education of school and of life.

The work of the Kindergarten comprises gift-lessons, occupations, movement-plays, games and talks with the children. The gift-lessons are given by means of a series of playthings called gifts which are put into the hands of the child to promote mental and manual discipline. After each lesson they are returned to their original form and are kept among other materials in the Kindergarten. The occupations, on the other hand—sewing, weaving, clay-modelling, drawing, paper-cutting and folding, pricking, interlacing of slats, etc.—being the epitomized industries of the world, introduce elements which are to be combined into wholes by the child and carried home as his own property.

It is often asked why the gifts were so called. Froebel studied growth in the natural world as symbolic of growth in the physical, mental and spiritual worlds. He said that everything on the earth was a gift of God, to be used as means to reveal man to himself, to reveal God to man, and to prepare for the fuller life to come. A few simple forms he selected as typical of these gifts in Nature, and called them "the gifts." These he used as the starting-point of the child's education.

The gifts are ten in number, beginning with the ball and concluding with any small seed used to represent a point. They take as the fundamental idea the development of the child's innate desire for activity. Every step is a logical sequence of the preceding one, and as the gifts begin with such simplicity of form and develop into complexities so gradually, it may easily be seen how the plan corresponds with the growth of the child. In an essay translated by Miss

THE GIFTS EXPLAINED.

Lucy Wheelock, of Boston, it is said : "A comparison of Froebel's play-gifts with those which from year to year competitive industry offers so richly—not exactly for the benefit of the world of children—first shows them in their true light. Almost all the playthings which we buy in toy-shops filled with all possible expense, are finished and perfect in themselves, often skilfully constructed objects whose beauty cannot be denied. Children stand amazed and delighted at the sight of a Christmas table ornamented with such gifts. But how long

ILLUSTRATION No. 1.

does the joy last? After a short time it changes, first to indifference, then to disgust; and economical parents put away under lock and key for a later time the things that are tolerably well preserved. What can the child do with playthings on which already the fancy of an artist has worked and has left almost nothing for the self-activity of the child? The only thing it can do with these is to take them apart and destroy them. But the punishments inflicted on such occasions show how many parents entirely misunderstand this expression of the instinct of activity so worthy of recognition, and the desire of the child for knowledge and learning. If one gives to an indulged child the choice of his play-material, he will see that a stick of wood will be the dearest doll, mother's foot-stool the coach of state, a little heap of sand material for cooking, baking, writing and drawing, and father's cane a darling pony. According to these experiences Froebel was anxious to make his gifts for play as simple as possible."

The first gift, which is for the most part introductory to the second, and which Froebel intended for use in the nursery, consists of six worsted balls in the six spectrum colors: red, orange, yellow, green, blue and purple.

The second gift consists of a ball, a cube and a cylinder, made of wood. This gift is the basis of the Kindergarten. From it are derived all the other gifts, and even the games and occupations will be found to be related to it. Froebel saw that the materials which God has provided are ever being used

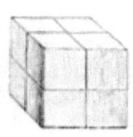 

ILLUSTRATION No. 3.

ILLUSTRATION No. 2.

by man for combinations into new wholes, and that in all inventions and industries these typical elements only reappear in new arrangements. Therefore, he took these three forms as epitomizing the universe. The ball stands for the earth, sun, moon and planets, all the vast wholes of Nature. Its opposite, the cube, is the simplest type of the mineral kingdom. As reconciling these contrasts and partaking of the qualities of both, appears the cylinder, the typical form of vegetable and animal life.

The third gift is a two-inch wooden cube, like the cube of the second gift, but divided once in each direction into eight one-inch cubes. This gift is a step in advance of the second; it satisfies the child's desire for investigation, representing both the whole and its parts. It is the first gift used for building.

The fourth gift is also a two-inch wooden cube, which is divided by one vertical and three horizontal cuttings into eight "bricks," each two inches long, one inch wide and half an inch thick. New dimensions of length and thickness are thus introduced.

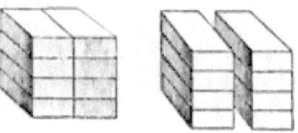

ILLUSTRATION No. 4.

The fifth gift, a three-inch cube, is more complex. It is made up of twenty-seven one-inch cubes, three of which are divided by one diagonal cutting into half-cubes or triangular prisms, and three more by two diagonal cuttings into quarter-cubes or smaller tri-prisms. Great dexterity and delicacy of touch are now required. The tri-prism appears as a new form, and the slanting surface becomes a reality, while designs

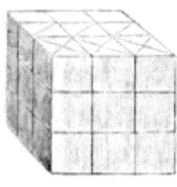 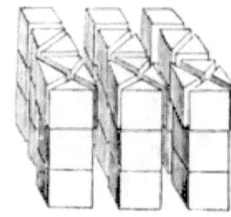

ILLUSTRATION No. 5.

so varied and so real are built that the child quickly learns to love his gift-lesson.

The sixth gift, a cube of the same size as the fifth, is divided into twenty-seven bricks of the same dimensions as those of the fourth gift; three, however, are cut lengthwise into halves and six breadthwise into halves, producing square prisms or columns

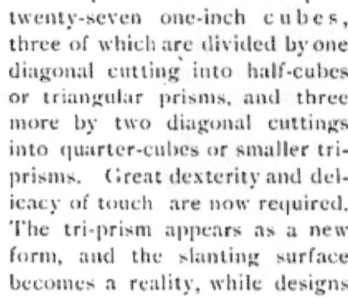

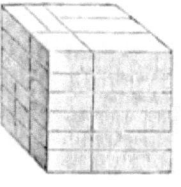 

ILLUSTRATION No. 6.

and half-bricks of two sizes. The columns of this gift enable the child to build high structures that suggest Grecian architecture, and are pleasing and diverting.

The seventh gift is composed of five planes made of thin pieces of polished wood in light and dark shades. These planes furnish lessons in elementary geometry, and cultivate the art of designing and a love of the beautiful by showing symmetrical forms. They are easily derived from the second gift.

ILLUSTRATION No. 7.

THE GIFTS EXPLAINED.

The eighth gift consists of steel rings in three sizes and corresponding half-rings. The rings represent the outlines of the ball, or the round face of the cylinder, and the half-rings corresponding portions of these objects. This gift is also used successfully in laying out interesting symmetrical patterns.

ILLUSTRATION No. 9.
....
ILLUSTRATION No. 10.

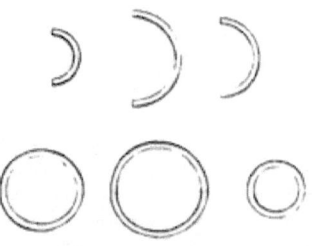
ILLUSTRATION No. 8.

In the ninth gift, sticks of different lengths are used to represent lines, the edges of the cube, or, in fact, those of any of the gifts having straight edges.

In the tenth gift small seeds serve as points, the parts of a line; and with them, as with the ninth gift, surfaces are indicated in outline.

THE FIRST GIFT.—The first gift, the ball, is to be considered as regards the thing itself and as to its adaptation to the child. Froebel in the beginning selected the red ball as the first gift, and afterward added to it the other five, thus showing the three primary colors, red, blue and yellow, and the three secondary, orange, green and purple, although it is not intended to teach the young child this classification of hues. The ball represents the wholes of Nature. It is a complete body that is always round, no matter from what point it is viewed. It is a universal plaything, was used by the Greeks and Romans, and is the basis of our national game.

Looking for the ball in Nature, we find that all the heavenly bodies are balls revolving with a circular motion about the sun as a centre. Ball forms are found in eggs and bird's nests, in the human head and eyes, in plant seeds, in flowers, such as the rose and its petals, and in many vegetables like the cabbage and the beet.

Circles or parts of circles appear in the tendrils of plants, in the curlings of smoke, in the windings of rivers, and in that beautiful arch of promise, the rainbow. Man uses

ILLUSTRATION No. 11.

a curved line in building a bridge, to gain greater strength, and in cutting a path to the summit of a mountain, that the ascent may be easier. The circle is emblematic of unity, immortality, eternity. Mrs. Peabody says that "every word in its origin has represented a particular object in Nature." So, we speak of the daily "round," of the "sphere" of one's influence, of a "ring" of conspirators, of the "cycle" of the years, of a "band" of workers, of the family "circle," all suggesting unity, a bond, a circle.

It was one of Froebel's great principles that the child is an epitome of the race, and as the race has been developed by symbols from the simple to the complex, from the concrete to the abstract, so the child's powers should be trained and enlarged. Nothing is more helpless than a young child. He gets his first knowledge of externality through the sense of touch. He has little perception of sound, and the first ideas gained through sight are those of light and darkness. He is early attracted by color and movement. As he must learn through his senses, the starting-point for his knowledge ought to be a simple object.

The simplicity of the ball, in connection with its universality in Nature and as a plaything, may be deemed an adequate reason for using it as the first gift. The child likes this simplicity, because he is not at first able to discern many qualities in an object, and he is also pleased with the ball's motions, which correspond with his own activity. Abbott suggestively remarks: "Give a baby a ball, and he will begin to study it as Nature dictates. He will look at it, feel it, turn it, squeeze it, suck it, smell it, throw it away, and crawl after it for a second study."

Froebel advises that while a baby is in his crib the ball be suspended by a cord where he can easily see it. After a while he will begin to distinguish it from the other objects around him, and, perhaps, his interest will be awakened by its bright color. If the ball is touched so that it swings, this motion will also appeal to him; he will follow the string and look for the cause of the motion. After he has formed some idea of locomotion, he will attempt to grasp the ball, because he wants to grasp it mentally. He will have a feeling of admiration, then a love of possession, and lastly understanding. We trace the steps as emotion, desire, thought, act. When the child first attempts to grasp the ball, he may not be successful, and will unconsciously ask, "Why did I not get it?" He will then measure the distance again and make a second attempt. This time he will, perhaps, be successful, and he will then have a feeling of gratified desire.

ILLUSTRATION No. 12.

He will next begin to form ideas regarding the form, size, weight, material, hardness, elasticity, color, and roughness or smoothness of the ball, through the senses of touch and sight. Knowledge will come by a perception of differences. After the child has had the red ball for some time, the blue and yellow ones may be offered. These clear primary colors will satisfy him, for color as well as language speaks to a child. The blue and yellow balls being different in color but alike in all other respects, a train of comparisons will

THE GIFTS EXPLAINED.

be started in the child's mind without his being confused by seeing too many differences.

No great distinction can be made between the use of the ball in the nursery and in the Kindergarten, as both the mother and the Kindergartner must be guided by the child's development. But each ball game should be connected with what has gone before, with something in the child's own life, and should be complete in itself. The mother may speak of the ball as "baby's ball," "the soft ball," "the nice, round ball" or "the quiet ball" (tapping it on a surface); and she may say with the child, inducing him to use his fingers:

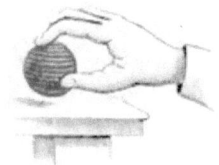

ILLUSTRATION No. 12 A.

ILLUSTRATION No. 13.

"Here's a ball for Baby;
Big, and soft and round;

ILLUSTRATION No. 14.

"Here is Baby's hammer,
Oh, how he can pound!

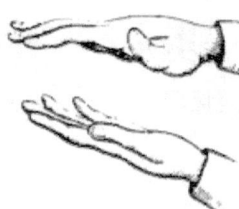

ILLUSTRATION No. 15.

"This is Baby's music,
Clapping, clapping so;

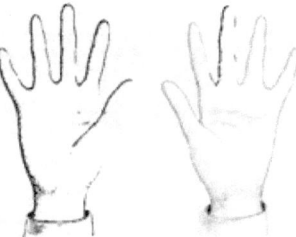

ILLUSTRATION No. 16.

"These are Baby's soldiers,
Standing in a row." *

A story may be told of bird-life, calling attention to the way the bird hops. Show how the child's little playfellow, the ball, can hop. Make a nest of the

---

* For the remainder of this selection, see *Nursery Finger Plays*, by Emilie Poulsson; published by the Lothrop Publishing Company, Boston, Mass.

left hand and put the ball into it with the right hand. With this repeat or sing the following, moving the hand to suggest the swaying of a bird's nest :

* " The little bird is in the nest,
So quiet and so still ;
I'll gently rock it to and fro
And love it well, I will."

Letting the ball hop, sing :

" The little bird hops in its nest,
So cosy and so warm ;
It tries to do its very best,
In sunshine and in storm.

" The little bird hops out its nest,
So cosy and so warm ;
It tries to do its very best,
In sunshine and in storm."

Now the little bird is old enough to fly, and its wings are so strong it wants to try them ; then the good mother and father birds, who have cared for it a long time, say " Chirp, chirp," which means " Try, try," and the little bird tries. After relating this, sing the following verses to the music given beneath (taking the ball-bird through the air in the hand and picking up crumbs) :

" Fly, little birdie, fly around,
And pick up crumbs from off the ground.
Fly, little birdie, fly around,
And pick up crumbs from off the ground.

" Fly, little birdie, fly up high,
Fly little birdie, near the sky.
Fly, little birdie, in your nest,
And have a quiet little rest."

Then the following lullaby may be sung :

" Close beneath thy mother's wing,
Birdie, lay thy little head ;
I will watch thy slumber, love ;
I will guard thy downy bed."

---
* Music for these lines is given in *Merry Songs and Games*, by Clara Beeson Hubbard.

THE GIFTS EXPLAINED.

"Nestle, nestle gently down,
　Close thine eyes to sleep, my dear,
　Safe within our Father's love,
　You and I have naught to fear."

Interest the child early in bird and animal life. Let him hop like a bird, and skip and jump as a lamb does. Tell about the family life of animals. Show a bird's nest; tell how the bird weaves her house round inside like a ball, and fit the ball into the nest. Tell how the good sheep gave us the wool to make the ball. It was part of her thick, soft coat, but this was too warm for her in Summer, so she let the farmer cut it off. He took it to town and sold it to a factory man, who had it washed, combed and twisted into threads called yarn. These threads were knit to make the ball. Boys' coats and girls' dresses to wear in Winter are also made of this wool which the sheep gives. Show some wool, and, if possible, let the child see an entire fleece, which is always rolled into a ball when ready for sale, that he may know how much the sheep gives away at a time. Learn in this connection "The Lambs," from Miss Poulsson's *Nursery Fingers Plays* :—

ILLUSTRATION No. 17.

"This is the meadow where all the long day
　Ten little frolicsome lambs are at play," etc.

The ball may be made of clay. To develop the child's hands, give him as large a piece of clay as he can well hold. Let him roll it between his palms gently (if rolled too fast, the water will be absorbed by the hands and the clay will crack), until it looks like the ball. Do not expect too much as to shape at first, and be careful not to tire the child. Let him also make a bird's nest, with little balls for eggs, and, if he likes, a bird to sit on the nest. These will all be life-like and real to him. Fire-brick clay is suitable for the purpose and can be obtained from any potter, and when bought in this way it is quite inexpensive. It should be kept in a covered stone jar, and the pieces may be used again and again if always put back into the jar and covered with water. After each using

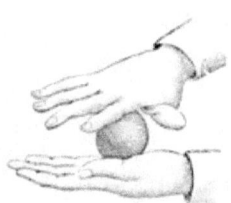

ILLUSTRATION No. 18.

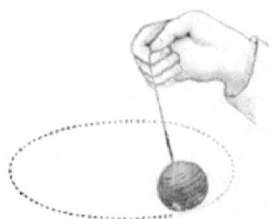

ILLUSTRATION No. 19.

pour off the water and renew it several times, to cleanse the clay from any impurities that may have been absorbed from the hands. Allow it to dry sufficiently so it will not be sticky, and cut it off with a piece of cord.

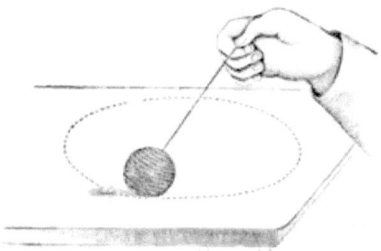

ILLUSTRATION No. 20.

Bring out the idea of round objects and of red objects—red balls, red apples, cranberries, the red sun at sunset, etc. Follow this by mentioning things that go round, as wheels or spinning tops. Show that the ball will go round and round. Hold the string and let the ball describe a circle in the air or on a table.

"Round and round it goes, swinging on a string,
Round and round and round and round, while we gaily sing."

Let the child turn his hand and arm round and round, making a circle in the air.

Move the string of the ball *up* and *down*, and let the ball *sink* and *rise* while some rhythmic song is sung. Ask the child to name something that goes *up* and *down*, as a window sash or elevator. Move the hand *up* and *down*. Sink and *rise* on the toes. Cultivate language by asking appropriate questions and having the child answer, "My ball goes *up* and *down*." "Susie's ball goes *up* and *down*." "The elevator goes *up* and *down*." Use terms to describe all the motions of the ball in the same way, developing correct speech after the object itself is understood. Also call attention to edges that run *up* and *down* in stationary things.

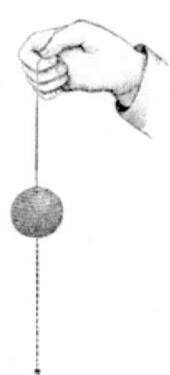

ILLUSTRATION No. 21.

These exercises may be repeated with the blue, yellow, orange, green and purple balls, the primary colors being given first, and then the secondary. Tell stories that emphasize the colors. Make a collection of things in all the different hues, and allow the child to classify them, putting all the red objects together, then all the blue ones, and so on. This will furnish amusement for a long period, and will at the same time cultivate classification.

Sing the "Fruit Selling Game:"

"I am a little grocer,
With fresh ripe fruit to sell,
And if you please to buy from me,
I'll try to serve you well."

THE GIFTS EXPLAINED.

"I've apples green and cherries red,
And yellow lemons too;
And plums and grapes and oranges,
Which I will sell to you."

The child will find the color game very interesting. Place the six colored balls in a circle; let the child close his eyes while you take one ball away and put it out of sight. Then bid the child open his eyes and guess which color has gone. During this game sing:

WHEN WE'RE PLAYING TOGETHER.

1. When we're play-ing to-geth-er, We are hap-py and glad;
In bright or dull weath-er We nev-er are sad.

2. Now tell, little playmate,
Who has gone from our ring;
And if you guess rightly,
We will clap as we sing.*

The child may hold out his right hand, right foot, left hand, left foot, and repeat the following lines, adapting them properly to each motion:

"I put my right hand in,
I put my right hand out;
I gave my right hand a shake, shake, shake,
And I turn my right hand about."

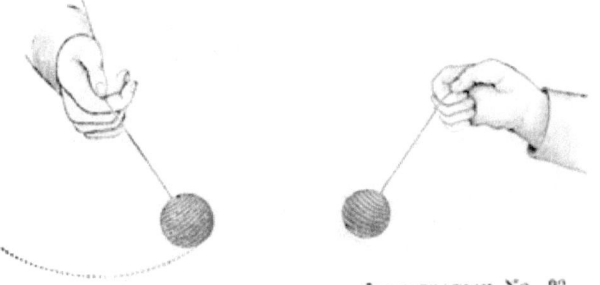

ILLUSTRATION No. 22.   ILLUSTRATION No. 23.

* From *Songs and Games for Little Ones*, published by The Oliver Ditson Co., Boston and New York.

THE PENDULUM.

Come and see, come and see, how mer-ri-ly the clock doth go. The pen-du-lum swings to and fro, and nev-er from its place doth go, Swings forward first, and then swings back, al-ways tick and always tack; Tick, tack, tick, tack, tick, tack, tick, tack, tick, tack, tick, tack, tick, tack, tick!

All of these bodily motions may be performed to music as a series of gymnastics.

Follow this by motions *right* and *left*. The balls swing *right* and *left*. The pendulum swings *right* and *left*, to and fro. This develops the idea of time and order. Tell something of day and night. Give songs about the sun.

Position of *front* and *back* will be gained from the ball.

> "From front to back now swing,
> You pretty little thing.
> Swinging, swinging, swinging still,
> Swinging with a right good will;
> From front to back now swing,
> You pretty little thing.

Show the child pictures of things representing the ball. Let him collect such pictures, cut them out and paste them in a scrap-book. Suit the lessons to the season of the year. In the Spring sing songs of the robin and blue bird, of building nests and of eggs hatching. In the Autumn sing "The brown birds are flying like leaves thro' the sky;" and in Winter, "The chilly little chickadees."

As soon as the child is old enough to enjoy and understand it, mix colors before him. Show him that blue and yellow make green, that red and blue make purple, that red and yellow produce orange. If the blue and yellow papers are held together in the light of a window, the green tint may be plainly seen. These papers show the colors extremely well, and give much pleasure to the child. The relationship of the primary colors to the myriad hues of nature and art cannot be too thoroughly impressed upon the child's mind.

The balls are very easy to make. There may be some difficulty at first to get them quite round, but that is soon overcome. Germantown yarn is the best and cheapest material for the outside covering and half a skein is more than enough for one ball. Do not think that any shade of red, blue, yellow, etc., will do. Be sure to get the clear color in each instance, and not a shade or tint. Use a steel needle of rather small size to make the covering. Form a center by firmly crushing a piece of paper, and about this wind old yarn, or, if a very soft ball is desired, wool batting cut into strips. Make this inside ball about four inches in circumference, and then crochet the covering.

We might continue almost without end to tell of the devices which the mother or Kindergartner can provide for the development of the child with the help of the ball, which is seemingly a simple plaything but when rightly used becomes a means of education. All the child's strength is exercised in this training, while his mind and soul expand in a natural and harmonious way. Some of the results attained are love of Nature and God's works ; ideas of color, motion, form, texture, impressibility, position, order and time ; and training in physical culture, language, attention, memory and classification.

For further reading on the first gift see :

Nursery Finger Plays,	by Emilie Poulsson.
Merry Songs and Games,	by Mrs. C. B. Hubbard.
Songs and Games for Little Ones,	by Misses Walker and Jenks.
The Kindergarten Guide,	by Madame Kraus-Boelte.

THIRD PAPER.

THE SECOND GIFT.

FROEBEL'S second gift to the Kindergarten is composed of a wooden ball, cube and cylinder. The gift includes the entire Kindergarten system, and also exemplifies Froebel's universal law, the *law of unity*. As has already been said, the ball represents the vast wholes of Nature, the planetary system. Examining the earth, man finds the cube as the simplest type of the crystals ; and to reconcile these opposites—the ball and cube—there is the cylinder, which typifies the form of life in man and in the vegetable kingdom and is used by man in his inventions. If this second gift and the law of unity which it embodies are fully understood, a guide will be found for the full and free development of the child, and the mother and Kindergartner cannot go far astray. In all that relates to the Kindergarten it is wise never to lose sight of first principles.

In considering the second gift, we will examine some phases of the law of unity, will show how the other gifts follow from this one, and will take up the practical use of the gift in the nursery and Kindergarten. These thoughts may at first seem dry and uninteresting, but it is only by studying the laws and principles upon which Froebel based the Kindergarten that we can obtain a true insight into his theory. Without this insight the Kin-

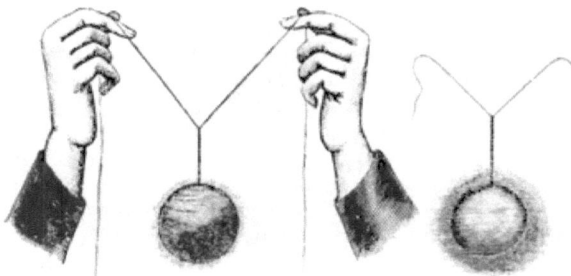

ILLUSTRATION No. 24.

dergarten becomes a mere routine, and is then rightly opened to the ridicule which has sometimes fallen upon it. Froebel denominates the law of unity in various ways, as, the law of contrasts and their connection, the law of harmony or equilibrium, and the law of related opposites; but the expression, "the law of unity," seems to convey most clearly what he had in mind. Students of Nature have for many years seen how this law operates in all her works, but Froebel, while studying crystals in the University of Jena, discovered that it could be applied to education.

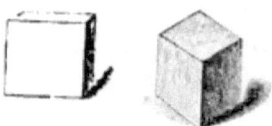

ILLUSTRATION No. 25.

The astronomer, regarding the heavenly bodies, finds that they all revolve in regular order about one common center, the sun, being kept in place by forces that pull equally in opposite directions, namely the centrifugal and centripetal forces. Newton wondered what held the apple fast to its parent stem, and

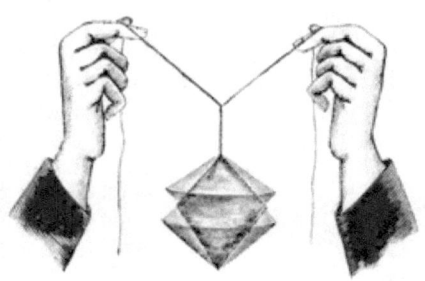

ILLUSTRATION No. 26.

when he saw it fall to the ground, he decided that as the force which pulled it up was weakened by the ripening of the stem, the apple was able to obey the

THE SECOND GIFT.

stronger pull and sought its way toward the centre of the earth. The philosopher said, "We will call this the law of gravitation," but it was only an illustration of the centrifugal and centripetal forces, both of which enter into the law of unity.

In the chemical world the law of unity is exemplified in the connection of opposites, as in the attraction and affinity of molecules, in magnetism, and in the positive and negative poles of electricity. In music we find the law operating to produce harmony and the relation of tones. God connects all things like links in a chain. Those great related opposites, the earth and sun, would be useless if unity had not been established between them by the atmosphere as a means of communication. The sun shines upon the ocean and causes it to give forth some of its moisture to the air. The moisture gathers into clouds, which are carried along by the winds until they strike some mountain-side or meet a colder current of air, when the moisture is precipitated in drops of water to the earth. The water is collected in the loose ground of woody places and forms a brook, the brook throws itself into a river, and the river finds its course at last to the ocean from which the water originally started. By this chain of cause and effect, the ever-recurring process of unity, the earth is aided in her work of growth and reproduction.

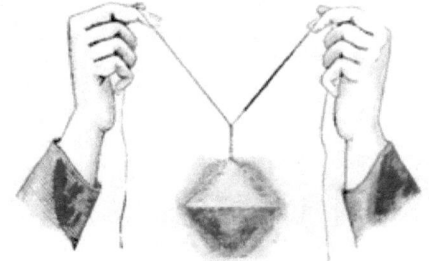

ILLUSTRATION No. 27.

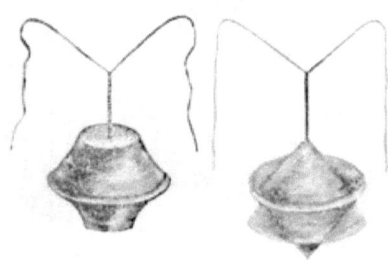

ILLUSTRATION No. 28.

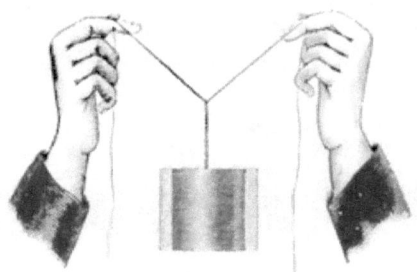

ILLUSTRATION No. 29.

The law of unity is constantly met with in our daily life. The finest railroad train cannot carry us in security to our destination if anything disturbs the unity of all its related parts. Let one piece of steel be removed from its place, and the entire train must be brought to a stop. The well-remembered disaster at Ashtabula was due to the fact that the frost had broken the attraction that held together the particles of iron composing the bridge.

The law of unity may be traced in innumerable ways—in every product of Nature, in man's arts and industries, in his processes of thought, in the records of the past, in the departments of study, in human society, in church and state.

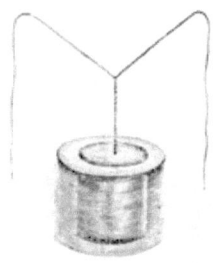

ILLUSTRATION No. 30.

Everything is the related opposite of something else, and each is made for the other.

Froebel says, "The schoolmaster is the person who is in a position to demonstrate the unity of things, and a school becomes a school, not by teaching and imparting a mere variety and multitude of facts, but only by emphasizing the living unity that is in all things." When Froebel's law is recognized by educators, inquiring minds will not be given isolated facts that only make them hunger for more. History will not be "a mere patchwork of battle-scenes," but a chain of causes and effects. Geography, botany, chemistry, philosophy and geology will no longer be treated as separate studies that leave the pupil with a mass of facts which prove of little practical benefit, because they are unrelated. In everything the true Kindergartner does, she observes the law of unity.

The opening exercises are conducted with the little ones seated in a circle, the type of unity. Each individual is thus merged into a larger organism. He is put into social relations and learns consideration for others, which is one of the keynotes of society. He sings "Good Morning to the Merry Sunshine," recognizing the sun as the source of life on the material plane, and is thus led, through the symbol, to God, the symbolized, the Giver of all life.

ILLUSTRATION No. 31.

In the march and gymnastic exercises he learns the unity and rhythm of motion. Looking at his clothing, he is carried back to the cotton-plant, to the flax from which the linen was made, to the wool from the sheep, or to the floss of the silk-worm, according to the texture of the garment, and he connects these opposites with the long line of means that is between.

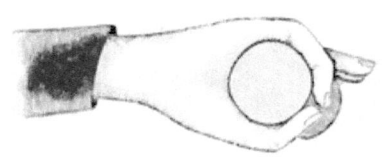

ILLUSTRATION No. 32.

In *The Kindergartner and the School*, Miss Brooks says: "Following Froebel's law, the Kindergartner will handle the children skilfully because she will do it chiefly by indirectness. She will repress the too noisy activity of some wide-awake boy by making him responsible for the happiness of another child younger or weaker than himself; or she will subdue voices that are loud or harsh, not by calling attention to them, but by leading the children to listen to and imitate sweet sounds. She will arrange to alternate activity and rest, merry play and quiet work;

THE SECOND GIFT.

in short, she will seek in everything to apply Nature's great law of equilibrium, the *law of unity*." Longfellow expresses the thought of unity when he says in *Endymion*:

> "No one is so accursed by fate,
> No one so utterly desolate,
> But some heart, though unknown,
> Responds unto his own."

Let us now consider how the other gifts follow from the second. In the first gift, the six worsted balls, the child becomes familiar with the ball form, its activities, and the qualities of softness and roughness. His only comparison lies in the difference of color. When he is presented with the ball of the second gift, he recognizes his old playfellow, but perceives that it looks, feels and sounds different; and he is told that this ball is made of wood, that it is smooth and hard, and that it makes a noise when struck against the table. As the mind develops through the perception of differences, so the child receives the cube after the ball, and connects these opposites with the cylinder.

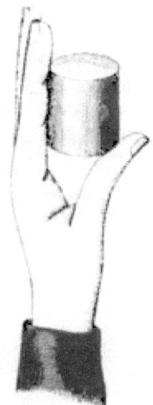

ILLUSTRATION No. 33.

Analyzing the second gift, we first take the ball. The ball has but one face, which is curved in every direction. If the finger is passed about it, it will outline either a great or a small circle. The ball can rest only on one point. (Illustration No. 24.)

The cube has six faces, twelve edges and eight corners. It stands on a face, and is inclined to rest, while the ball is formed for motion. The cube can be made to slide on a face. If a string is fastened to one corner or the middle of an edge and the cube is twirled, the latter will present the appearance, when viewed from the side, of a double cone or top. When looked down upon, its edges and corners will seem to slip away, and we will see a point in the centre surrounded by a circle. When the cube is twirled from the centre of a face, it will look like a cylinder when viewed from the side, and will show a shadowy circle outside a smaller solid one when looked at from above. (Illustrations Nos. 25 to 30.)

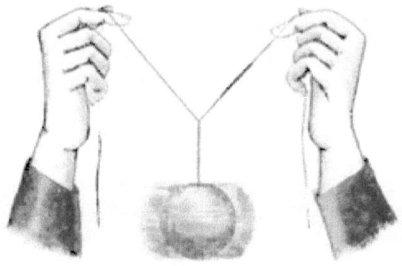

ILLUSTRATION No. 34.

The cylinder represents both the ball and the cube. It has one curved face, two flat faces and two curved edges. It can roll like the ball, and stand and slide like the cube. The outlines of the flat faces form circles. If the finger is passed about the curved face, it will trace a circle, but if drawn up and down on the curved face, it will indicate a straight line. The ball rests on a point, the cube on a face, and the cylinder either on a face or on a line, which is made up of a succession of points. (Illustrations Nos. 31 to 34.)

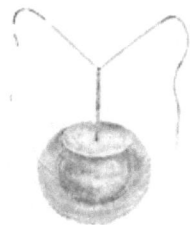

ILLUSTRATION No. 35.

When the cylinder is twirled from the middle of a curved face, it resembles a ball with a shadowy rim about it when observed from the side, and a ball with a shadowy rim flattened at the top when viewed from above. Twirled from the edge of a flat face, it looks like a cone when seen from the side, and like a ball when looked down upon. (Illustrations Nos. 35 to 37.)

Thus the ball is seen in the cylinder, the cylinder in the cube, and the double cone in both the cube and the cylinder; and this suggests Froebel's law—That each new plaything the child receives should be evolved from what he has had before and should contain the latter.

The third, fourth, fifth and sixth gifts are derivations from the cube of the second gift. The seventh gift is easily worked out from the face of the cube. The rings of the ninth gift show the outline of the circular face of the cylinder, the circle described by passing the finger around the ball, or the rim seen when the cube is twirled. The tenth gift, the representation of the point, may be derived from the point on which the ball rests or the termination of any line in the cube. Thus it is seen that the second gift contains all the others.

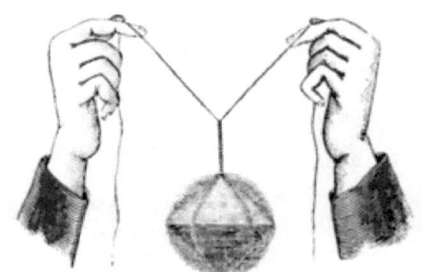

ILLUSTRATION No. 36.

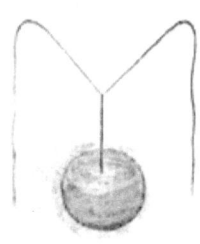

ILLUSTRATION No. 37.

Froebel's idea is misconceived when all curved figures, as ellipsoids, ovoids, etc., are introduced into the second gift, for the latter then degenerates into a lesson in form. The occupations and games are intimately connected with the second gift. The square and circle are used in paper folding and cutting. The law of opposites exemplified by the ball and cube is followed in designing. Circles and squares of paper are pasted to form patterns; balls, cubes and cylinders are strung together in chains; and in many ways the unity of nature is shown by bringing together seemingly disconnected opposites and finding the connections. The child sees more in the gifts as his mind unfolds, and from them he is led to a realization of the fact that nothing is wholly unrelated.

Froebel saw that everything in nature follows the law of evolution; the

THE SECOND GIFT.

child is no exception. As the child contains the germs of the future man, which germs are to be unfolded in a regular order, Froebel put the germs of the Kindergarten in the second gift, and evolved the other gifts from it in an orderly way corresponding with the development of the child. The child is at first in a purely symbolic stage. His imagination allows him to see anything he likes in his ball, cube or cylinder. He plays that the ball is a bird, the cube a house or cart, the cylinder the baker's rolling-pin, as fancy dictates. Froebel classed the first and second gifts together and named them the "Nursery Set." Here things are symbolized. This is analogous to the development of the human race. The Indians used pictures to express thought; the Egyptians cut hieroglyphics on monuments; Christ used material things to symbolize himself and his mission when he said, "I am the bread of life," "I am the light of the world," "I am the true vine, and my Father is the husbandman."

Man is put on this earth to work out for himself a degree of perfection for the life to come. Natural things have reference to the spiritual, and God intends that we shall be led from the created thing to the Creator. Therefore, the child is to be surrounded by Nature. Poets feel the power of symbolism. Bryant expresses it in his lines to "The Fringed Gentian," and another poet teaches a lesson which he sees reflected in the lovely flowers of the arbutus that shed their fragrance while hidden under the withered leaves of the old year:

> "Walk life's dark ways, it seems to say,
> With love's divine foreknowing,
> That underneath the withered leaves,
> The sweetest flowers are growing."

Froebel would have us bring the children into loving relations with ourselves and with Nature, and in this connection he says, "Children must first read the book which God himself has given to humanity to read in its childhood—namely, the world which he has created and in which he has manifested his divine thoughts."

We may now take up the practical use of the second gift. The child is first shown the ball, which he recognizes as having the same form as his first playfellow. He feels of it and is told that this is a smooth ball, and he compares it with the rough ball and other rough and smooth objects. This ball is also hard, is noisy, and is made of wood. Comparisons are made gradually, and other hard, wooden, quiet and noisy things are found and talked about. The child learns the new word, *sphere*. The games for the first gift may be played again, as for instance, the following:

> "Roll over, come back here, so merry and free,
> My playfellow dear, who shares in my glee." *

After the ball, the cube is shown as the greatest contrast; but, as Froebel says, "Children should never be left alone with disconnected opposites," and

---
* Madam Kraus in her *Kindergarten Guide* gives many rhymes and songs for the first and second gifts.

the cylinder must soon be added to these. Talk about the cube's faces, corners and edges. Bring out positions—front, back, top, bottom, right and left, always mentioning the opposites. Let the child find the corner at the right-hand side in front, and its opposite at the left-hand side at the back. Let him take the cube in his hand and feel the smooth, square faces and the sharp corners and edges which were not found when the ball was held. Let him compare it to a house, a cart or a box.

Introduce the cylinder, and note its points of similarity and difference as compared with the ball and cube. It combines the motion of the ball with the rest of the cube, and it has flat faces and a curved surface. The child may compare it with a rolling-pin, a boiler, a tree-trunk, or part of his own body. Give the names ball, cube and cylinder, and when the child knows the forms and can call them by name, test his knowledge by allowing him to feel the forms without seeing them. Ask him to name the forms, and to tell why he

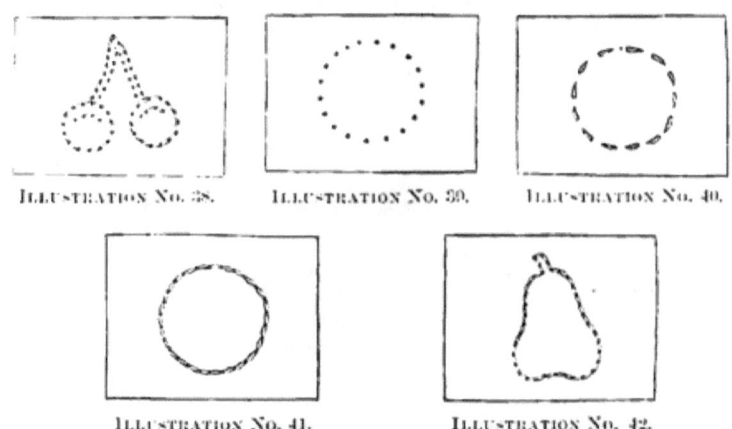

ILLUSTRATION No. 38. ILLUSTRATION No. 39. ILLUSTRATION No. 40.

ILLUSTRATION No. 41. ILLUSTRATION No. 42.

knows what they are without seeing them. This practice will increase both the perceptive powers and the memory.

The ball, cube and cylinder may be modeled in clay, and also forms that lead out from them, such as apples, boxes, rolling-pins, bottles, etc. For the cube, roll the clay between the palms of the hand still it begins to look like a ball, and then pat the sides on a smooth surface. Follow the same general plan for the cylinder, patting the ends, rolling the sides, and taking care that the ends do not become hollowed.

Sewing may now be commenced. For it, use stiff white Bristol paper or the best quality of manila. First, take a piece four inches square, and upon it draw a circle two and a half inches in diameter by using a string and pencil, or by placing some round object on the card and drawing round it. Prick this circle with a small hat-pin, laying the card on a piece of thick cloth, and let

THE SECOND GIFT.

the child sew through the holes, at first leaving out every other stitch, or, as we say, "leaving the gates open." After he has sewed, perhaps, two cards in this way, he may sew round them again and "close the gates." Always insist that

ILLUSTRATION No. 43.

the sewing shall be neat and regular on the wrong side, and in case of careless work, have the stitches taken out and done over, that no untidy habit be formed.

ILLUSTRATION No. 44.

Circles may be sewed in each of the six colors, and then the three primary colors may be used for three small circles on one card, and also the secondary colors. Next, the six colors may be used on one card in circles placed one within another, the colors being arranged in their regular order—red, orange, yellow, green, blue and purple. The various straight lines may also be thus taught, and so may designs that follow from the straight line and circle. The ingenious mother or Kindergartner can devise patterns, and the child may invent by using discarded pasteboards that have held buttons. (Illustrations Nos. 38 to 42.)

ILLUSTRATION No. 45.

Balls, cubes and cylinders are manufactured for stringing on shoe-strings. These seldom lose their interest, and memory may be unconsciously cultivated by their use. All the balls of one color may be strung together, or all the cubes or cylinders; or blue and red balls may be arranged in alternation, or the six colors in their

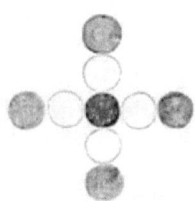

ILLUSTRATION No. 46.

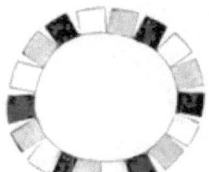

ILLUSTRATION No. 48.

ILLUSTRATION No. 47.

order; or a cube, a cylinder and a ball may be strung in regular order in the six colors. The balls may be made by soaking dry peas, piercing them, and coloring them with aniline dyes. The cylinders can be made of elder stems, and the cubes by procuring a square stick one inch or half an inch each way, and sawing it into suitable lengths. (Illustrations Nos. 43 to 45.)

Small circles and squares may be cut from colored paper and pasted in patterns, which the older children may draw and cut out with blunt-pointed scissors. This work affords excellent training for both eye and hand. (Illustrations Nos. 46 to 48.)

"Mr. Cube stands firm and he never falls,
With his corners and his edges and his six square walls.

"The little ball rolls round him; he is full of fun,
And he's not a bit afraid, for he knows the cube can't run.

"Now here comes the roller, standing straight and tall;
You better keep away, you roguish little ball.

"But the ball keeps on rolling; he doesn't stop to play,
Till the roller tries to catch him, and then he runs away."

FOURTH PAPER.

THE THIRD GIFT.

OUR treatment of this gift will include a brief review of principles, a description of the gift and its proper handling, a comparison of it with the second gift, and a consideration of its adaptation to the child, of its use in "sequences" of knowledge, life and beauty, and of its psychology.

From the foregoing papers we may evolve the following principles:—

The New Education involves the heart as well as the mind and body, or is a setting free of all the powers in an orderly and harmonious way.

Development begins with the child's birth; therefore, his education must begin then.

Each stage of development depends for its own perfection on the perfection of the stages before it. Viewed from this standpoint, the early development is of much importance.

Physical, spiritual and mental development proceed together, not separately. But the child's first manifestation (motion) is physical, and for that reason early development deals with the physical, and influences the child spiritually and mentally through the exercise of his senses.

The child's instinctive utterances furnish the key to the right mode of procedure. As color and movement appeal to the child very early, the ball, by its bright hue, extreme simplicity and various activities, seems most suitable for the first plaything.

The second gift is the basis of the Kindergarten system, while the *law of unity* it exemplifies furnishes a guide for both theory and practice, because it leads along the lines of Nature.

The first and second gifts are classed as the "Nursery Set," for, as selected

THE THIRD GIFT.

symbols, they answer to the early symbolic stage of the child. The race has developed by experiences and experiments from ignorance to culture, and the individual follows the same method. In this process he uses symbolic or material things as an aid to the understanding of the intellectual.

The third, fourth, fifth and sixth gifts Froebel denominated the "Building Gifts," and in taking up the third gift we deal with the first of this second series. These four gifts meet the child's instinctive desire for investigation and construction.

The third gift (illustration No. 49) comes packed for use in a dark-colored cubical wooden box measuring about two inches and a half each way and furnished with a sliding cover. The tables at which the children sit for their gift and occupation work have their surfaces ruled in one-inch squares that are very helpful in measurement and position. For the use of the gift in the home, a sheet of blotting-paper or a piece of dark muslin to fit the little one's table may be ruled in squares and, when needed, tied upon the table from underneath with strings. The gift can be made at home or by a carpenter.

ILLUSTRATION No. 49.

As soon as the box containing the gift is presented, the child recognizes it as another cube, and it is well to talk about it and compare it with other boxes. Place the box at the edge of the table with the top down, draw out the cover, lift the box, put the lid diagonally inside, and place the box where it will not interfere with the lesson. Move the gift four inches back from the edge of the table.

At first the Kindergartner has but one cube, in order to concentrate the attention of the children. Counting up to twelve has already been given in teaching the edges of the second-gift cube, and when the third gift is presented to the children, this same order should be preserved. After the lesson is finished and the large cube rebuilt (never put the small cubes singly into the box), place the gift on the lid, put the box over it, and invert carefully. Slide in the lid, and put the box away before any other work is commenced. In this way children may be taught to gather up their playthings and will simply consider such care part of the play.

ILLUSTRATION No. 50.

ILLUSTRATION No. 51.

A two-inch cube of wood is before us, being similar in material and size to the cube of the second gift, but differing in that it is divided into parts. (Illustrations Nos. 50 and 51). One horizontal and two vertical cuttings separate it into eight one-inch cubes, and it is, therefore, one step in advance of the first cube. As a whole it differs from the first cube only in divisibility; its parts are cubes which differ from the first cube only in size, each being like the whole cube, but smaller.

While the third gift is associated with the second on account of its similarity in size and material, and the child is interested because of this likeness, his attention is fixed and kept by the contrast between the two gifts. Thus, he is taken in a natural way from what he already knows into a wider field of knowledge. The similarity is sufficient to keep in mind the connection between the two playthings, and the contrast is great enough to sustain the little one's interest. The child compares the second and third gifts in regard to faces, corners, edges, direction and element of rest, and in this way his memory is tested and he is also led to commence a classification of objects by deciding that all bodies of similar proportions and qualities must be cubical in form. This influence is likewise exerted when he is examining the parts, since each is the exact counterpart of the whole cube save in size.

The gift is perfectly adapted to the child's limited physical strength. He can learn to handle it lightly and easily, thus gaining both delicacy and precision of touch. Ideas regarding correctness of form, position and order are gained, and exactness of language and accuracy and minuteness of description are insensibly acquired. It is said that the study of botany is especially valuable, because it sharpens the powers of observation and trains the mind for accurate description and systematic classification; Froebel has put much of this quality into his gift-work and begins to exert it upon the young mind.

The third gift is given to the child when his desire for investigation is first manifested. Without a division of a substance into its parts, the best knowledge cannot be attained; so the child is encouraged to follow his instinctive wish to see the construction of things. He is delighted to take his cube apart, examine the pieces, and build them up again, or, by rearranging, discover new qualities and uses. He may do all this without adding to his destructive tendency, and he does not meet with the disappointment he finds in his other playthings, when, having taken them apart, he finds he cannot put them together again. The desire to look at the interior of things is the germ of the fullest development, the beginning of the formation of the scientific mind. Froebel traced this manifestation to see what it indicated in man, and upon the facts discovered he based the Kindergarten gifts and occupations.

Children reproduce in play what they see and know. In this way, the third gift gives much pleasure, because it can be used for building purposes. The child may embody his desire for possession or property by making a garden and building a wall around it, and a house to live in. That this building play might have a purpose and lead to orderly thinking, Froebel devised what is called the "sequence." The word itself is derived from the Latin verb *sequor*, to follow after, and means a following from what went before, each point being a step in advance of the previous one; and if from any given point the steps are retraced, the first will be again reached.

There are three classes of sequences: First, those that represent *forms of knowledge;* second, those that represent *forms of life;* and third, those that represent *forms of beauty.*

Forms of knowledge are forms illustrating mathematical facts, as number,

THE THIRD GIFT.

proportion, order, etc. *Forms of life* are models representing living objects or articles seen in daily life. *Forms of beauty* are symmetrical patterns that are not necessarily forms of knowledge or of life, but may, however, be both. By the use of the gift in sequences, the child is led into the living world around him.

FORMS OF KNOWLEDGE.—The first idea of the third gift is a whole that can be divided into its parts, and it thus gives a conception of the whole, of its parts, of comparative size, and of the properties and relations of numbers. The terms *front, back, right, left, top* and *bottom*, and the naming of opposites are reviewed, and also the directions of the different lines. The cube is divided into

ILLUSTRATION No. 52.

ILLUSTRATION No. 53.

ILLUSTRATION No. 54.

halves in every way, so that it has top and bottom halves, right and left halves and front and back halves. (Illustrations Nos. 52, 53 and 54.) These are all

ILLUSTRATION No. 55.

ILLUSTRATION No. 56.

ILLUSTRATION No. 57.

measured in their three dimensions. The halves may be divided into halves, producing quarters of the whole cube. (Illustrations Nos. 55 and 56.) Also show that two-fourths equals one-half and that three-fourths is greater than one-half or two-fourths. (Illustrations Nos. 57 and 58.)

ILLUSTRATION No. 58.

ILLUSTRATION No. 59.

ILLUSTRATION No. 60.

Divide the quarters into halves, forming eighths (illustration No. 59), and show that two-eighths equals one-quarter, and that one-half of one-quarter is one-eighth (illustration No. 60); also that eight-eighths equals one whole, and four-eighths one-half. Lessons in addition and subtraction may be taught, as, that one plus one equals two, two plus one equals three, and one from two leaves one. Multiplication and division of twos may be taught up to twelve by grouping the twos. Much of this work must necessarily depend upon the growth of the child, the instructor being careful not to force him, and making sure that what has preceded is understood before new steps are taken. Teach the children to use correct language in their answers, and encourage them to investigate and tell the results.

To acquaint the children with the parts, give a simple sequence thus: Draw the front half two inches away from the others and consider the result as the walls on the two sides of a country road. Measure their height and length, and tell a short story about the road. Push the halves together, and separate them again, right and left, to make another road crossing the first. Put them together, and remove the top half two inches to the right, thus forming two tables for a tea-party. Find how wide, how long and how high they are.

To bring out the number and positions of the faces, call the cube a house, and tell what can be seen from the top, from the front, from the back and from the right and left sides. Show the edges and their directions by building floors, walls and columns of different heights and lengths, front and back, right and left, up and down; as, a floor four inches long, two inches wide and one inch high, or a column whose upper and lower faces are squares, and whose sides are oblongs eight inches high, four inches high, or two inches high, making four of the last. Locate the corners, as, two in front on top, two at the back on top, two in front at the bottom, and two at the back at the bottom. (Illustrations Nos. 61, 62 and 63.) Now find the opposite corners.

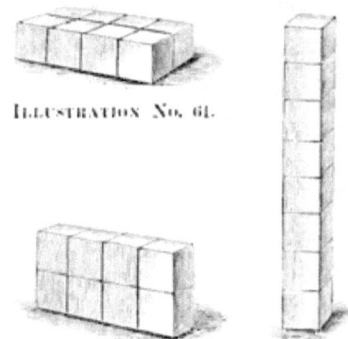

ILLUSTRATION No. 61.

ILLUSTRATION No. 62.   ILLUSTRATION No. 63.

LIFE SEQUENCES—Precision, order and regularity should be insisted upon. As far as possible have the steps taken from dictation rather than by imitation, to cultivate attention and concentration. First show the ways cubes touch each other, as face to face, right and left, front and back (illustration

ILLUSTRATION No. 64.   ILLUSTRATION No. 65.   ILLUSTRATION No. 66.   ILLUS'N No. 67.

No. 64), edge to edge, corners front, faces front right and left, front and back (illustrations Nos. 65 and 66), edge to center of face at right, left, front and back (illustration No. 67).

THE THIRD GIFT

To add to the interest, connect a simple story with the forms built, or let one child tell of something he has seen, and illustrate the account by building the object. Let the children invent and tell a story about the form. All the cubes are to be used in building, as otherwise the relation between the parts would be destroyed. Build walls and platforms and measure them. Do not describe the figure to the child before building, but let him build and notice

ILLUSTRATION NO. 68.

ILLUSTRATION NO. 69.

what he has done. Follow the same two rules for yourself. Begin with doing, and notice what you have done; and try to impart some ideas of relative position, as, near together or far apart, or of contrasts like high and low, crooked and straight, parts and the whole.

The following is a life sequence:

First, *A cube*.—(Illustration No. 68.)

Second, *Two square platforms*.—Top half of cube two inches to the right of the bottom. (Illustration No. 69.)

ILLUSTRATION NO. 70.   ILLUSTRATION NO. 71.   ILLUSTRATION NO. 72.

Third, *A long platform*.—Join halves. (Illustration No. 70.)

Fourth, *A broad chair*.—Two right-hand cubes on top of two left-hand cubes. (Illustration No. 71.)

Fifth, *Two chairs*.—Divide in halves right and left. (Illustration No. 72.)

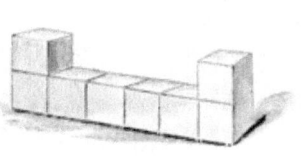

ILLUSTRATION NO. 73.   ILLUSTRATION NO. 74.

Sixth, *A couch*.—Turn and join seats. (Illustration No. 73.)

Seventh, *An engine*.—Top right-hand cube on top of cube at the left hand. (Illustration No. 74.)

Eighth, *A church.*—Right-hand cube on top at left; next two right-hand cubes on top of two cubes touching them. (Illustration No. 75.)

Ninth, *Opening in wall for cannon.*—Cube on top at left hand to be put on top at right hand. (Illustration No. 76.)

ILLUSTRATION No. 75. ILLUSTRATION No. 76. ILLUSTRATION No. 77.

Tenth, *A clock.*—Take up cube in the center and place in opening, edge down. (Illustration No. 77.)

Eleventh, *A window.*—Take up three top cubes as they stand, place upper one in corner formed by the other two, and arrange the latter on their edges on remaining cubes. (Illustration No. 78.)

Twelfth, *A tunnel.*—Take off three on top and one out of center, build up the two columns three inches high, and place the two remaining cubes across the top. (Illustration No. 79.)

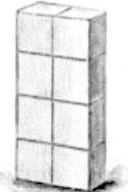

ILLUSTRATION No. 78. ILLUSTRATION No. 79. ILLUSTRATION No. 80. ILLUSTRATION No. 81.

Thirteenth, *A monument.*—Take two from top, add one to each column, and move the columns together. (Illustration No. 80.)

Fourteenth, *A cube.*—Take off top half, and place it in front of the lower half. (Illustration No. 81.)

When a story is told the sequence may illustrate the story, or the story may be used simply to lend interest to the sequence; it is also an open question among Kindergartners as to whether sequences by dictation should predominate, or the children should be urged to invent their own sequences. The following very simple story will show mothers how a narrative may be connected with the above sequence;

A VISIT TO GRANDMAMMA.—Willie is a little boy who lives in a large city. He is a very good friend of mine and often tells me about his new playthings

THE THIRD GIFT.

and where he has been and what he has seen. One place that he never grows tired of is his grandmamma's house in the country. Grandmamma is quite an old lady, with white hair, and wears a cap; but she has a bright smile and a warm heart, and enjoys making happy all the children who visit her. Willie paid her a long visit last Summer, and now that he has returned to the city, he likes to build with the cubes, different things in grandmamma's house and barn and in the quaint old town near which she lives. He says the *cube* looks like the square, old-fashioned house (*dictation*). The *two square platforms* belong to the scales for weighing potatoes, grain, apples—and little boys, too, when the new milk and fresh country air make them grow a great deal (*dictation*). The *long platform* is in the barn. Here the loads of hay are weighed, and the fat oxen (*dictation*). Grandmamma has a *broad chair* (*dictation*), *two little chairs* (*dictation*), and a *large mahogany couch* in the sitting-room (*dictation*). This couch is so long and broad that it makes a very comfortable place to sleep on. Willie often takes a nap there when he is tired from playing in the hay. The *engine* (*dictation*) for the train running through the town looks something like this form of cubes, and the *church* looks like this (*dictation*), with its

"Bell in the steeple,
Calling all the good people."

The most curious thing, though, is the *wall with cannon-openings*, high above the town (*dictation*). This was built years ago in time of war to prevent the enemy's ships from sailing up the river near by. One large building in the center of the town has a *town-clock* (*dictation*), and the new library has a handsome colored *window* in front (*dictation*). When Willie came to the city through the *tunnel* (*dictation*), with high walls like the walls of the *cube* (*dictation*), it seemed a long time before he could go again to grandmamma's house.

SEQUENCES.—The law of unity, here operating as the law of opposites, is distinctly brought out in forms of beauty, for all the changes of form are to be made by opposites; that is, if a cube is moved in front, a corresponding move must be made at the back. In this way symmetrical patterns are laid and a love of the beautiful is cultivated. These forms, being only one block in height, represent outlines of surfaces and are each formed, according to the rules of drawing, around some point as a base or center. Notice the spaces enclosed.

The sequences given in this paper are very simple, but by working with the gift, the child will continually find new combinations. These combinations are exhaustively treated in Madam Kraus's *Guide* and in Wiebe's *Paradise of Childhood*. Here is a sequence of beauty:

Form hollow square, face front, by placing the two cubes on top at the right, at the side, touching; the two on top at the left, in front, one right and one left, with their faces touching; and draw out center cube. (Illustration No. 82.)

ILLUSTRATION
No. 82.

Turn the cubes in the corners by opposites diagonally. (Illustration No. 83.)

Pull out the inside cubes by opposites, at the front, back, right and left, till they are even with the others. (Illustration No. 84.)

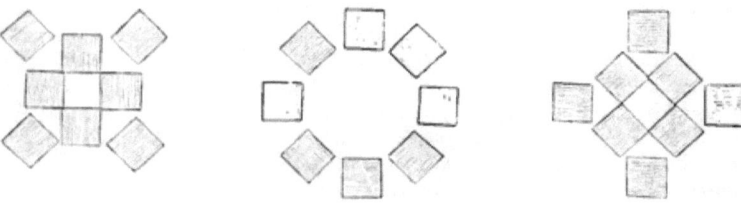

ILLUSTRATION No. 83.   ILLUSTRATION No. 84.   ILLUSTRATION No. 85.

Push in the cubes at the corners till their edges meet, leaving a square with corner front, in the center. (Illustration No. 85.)

Turn the cubes at the front, back, right and left into the vacant spaces before them, with corners front. This forms a hollow square with corner front. (Illustration No. 86.)

ILLUSTRATION No. 86.   ILLUSTRATION No. 87.

Pull out the cube in the middle of each side till it touches at the corners. (Illustration No. 87.)

Turn by opposites the cubes of the new sides formed, till they stand faces out instead of corners. (Illustration No. 88.)

ILLUSTRATION No. 88.   ILLUSTRATION No. 89.   ILLUSTRATION No. 90.

Push the cubes just turned into the center, till their corners touch. (Illustration No. 89.)

Turn corner cubes into corners. (Illustration No. 90.) This brings us back to the first step. Then rebuild according to these directions reversed. In giving the above, dictate position of one cube and then that of its opposite.

The formulæ of the second and third gifts are those given by Mrs. Hubbard:

The outside of anything is called its surface.

Surfaces are of two general classes, plane and curved surfaces.

The various divisions of a surface are called the faces of that surface.

The sphere has one curved face.

The cylinder has one curved face and two plane faces.

The cube has six plane faces.

The sphere is always the same.

The cube turned on its face looks like a cylinder.

The cube turned on its corner looks like a top.

The cube turned on its edge looks like a cylinder with a circle around it.

The cylinder turned on its plane face remains a cylinder.

The cylinder turned on its curved face looks like a sphere.

The cylinder turned on its edge looks like a top.

The cylinder has two changes and the cube three changes; the sphere never changes.

The cube has six faces, eight corners and twelve edges (number).

The cube has one face above, one below, one in front, one at the back, one at the right and one at the left.

The cube has eight corners, four above and four below.

The cube has twelve edges, four running up and down, four running from front to back, and four running from right to left.

The cube has two corners above in front.

The cube has two corners below at the back.

The cube has two corners above at the back.

The cube has two corners below in front (position).

The cube has two edges running up and down in front.

The cube has two edges running up and down at the back.

The cube has two edges running from front to back on top.

The cube has two edges running from front to back at the bottom.

The cube has two edges running from right to left on top.

The cube has two edges running from right to left at the bottom.

The faces of the cube are plane.

The faces of the cube are equal.

The faces of the cube are square.

Definition.—A cube is a solid having six equal square faces.

The square has four sides and four angles. (Quadrilateral.)

The opposite sides of the square are parallel. (Parallelogram.)

The angles of a square are right angles. (Rectangle.)

Definition.—A square has four equal sides and four right angles.

The oblong has four sides and four angles. (Quadrilateral.)

The opposite sides of the oblong are parallel. (Parallelogram.)

The angles of the oblong are right angles. (Rectangle.)

The opposite sides of the oblong are equal, but its adjacent sides are unequal.

Definition.—The oblong has four sides and four right angles, and its opposite sides are equal, but its adjacent sides are unequal.

Parallel lines are straight lines which have the same direction.

An angle is formed by two lines meeting or crossing each other.

An angle like the angle of a square is called a right angle. When a vertical and horizontal line meet they form a right angle.

An angle smaller than a right angle is called an acute angle.

An angle larger than a right angle is called an obtuse angle.

Summing up the faculties that are exercised by the third gift, we find them to be analysis, synthesis, attention, imagination, perception, conception, formative and expressive powers, language, social relations, and mathematical appreciation of size, form and position. First, the child's attention is gained by likeness to and contrast with the second gift, and is kept by a story connecting the forms through the force of interest and novelty. He is led out into the living world, there to take notice of objects by comparison and to learn of their properties by induction. It is necessary to observe relations in order to have clear perceptions, which are the foundation of conception. He proceeds from a conception of a cube as a unit to an understanding of the parts of which it is composed, and thus gains analysis; and the analyzed parts he rebuilds into the original or new wholes, ending his anaylsis in synthesis.

His comparisons with the second gift test his memory in calling up the points of similarity, and also develop the power of classification and generalization by leading him to decide that bodies of similar proportions and qualities must be cubical in form. The child takes the cube as a whole from the box and returns it in like manner, thus giving lessons in order and precision. All the parts of the gift are used to show how things are mutually related, how each is needed to complete the whole; each has its appointed place.

> Nothing useless is or low,
> Each thing in its place is best;
> And what seems but idle show
> Strengthens and supports the rest.
> LONGFELLOW'S *Builders.*

The child is happy in playing with his gift, and seeks to embody his own ideas in tangible form. Both his formative and expressive powers are exercised. He invents and represents objects, clothing them with life, and thus developing originality and imagination. Forms of knowledge help to develop judgment and reasoning through the exactness of statements involved; and through the forms of beauty is gained a love of the beautiful. The child seeks the origin of beauty and is led to God, the first great Cause, and his spiritual nature is thus appealed to.

The will is cultivated through pleasure, because he sees that an orderly way is the best and quickest way to gain the desired end, that greatest liberty comes through obedience to law. Socially, he learns self-control, patience, persever-

THE FOURTH GIFT.

ance and sympathy by contact with his playfellows ; and in all this he believes he has free choice. "The Kindergarten institution is eminently fit to educate *free* citizens of a *free* country."

For further reading on the third gift see: *Paradise of Childhood*, by Edward Wiebe; *The Kindergarten Guide*, by Mme. Kraus-Boelt.

FIFTH PAPER.

THE FOURTH GIFT.

ILLUSTRATION No. 91.

THE fourth Kindergarten gift (see illustration No. 91) is another two-inch wooden cube of the same size as those of the second and third gifts. This cube is divided by four cuttings into eight parallelopipeds. These cuttings will be designated as one vertical and three horizontal, three vertical and one horizontal, or four vertical, according to the position of the gift. (Illustrations Nos. 92 and 93.) The position usually adopted in starting is the one arranging one vertical and three horizontal cuts. For convenience, the parallelopipeds will be called bricks, because their dimensions are in the same proportions to one another as are those of a building brick, the latter being two inches thick, four inches wide and eight inches long, while each brick in the gift measures one-half inch, by one inch, by two inches. Thus, the width is twice the thickness and the length twice the width, or four times the thickness. (Illustration No. 94.)

The fourth gift follows the third in a logical way. (Illustrations Nos. 95 and 96.) Both are made of the same material, wood, and they are alike in shape, weight and bulk. Both are wholes divided into eight equal parts, to be used for new combinations and constructions. The third gift has parts that are each like the whole in form and proportion, but the parts of the fourth gift are unlike the whole, and their dimensions are unequal. The

ILLUSTRATION No. 92.

ILLUSTRATION No. 93.

ILLUSTRATION No. 94.

ILLUSTRATION No. 95.

ILLUSTRATION No. 96.

unequal dimensions, the new use of one-half, and the laws of balance and communicated motion are the main characteristics of this plaything, and these characteristics are best learned by experiences through play. By a carefully directed handling of the gift, the thought embodied in it may be brought to the child's consciousness. He really *knows* the form as regards faces, dimensions, proportions and the relation of parts to the whole; he can use the material intelligently and creatively; but he is not to be called upon to formulate or abstract this knowledge.

The faces of both the third and fourth gifts, as wholes, are square. Their lines are all right lines, and, therefore, their angles are all right angles. With the third gift the square faces are so constantly before the child that he soon gains a true conception of a square, while the use of the gift gives him experience of a form not square; and this leads up to the fourth gift. The latter is suggested in the third by the union of two cubes face to face, which form a parallelopiped of the same length, width and height as two bricks of the fourth. Two cubes are equal in volume to two bricks; therefore, one cube is equal to one brick. This will come to the child from his handling of the two forms. He will see that if a brick be cut in half breadthwise and one part placed above the other, the cube will be formed. This may be illustrated in clay or soap. The wholes of both gifts are equal, and so are the halves, quarters and eighths; therefore, solids may be equal, though differing in form. (Illustrations Nos. 97 and 98.)

ILLUSTRATION No. 97.

ILLUSTRATION No. 98.

The faces of the third and fourth gifts differ, as indicated by the following statement:

In the third gift—

    Top and bottom faces are respectively four squares.

    Front and back faces are respectively four squares.

    Right and left faces are respectively four squares.

Therefore, all the faces are squares.

In the fourth gift—

    Top and bottom faces are respectively two oblongs.

    Front and back faces are respectively eight oblongs.

    Right and left faces are respectively four oblongs.

Therefore, all the faces are oblongs. All the faces of each brick are oblongs of various sizes, and the child must be brought to see this clearly to fix the concept of an oblong in his mind.

It has been shown that the divisions of both gifts are alike in volume. In appearance—

    The halves of the fourth gift are like the halves of the third gift.

    The quarters of the fourth gift are like the quarters of the third gift, but

    The eighths of the fourth gift are unlike the eighths of the third gift.

A cube of the third gift is a rectangular prism having six square faces. A brick of the fourth gift is a rectangular prism having six oblong faces. The brick, like the cube, has six faces, eight corners and twelve edges. The faces of the brick are in three pairs: two broad faces, two long, narrow faces and two short, narrow faces.

THE FOURTH GIFT.

The broad faces are two inches long and one inch wide.
The long, narrow faces are two inches long and half an inch wide.
The short, narrow faces are one inch long and half an inch wide.

The fourth gift exceeds the third in possibilities of position. The cube can only stand, and it presents either a square face or a corner. While the cube is always the same height, the brick can be tall, short or medium. Like the child, it can stand, sit or lie down. Each brick can be placed in nine different positions. These positions are: standing, lying and sitting (illustrations Nos. 99, 100 and 101), three of each. The brick may *stand* with its broad face,

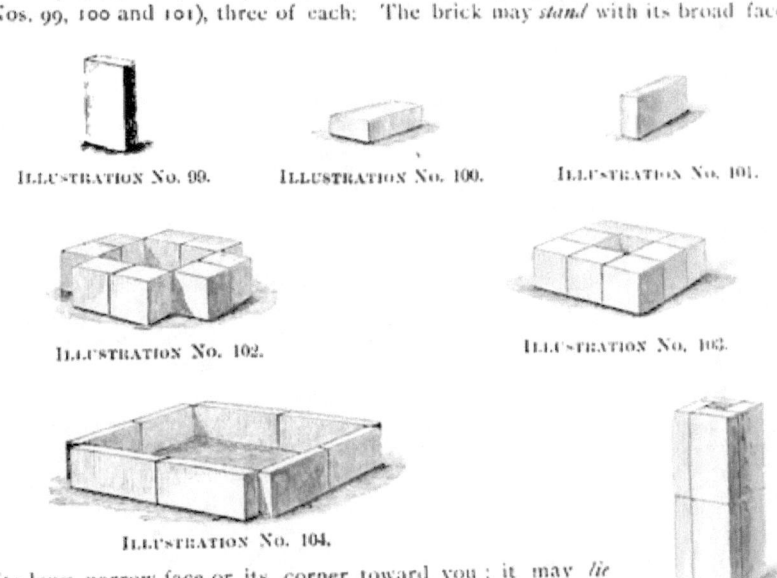

ILLUSTRATION No. 99. ILLUSTRATION No. 100. ILLUSTRATION No. 101.

ILLUSTRATION No. 102. ILLUSTRATION No. 103.

ILLUSTRATION No. 104.

ILLUSTRATION No. 105.

its long, narrow face or its corner toward you; it may *lie* with its long, narrow face, its short, narrow face or its corner toward you; it may *sit* with its broad face, its short, narrow face or its corner toward you. These positions include the directions, right and left, front and back, up and down and diagonal, previously presented, and they give a more distinct meaning to the terms perpendicular and horizontal.

In the cubes of the third gift the measurements are confined to one inch, while in the bricks of the fourth gift the two new measurements of two inches and a half inch appear. In the third gift the number three is brought out in the three cuttings, and in the fourth this is emphasized in the three horizontal cuttings, three vertical cuttings (when on long, narrow faces) and three pairs of faces in each brick.

The fourth gift also possesses advantages for the enclosure of space. The largest quadrilateral enclosure possible with the third gift is four square inches (illustration No. 102), and the smallest is one square inch (illustration No. 103).

The largest enclosure possible with the fourth gift is sixteen square inches (illustration No. 104), and the smallest is one-quarter square inch (illustration No. 105).

By placing the bricks of the fourth gift on their short, narrow faces, one upon another, we can form a pile sixteen inches high (illustration No. 106); by placing them on their long, narrow faces, a pile eight inches high (illustration No. 107); and by placing them on their broad faces, a pile four inches in height (illustration No. 108). In the third gift the piles can be no less than one inch (illustration No. 109) or more than eight inches (illustration No. 110) in height. In the fourth we can get a height of half an inch (illustration No. 111), of one inch in two ways (illustrations Nos. 112 and 113), of two inches in three ways (illustrations Nos. 114, 115 and 116), of four inches in two ways (illustrations Nos. 117 and 118), and of eight inches in two ways (illustrations Nos. 119 and 120).

The law of equilibrium may be explained by placing the center of the broad face of one brick across the end of another. (Illustration No. 121). Communicated motion may be illustrated by standing the bricks in a row and then pushing the last or first towards the one next it. (Illustrations Nos. 122 and 123.) The greater possibilities of the fourth gift lead the child to further development, to a greater knowledge of form and number, and he can make better constructions in his building.

Forms of life, beauty and knowledge apply to this gift as to the third. The three call for doing, feeling and thinking. The rule given last

ILLUSTRATION No. 106.   ILLUSTRATION No. 107.   ILLUSTRATION No. 108.   ILLUSTRATION No. 109.

month as to the opening of the box applies also to the fourth gift. The latter should stand as a whole before the child; he should begin his work with it as a whole, and he should return it to the box as a whole. This rule, with the use of all the parts, and the working of opposites, must be strictly observed in the gift work.

In presenting the fourth gift, the two boxes may first be compared. They are alike. Then observe the resemblance between the gifts as wholes, as halves,

THE FOURTH GIFT.

as quarters and as eighths, and bring out the distinguishing peculiarities. Let the children measure and compare the new surface and find and talk about other oblong things, as tables, books, mats, pictures, etc. The brick is made of wood, and wood comes from a tree. Examine all the faces of the two gifts as wholes. Give exercises on the different positions of a single brick, on the ways bricks may touch each other, and on the various positions of quarters and halves, as well as the positions of the whole gift. Compare two bricks with two cubes, to lead the children to see that one brick and one cube are equal. Compare the heights of the piles formed with the two gifts, beginning with one cube and one brick, and leading up to the pile eight inches high in the third gift and that sixteen high in the fourth. Also give the enclosing of space, the covering of space and the building of walls.

Find edges on top running front and back; also at the bottom; at the right and left running up and down; front and back running up and down; right and left. Let the children fix the corners, as: two on top in front, two on top at the back, two below in front, two below at the back. Work with the fourth gift cultivates exactness and precision as to position and close attention to language. From twenty minutes to half an hour each day is sufficient time for the gift lesson. The concentration required would be harmful if too prolonged. After the lesson the children should be allowed a short time to make what they choose and should be encouraged to invent.

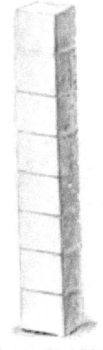
ILLUSTRATION
No. 110.

Moral and social relations may be cultivated by letting the children work as a community, one building a school, another a railway station and another

ILLUSTRATION
No. 111.

ILLUSTRATION
No. 112.

ILLUSTRATION
No. 113.

ILLUSTRATION
No. 114.

a church or a store. Each child thus makes something for the common good of all. Explain moral obligations and interdependence.

To make the gift at home, procure from a carpenter a stick eighteen inches long, one inch wide and half an inch thick, and saw it in two-inch lengths. The extra length allows for waste in sawing.

Sequences will be given principally by dictation. The following sequence shows how the games and songs may be illustrated in the gift work:

"This is the meadow, where all the long day,
Ten little frolicsome lambs are at play.

These are the measures the good farmer brings
Salt in, or corn-meal and other good things.

This is the lambkins' own big water-trough,
Drink, little lambkins, and then scamper off.

This is the rack where in Winter they feed ;
Hay makes a very good dinner indeed.

These are the big shears to shear the old sheep ;
Dear little lambkins their soft wool may keep.

Here with its big double doors shut so tight,
This is the barn where they all sleep all night." *

Open the box in the usual way, and arrange the gift to show one vertical and three horizontal cuttings, with the short, narrow faces front. Take the right-hand brick on top and place it on its long, narrow face, with the broad face front, four inches back from the edge of the table. Now place the left-hand brick on top four inches back of the first one and in a corresponding position. Lay the next two bricks respectively at the right and left on their long, narrow faces, with the short, narrow faces front ; and the next two diagonally on their long, narrow faces, one at the right-hand corner at the back and the other at the left-hand corner in front. There will then be only two places not filled in the fence, one at the right-hand corner in front and the other opposite it at the left-hand at the back ; close these gaps in the fence with the last two bricks on their long, narrow faces, and let all the bricks touch at their corners. This will make a strong fence around the *meadow* for the little lambs. (Illustration No. 124.)

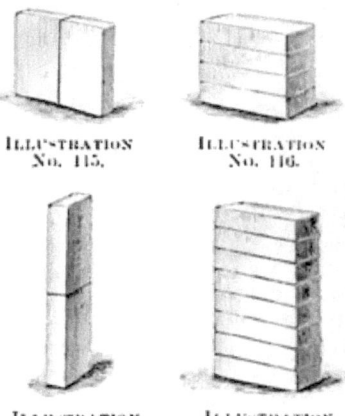

ILLUSTRATION No. 115.   ILLUSTRATION No. 116.
ILLUSTRATION No. 117.   ILLUSTRATION No. 118.

Soon the farmer comes to feed them. To build the measures for the salt and corn-meal, first find the brick at the right-hand side, place the one next it at the back so that it will stand right and left, with its short, narrow face touching the broad face of the first brick. Now find the one touching the latter in front, and turn it like the one just placed. These three bricks make the sides and back of one measure. For the bottom, slip the brick that stands in front of the fence in between the two sides on its broad face. One measure is now finished, and another must be made like it, of the bricks that form the left side of the fence. These are the *measures*. (Illustration No. 125.)

When the lambs are thirsty, make the *water-trough* by joining the two measures. (See Illustration No. 126.)

For the *hay-rack*, leave the bottom of the trough for the rack ; stand the

---

* *Nursery Finger Plays*, by Emilie Poulsson, published by Lothrop Publishing Company, Boston, Mass. Idea of sequence from *The Kindergarten Magazine*, March, 1891.

THE FOURTH GIFT.

two bricks in front and the one at the right end on their long narrow faces, with one end of each on the bottom bricks, and equal spaces between them; and place the ones at the back of the trough for the little stalls at the back. (Illustration No. 127.)

Now when it is time to shear the old sheep, take the two bricks in front, stand them on their long, narrow faces, and join them by their broad faces at the right.

ILLUSTRATION No. 119.   ILLUSTRATION No. 120.   ILLUSTRATION No. 121.

Put together the two at the back in the same way, and join to the first two by the short, narrow faces, all running right and left. This is the handle of the shears. Take the two bricks lying down, turn them on their long, narrow faces, join by their short, narrow faces, and join to the right-hand corner in front of the handle. Place the remaining two bricks in a like position at the left-hand corner. These are the big *shears*. (Illustration No. 128.)

ILLUSTRATION No. 122.

ILLUSTRATION No. 123.

The lambs go to the *barn* at night. Stand on end the bricks that make the blades of the shears. Join two by their long, narrow faces and place them four inches back from the edge of the table for the front of the barn, and put the other two in the same way a little less than an inch back of these for the back of the barn. Find the right-hand bricks of those left on the table, and put one of these on its short, narrow face at the right end of the barn, and the other similarly at the left end, to close the ends. Join the remaining two bricks by their short, narrow faces, and lay them across the top. Now the barn is tight and warm, with its big double doors in front. (Illustration No. 129.)

ILLUSTRATION No. 124.

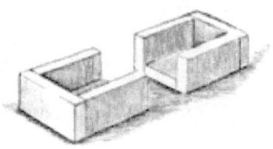

ILLUSTRATION No. 125.

ILLUSTRATION No. 126.

ILLUSTRATION No. 127.

ILLUSTRATION No. 128.

ILLUSTRATION No. 129.

To rebuild the cube, make a little square of the two bricks on top of the barn; form another square of those at the right and left, and place it on top of the others; then add those at the front and at the back.

SEQUENCES.—The object of the gift lesson is to arouse the child to voluntary action and effort and to leave him with suggestions of things to do and to be. To attain this object, the various Kindergartens are working toward a greater inventiveness and spontaneity on the part of the child, with less dictation from the Kindergartner.

The fourth gift is in many ways superior to the third for building, but the two may be used together to good advantage, the third providing solid foundations. One of the most suggestive sequences pertaining to the fourth gift is the "baker sequence," which originated in the West. This could follow a lesson and game on trades, and would help to teach respect for the various occupations, and also the interdependence of people. First show grains of wheat. Then fill a glass with water, tie a piece of netting over the top so it will just touch the water, lay the grains upon the netting, and set the glass in a sunny window. Let the children closely watch the tiny roots sprout downward and the blade shoot upward. This can also be shown with other seeds, such as corn, lima beans, etc., and will form an interesting beginning for science lessons. If the grains of wheat are planted in a field and receive proper care, sunshine and rain, they will grow, blossom and bear seed.

Next show the full-grown spear of wheat, calling attention to the strong coverings that are provided to protect the grains from rain, insects and birds. Also describe the ploughing and harrowing of the field, and follow this talk with the song, "There was a Field that Waiting Lay," from Miss Poulsson's *Finger Plays and Nursery Songs*, or the following from the same book:

> "In my little garden bed,
>   Raked so nicely over,
> First the tiny seeds I sow,
>   Then with soft earth cover.
>
> "Shining down the great round sun,
>   Smiles upon it often.
> Little raindrops, pattering down,
>   Help the seeds to soften.
>
> "Then the little plants awake,
>   Down the roots go creeping,
> Up they lift their tiny heads,
>   Through the brown mould peeping.
>
> "High and higher still they grow,
>   Through the Summer hours,
> Till some happy day the buds
>   Open into flowers."

After telling how the wheat becomes ripe and ready for cutting, give from *Merry Songs and Games* the songs of "The Farmer," and "Round and Round It Goes," for the mill-wheel and the miller. The "Baker Song," (music by Miss Eva B. Jones) to be given with the sequence, runs thus:

BAKER SONG.

Now, my child would have us bak ing. Let us cakes of her own mak ing.
Pat the cakes so soft and white. Make them round and smooth and light.

Talks and plays, of which the above gives only the most meagre suggestion, could be filled in and carried on in the home, and the different employments of everyday life could furnish the subjects. Children love to stand by and see the bread being kneaded or the cookies rolled out. If the baking table is near a window, why not have a glass of wheat growing there? The wonderful things of plant life teach impressive though voiceless lessons of Divine appointments

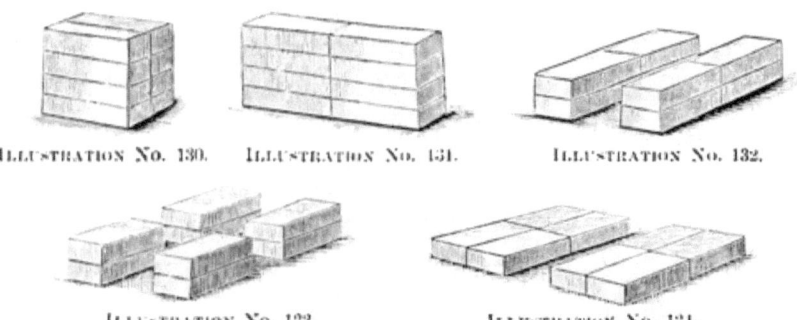

ILLUSTRATION No. 130.   ILLUSTRATION No. 131.   ILLUSTRATION No. 132.

ILLUSTRATION No. 133.   ILLUSTRATION No. 134.

to both old and young. Some mothers may say, "We are too busy to give our children such attention," but is it not just as necessary to direct your children's moral and social natures as it is to clothe and feed their bodies? Remember that companionship with children keeps the heart young, while a study of the workings and repose of Nature helps to lift one up above "personal cares and anxieties into the big, warm Quiet which is always waiting for those who seek it."

THE FOURTH GIFT.

THE BAKER SEQUENCE.—The cube standing with the cuttings right and left represents the *shop*. (Illustration No. 130.)

ILLUSTRATION No. 135.

ILLUSTRATION No. 136.

ILLUSTRATION No. 137.

ILLUSTRATION No. 138.

ILLUSTRATION No. 139.

Move the front half of the cube round to the right so that the short, narrow faces touch each other. This will form the *shelves* in the shop. (Illustration No. 131.)

Take off the top half of the shelves, place it two inches in front, and turn both halves to run front and back, for the *two counters*. (Illustration No. 132.)

ILLUSTRATION No. 140.   ILLUSTRATION No. 141.

ILLUSTRATION No. 142.

ILLUSTRATION No. 143.

Move the front half of the right-hand counter one inch to the front, and do the same with the left-hand counter, to form *loaves of bread*. (Illustration No. 133.)

Join the two loaves of bread in front by their long, narrow faces. Do the same with the two at the back. Take off the top half of the front, and place it in front of and just touching the lower half. Do the same at the back, and move this oblong along two inches or more to the right of the other one. In this way will be formed the *baking sheets*. (Illustration No. 134.)

ILLUSTRATION No. 144.   ILLUSTRATION No. 145.   ILLUSTRATION No. 146.

Join the baking sheets by their long, narrow faces for the *moulding board*. (Illustration No. 135.)

Turn the moulding board with the long, narrow faces front. Move the two bricks at the back at the right side around so that they touch the two in front of them by their short, narrow faces. Then take the two at the left at the back, and place one at the middle of each end of the oblong formed by the six bricks in front, letting them touch by their short, narrow faces. This makes the *rolling-pin*. (Illustration No. 136.)

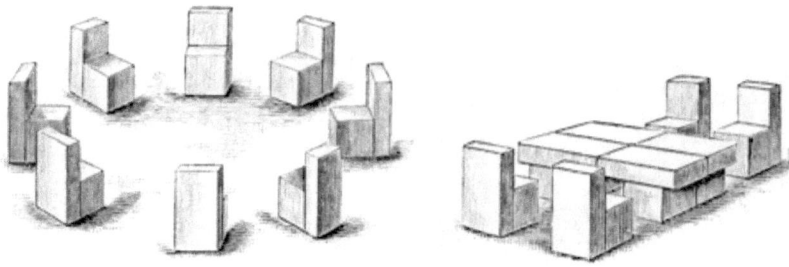

ILLUSTRATION No. 147.   ILLUSTRATION No. 148.

Now remove the two bricks at the ends, place them together by their short, narrow faces, and lay them on their long, narrow faces and touching the two bricks at the right hand at the back in the oblong. Place the two in front in a corresponding position in front, and stand one of the two remaining bricks at each end, letting its broad face touch the other bricks. This makes the *mixing pan*. (Illustration No. 137.)

Move the right-hand portion of this structure one inch to the right. Take the end brick of the left-hand part, and place it at the left end of the right-

THE FOURTH GIFT.

hand part, having it touch by its broad face. Then draw out the middle brick of the three at the left and lay it across the right-hand part for a seat. This makes the baker's *wagon* ; the two bricks at the left are his *horses*, and should be moved back to touch the wagon. (Illustration No. 138.)

ILLUSTRATION No. 149.

ILLUSTRATION No. 150.

Now stand the seat on its short, narrow face at the left hand at the back, with its broad face front. Join the two bricks that represent the horses by their long, narrow faces, and stand them at the back on top of the wagon next to the first brick and in a similar position. This is the baker's *money-box*. To close it, lay the lid down. (Illustrations Nos. 139 and 140.)

Rebuild the cube.

SEQUENCE IN THIRD AND FOURTH GIFTS, COMBINED.

Have the two gifts standing side by side on the table. (Illustration No. 141.)

ILLUSTRATION No. 151.

Remove the top half of the third gift, and place it in front of and touching the lower half. Take the two top bricks from the fourth gift, and place them on their short, narrow faces at the left side of the cubes toward the back, and touching. Stand the next two bricks on the right side opposite the ones just placed. Place the next two on the left side in front of the first two, and the remaining two opposite. The resulting structure is a *draw-bridge*. (Illustration No. 142.)

Divide the draw-bridge in halves right and left, to form *side car seats*. (Illustration No. 143.)

Move the entire left-hand half around to the right so that the two rows of bricks will touch by their broad faces. The bricks will thus run between the cubes, forming the backs of the *middle car seats* in a train. (Illustration No. 144.)

Take out the two lines of bricks, join them by the ends to make a square, and lay aside. Move the rows of cubes about an inch and a half apart, and lay the square of bricks across the top. This makes a *covered tunnel*. (Illustration No. 145.)

Remove the four bricks from the top in front, and stand each of the two cubes in front on top of the one immediately back of it. Take two of the bricks just removed, join them by the ends, and lay them across the cubes in front. Lay another brick on its broad face in the middle on top of the two just placed, and at the center stand the last brick, with its broad face front. This ingenious arrangement is a very good imitation of a *station*. (Illustration No. 146.)

From the station form a *Kindergarten ring*. Stand all the bricks upright in a circle for the backs of the Kindergarten chairs, and place a cube in front of each for a seat. (Illustration No. 147.)

Reserve four of the chairs. Make a table from the other four by arranging the cubes in two pairs about an inch apart, and laying the four bricks across the top. Result, a *table and four chairs*. (Illustration No. 148.)

Use all the bricks to make a platform four inches long, two inches wide and one inch high. Form another platform as long, wide and high, of the cubes. Place the *two platforms* side by side. (Illustration No. 149.)

ILLUSTRATION No. 152.

ILLUSTRATION No. 153.

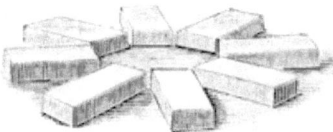

ILLUSTRATION No. 154.

ILLUSTRATION No. 155.

ILLUSTRATION No. 156.

ILLUSTRATION No. 157.

To rebuild the gifts, place the front half of each platform on top of the back half. (Illustration No. 150.)

Many other pleasing and natural forms may be built with the two gifts used together. The *fireplace* shown at illustration No. 151 is a good example of the possibilities of the simple bricks and cubes.

SEQUENCE OF BEAUTY.—Make a pin-wheel form of the eight bricks laid on their broad faces, placing two in front, two at the back, two at the right and two at the left, with a space one inch square at the center. (Illustration No. 152.)

Turn the bricks in the corners diagonally. (Illustration No. 153.)

THE FIFTH GIFT.

Pull out the bricks at the front, back, right and left until an octagon is formed in the center. (Illustration No. 154.)

Push in the bricks at the corners until they meet. (Illustration No. 155.)

Turn the brick directly in front around until it runs parallel with and touches the one next it on the right. Place its opposite at the back in a similar position, and do the same at the right and left. This gives a pin-wheel form with a corner front. (Illustration No. 156.)

ILLUSTRATION No. 158.

Pull the upper brick at the right-hand corner in front out one inch, and do the same with its opposite at the back. Then pull the lower brick at the left side in front out one inch, and do the same with its opposite at the back. The resulting design has a square cross at the center. (Illustration No. 157.)

Turn the bricks at the front, back, right and left about until they run true and the inner ends form an octagon. (Illustration No. 158.)

Push in the bricks at the front, back, right and left until they join at the center. (Illustration No. 159.)

ILLUSTRATION No. 159.

ILLUSTRATION No. 160.

Turn the brick in the left-hand corner in front around until it touches and runs the same as the one in front ; and do the same with the opposite brick. Then turn the brick in the right-hand corner in front, and also its opposite. This brings us back to the form with which we started, and from which the cube may be easily rebuilt. (Illustration No. 160.)

For further reading in regard to the fourth gift see : *Nursery Finger Plays*, by Emilie Poulsson ; *The Idea of Sequence*, in the *Kindergarten Magazine* for March, 1891.

SIXTH PAPER.

THE FIFTH GIFT.

FROEBEL, when studying the universal plays of childhood, noticed the desire to build and provided suitable materials to meet this instinct of the child to imitate what he sees in the world around him. Each stage of development demands particular activities and amusements. The child likes to pull things apart, and then, if possible, to put them together again, or else to make something novel that will express the pictures of his imagination. Thus he discovers new qualities and uses and so enlarges his experience.

The fifth gift, the subject of this paper, is the third of the building set. It is a three-inch wooden cube divided by four vertical cuts (two front and back and two right and left) and two horizontal cuts; in other words, the cube is divided twice in each of its dimensions, the result being twenty-seven one-inch cubes. (Illustration No. 161.) Three of these one-inch cubes are each divided by

ILLUSTRATION NO. 161.

ILLUSTRATIONS NOS. 162 AND 163.

one diagonal cut into half-cubes or triangular prisms (illustration No. 163), and three more are each divided by two diagonal cuts into quarter-cubes or smaller triangular prisms. (Illustration No. 162.) The divisions are, therefore, twenty-one whole cubes, six half-cubes, and twelve quarter-cubes, thirty-nine parts in all.

Owing to its one-inch cubes, the fifth gift appears as an elaboration and evolution of the third gift, but where the third was divided once in each direction, this gift is divided twice. The third is formed of eight cubes, while the fifth is made up of twenty-seven; but though the fifth gift is seen to have some points of resemblance to the third, on no account is it to be considered as an enlarged third gift.

The fifth gift is like the fourth in material, and one brick of the fourth, and one cube of the fifth are equal in volume. Moreover, the fifth is similar in the oblong surface, which is brought out in two sizes in the half and quarter-cubes.

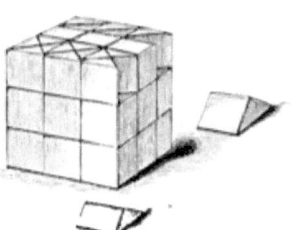

ILLUSTRATION NO. 164.

The division of three cubes into halves and three into quarters gives a new solid, the triangular prism. Each of the half-cubes is a triangular prism having five faces—one oblong, two triangular and two square. The twelve quarter-cubes are triangular prisms one-half the size of the half-cubes, and each has one square face, two oblong faces and two triangular faces. (Illustration No. 164 shows half and quarter cubes.) We also have a new square prism when two quarter-cubes are joined by their square faces. (Illustration No. 165.)

THE FIFTH GIFT.

Heretofore only vertical and horizontal lines and surfaces have been represented, but now these are joined by the *slanting* line and surface, which connect them. The slanting line and surface were anticipated in the third and fourth

ILLUSTRATIONS NOS. 165 AND 166.   ILLUSTRATIONS NOS. 167 AND 168.

gifts when side touched edge, and when one cube was hung edge downward between two others, but in the fifth gift the slanting direction is permanent. (Illustration No. 166.)

The use of the slanting line with the vertical and horizontal lines gives a new angle, the acute of 45 degrees; adding this acute angle to a right angle in either half or quarter cubes gives still another new solid of two sizes, the rhomboidal prism. (Illustrations Nos. 167 and 168.)

THE NEW NUMBER.—The third and fourth gifts brought out the number two and its multiples. The fifth gift, while it incidentally gives one of the former multiples, six, the number of the half-cubes, especially emphasizes three and its multiples, nine, twelve, twenty-seven and thirty-nine.

ILLUSTRATION NO. 169.

The gift is a three-inch cube. It has three horizontal layers, front and back, and three vertical layers, right and left. When the whole cube is divided by vertical cuts, front and back, each part contains uppermost one whole cube, one cube divided into halves and one cube divided into quarters.

THE NEW FRACTION.—This leads to the new fraction, one-third. The gift cannot be easily separated into halves, but can be very readily parted into thirds. (Illustration No. 169 displays thirds.) The thirds may be separated into thirds, which will be ninths of the whole. (Illustration No. 170.) Going further, the ninths may be separated into thirds, which will be twenty-sevenths of the whole. (Illustration No. 171.) Thus the mathematical possibilities or forms of knowledge disclose the whole, halves, quarters, thirds, ninths and twenty-sevenths, as

ILLUSTRATION NO. 170.

well as such combinations as three-ninths equal to one-third, six-ninths equal to two-thirds, two-fourths equal to one-half, nine-twenty-sevenths equal to one-third, etc., which give concrete work for the school.

THE FORMS OF LIFE.—The forms of life in the fifth gift approach very nearly to architectural designs, the half and quarter cubes aiding materially, with their slanting surfaces, to represent roofs, gable-windows and stoops, as well as square towers, etc.

ILLUSTRATION No. 171.

When the child built forms with the third and fourth gifts they merely suggested the outlines of the things represented. His cube was a house because it had four walls, a top and a bottom, and he was just as well satisfied as he would have been with a more perfect design. His impressions were too vague and imperfect for him to have especially noticed slanting roofs and chimneys.

ILLUSTRATION No. 172.

Owing to its many parts the fifth gift is much in advance of any of the former ones, and should not be given to very young children. It is difficult to handle and requires greater strength and control of the hands, for in the building the half and quarter cubes are often used as slanting roofs and projections or for square towers. These are sometimes changed on different faces without being taken out, or a triangular prism is stood over a square tower. Again, larger roofs are moved off in one handling; and all this necessitates dexterity and delicacy of touch, while it gives excellent training to the fingers.

ILLUSTRATION No. 173.

The intellectual advancement in perception, attention, imagination and language is also great when this gift is faithfully used. This fact is shown in the necessary directions given in building, for a half or quarter cube presents different appearances according to the positions and directions in which it stands. The use of the fifth gift likewise embodies good social training. At first one

THE FIFTH GIFT.

gift is given to every three children, each child having only one-third. Obedience and promptness are cultivated, and when three children put their work together to form some special object with the entire gift, kindly and sympathetic feelings must exist among them to aid in the work and prevent the temptation to destroy.

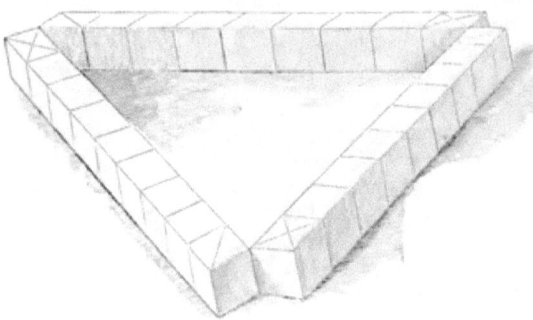

ILLUSTRATION No. 174.

Some one has said, "Two cannot work together except they be agreed," and that is the social world in a nutshell. Each child is stimulated to put forth his best efforts, and that without any place-taking, since well-doing is its own reward. The slower child is encouraged by his swifter companion, and the bright child is taught that his quick fingers are God's gift to him, to be used in helping others. The child contrasts himself with others, imitates and is imitated. In this way the Kindergarten gives what even the best home training cannot give—the companionships and competitions of life in the right spirit, and provides a firm basis for activity at school and in the world.

ILLUSTRATION No. 175.

THE FORMS OF BEAUTY.—The forms of beauty in the fifth gift include many geometrical shapes, besides various pleasing designs which may be used for conventional patterns in wall-paper, oil-cloth or tiling. The germ of the useful arts is thus fostered. Statistics of children who have been trained in this way show that more than a few artists have traced their first impetus back to the Kindergarten. As the Kindergarten also provides material for laying these designs in light and dark woods and for pasting them in colored papers, they may be kept in tangible form.

ILLUSTRATION No. 176.

Sequences in the forms of beauty may present either four-sided or three-sided figures. As a sequence would involve too many steps to give a fair idea of the pleasing effect, we will simply illustrate the ground form of each, and an example of what may be evolved from that ground form. (Illustrations Nos. 172, 173, 174 and 175.)

USE OF THE FIFTH GIFT.—The Kindergartner introduces the gift by showing only one, which stands on her own table. First she compares it with the third and fourth as to size. The cube divided into halves may next be shown, its different faces taught, dictations given as to placing it in different directions, and the new name, triangular prism, mentioned and commented on.

Exhibit and explain in the same way the cube divided into quarters, until the children know the names and the different faces and can place the faces in the various directions, make other sizes and lengths of triangular prisms of the parts, use them with a single whole cube, as at illustration No. 176 and make whole cubes from halves, and quarters into square prisms.

ILLUSTRATION No. 178.

ILLUSTRATION No. 177.

Next proceed to the thirds, giving the number of parts and the measurements, and bringing out the idea of one-third, two-thirds and three-thirds; and with older children the ninths and twenty-sevenths may be shown. The child must always build up his third or his whole cube. Time should be given with each lesson for free play, to encourage inventiveness; or a lesson might consist in requiring each child to build some particular thing suggested by his own ingenuity.

ILLUSTRATION No. 179.

In this as in the other gifts the rule applies, that each form follows in an orderly way from what has gone before; and in every case all the material is to be used. Froebel says: "No form is to be torn down that something new may be built up from the ruins. Orderly doing leads to orderly thinking." Keep the position of the half and quarter cubes as shown in the illustration of the entire gift. Thus, in the third, the whole cube is to be stood in the middle on top.

ILLUSTRATION No. 180.

SEQUENCES IN FORMS OF LIFE.—The following simple sequence shows the first use of one-third.*

AN EXCURSION TO THE SEA-SHORE.—Take one-third of the gift. Place it so it runs right and left, with halves on the right, quarters on the left, and a whole cube in the center.

ILLUSTRATION No. 181.

Gates to Pass to Ferry.—Draw the three right-hand cubes one inch to the

---

* Obtained from Miss F. E. Mann, of New York City, and originated by Miss Gertrude Noyes. The other sequences are original.

THE FIFTH GIFT.

right, and the three left-hand cubes the same distance to the left. (Illustration No. 177.)

Ferry-Boat.—Draw out the three middle cubes, and lay them on the table right and left between the two sides. (Illustration No. 178.)

Bath-Houses.—Remove the upper two right-hand cubes and the corresponding two on the left. Place one whole cube at the left end in line with the others, and locate the remaining whole cube in front of the middle two cubes in the row and touching them by a face. Make a long tri-prism of the two halves, and place it on the front

ILLUSTRATION No. 182.

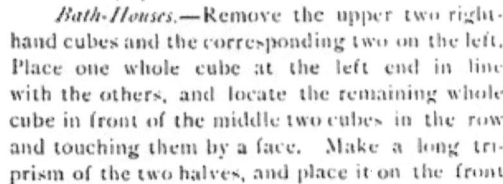

cube and over the meeting of the middle two cubes, with the three-cornered faces front and back and the square faces slanting right and left. Roof the cube at each end with a quarter cube, placing the latter with its square face downward and its triangular faces front and back. Roof the remaining cubes in like manner. (Illustration No. 179.)

Restaurant.—Lift the tri-prism formed of half cubes and stand it on one three-cornered face at one side

ILLUSTRATION No. 183.

to serve as a sign. Place the front cube over the crack between the middle two cubes. Move the right-hand cube with its roof in front of the next cube so the two touch by front and back faces, and treat the left-hand two in the same way. Join the two halves (which form the sign) by their square faces and place them on top of the middle cube, with the three-cornered faces front and back. Result, a restaurant with a yard for tables on warm days. (Illustration No. 180.)

ILLUSTRATION No. 184.

Animal Houses.—Remove the roof from the left-hand cubes, place the front left-hand cube on the back left-hand cube so it touches the tri-prism by an edge, and do the same at the right side.

Make a square prism of two quarters, and stand it on the left-hand cube; same at the right. (Illustration No. 181.)

Music Pavilion and Stand.—Draw the right-hand cubes one inch to the right hand, and the left-hand cubes similarly one inch to the left hand. The center piece forms the music stand, and the people may be supposed to sit in front of it. (Illustration No. 182.)

ILLUSTRATION No. 185.

ILLUSTRATION No. 186.

Observation Tower.—Lift off the top middle cube and the roof, stand the two lower cubes upright, and replace the top middle cube and roof. (Illustration No. 183.)

ILLUSTRATION No. 187.

ILLUSTRATION No. 188.

Gates.—Place the cubes of halves on the right-hand cubes and the cubes of fourths on the left-hand cubes. Close the gates to get the third with which we started. (Illustration No. 184.)

SEQUENCE No. 2.—This sequence is more complex. It shows how the forms built of one-third may be combined in parts, or all put together in one. Each child might also use an entire gift, building one form with a third, then the next and the next, producing a little village. Use only one-third of the gift in this sequence.

Front Elevation of the Town-Hall.—Remove the half and the quarter cubes. Place the half-cubes on their square faces upon the right and left hand whole cubes, touching the center cube by their square faces, and with their slanting faces sloping right and left. Make a square prism of two quarters, and stand it on top of the center cube, face front. Over this put a half-cube, made of two quarters, with the three-cornered face front. (Illustration No. 185.)

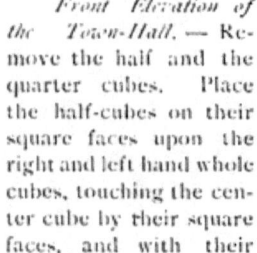

ILLUSTRATION No. 189.

ILLUSTRATION No. 190.

House.—Remove the halves and quarters; move the top cube one inch to the left, and on it stand a half cube with a three-cornered face front. Take two whole cubes from the right, and place them in front of the two at the left, right and left. Over one just placed make a roof with one half-cube, oblong face front. Put roof on right-hand back cube with one quarter-cube. Make door-steps in front with the three remaining quarter-cubes by putting two down on their square faces, with the three-cornered faces front, and dropping the third quarter-cube in between. (Illustration No. 186.)

ILLUSTRATION No. 191.

School with Two Entrances.—Draw away the door-steps. Turn the right-hand part of the house around until it runs right and left and touches the tower.

THE FIFTH GIFT.

Take the three quarter-cubes that made the door-steps. Put one on the extreme right-hand cube of the new building for a roof, with the oblong face slanting front. Make steps in front of the right and left hand cubes with the two quarter-cubes not yet used. (Illustration No. 187.)

Church.—Remove the quarter and half cubes. Stand the whole cube at the left in front on top of the tower back of it, and on this place one half-cube on its oblong face, with its three-cornered face front. Lay the other half-cube on the right-hand cube, with its oblong face downward, and its square face sloping front. Make a square prism of two quarter-cubes and place it on top of the middle whole cube, face front. On top of this place two quarter-cubes made into a half-cube. (Illustration No. 188.)

TO COMBINE :—

Large Church.—Put the house shown at illustration No. 186 in front of the town hall. (Illustration No. 189.)

ILLUSTRATION No. 192.

Hotel.—Join the small church to the left of the school, with the highest parts in the middle. On the left side is a small tower of two quarter-cubes. Use the two steps in the front to make a similar tower at the right, taking away the whole cube. Raise the building at the left with this whole cube. (Illustration No. 190.)

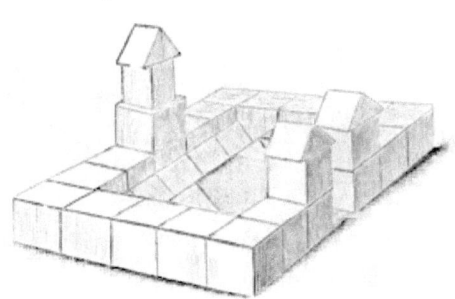

ILLUSTRATION No. 193.

If it is desired to use the entire fifth gift in one building, place the house (one-third) in front of the hotel, which is composed of the small church (one-third) and the school (one-third). Take the door-steps to raise the center tower. The result will be a college. (Illustration No. 191.) Other structures calling for the whole gift are *Front of Ferry-House* and *Poultry Yard*. (Illustrations Nos. 192 and 193.)

SEVENTH PAPER.

THE SIXTH GIFT.

The sixth gift (illustration No. 194) concludes the building set. As a whole it is like the fifth gift, being a three-inch wooden cube. Like the fifth gift, its first division consists of twenty-seven parts, but these parts, instead of being one-inch cubes, are blocks of the same size and proportions as the bricks of the fourth gift. Of these blocks, or bricks as we will call them, three are divided lengthwise into halves, making long, square prisms resembling columns; and six breadthwise into halves, or short, square prisms, called for the sake of convenience, half-cubes. Thus the parts are: eighteen bricks, twelve half-cubes and six columns, in all, thirty-six parts.

Illustration No. 194.

Illustration No. 195.

The columns of this gift were foreshadowed in the fifth gift when two quarter cubes were joined by square faces. (Illustration No. 195.) Although, as a whole, it most nearly resembles the fifth gift, the parts are most like those of the fourth gift. While it is not an enlarged fourth gift, it may be called its continuation.

For an easier and more systematic handling, Miss Brooks, of the Teachers' College, New York City, has devised the plan of laying the gift out in six layers. (Illustration No. 196.) Three of these contain three whole bricks and three half-bricks, or half-cubes, the last being made by a crosswise cut through the middle of a brick. The other three layers consist each of three bricks, one half-cube, as described above, and two long, square prisms, or columns made by a lengthwise cut through the middle of a brick. When spread out upon the table, the layers with three bricks and three half-cubes are in front, while the layers with three bricks, two columns and one half-cube are laid back. In building up the gift the layers alternate.

Illustration No. 196.

Illustration No. 197.   Illustration No. 198.

FORMS OF KNOWLEDGE.—Taking up the separate parts, we find that the

THE SIXTH GIFT.

bricks of the sixth gift are like those of the fourth, being two inches long, one inch wide and one-half inch thick. The half-cubes, or short, square prisms, are one-inch square by one-half inch thick. (Illustration No. 197.) They equal

ILLUSTRATION No. 199.

ILLUSTRATION No. 200.

one half-brick and also one half-cube. Two of them side by side form one brick. Two, one on top of the other, form one cube. The columns are two inches long, one-half inch wide and one-half inch thick. (Illustration No. 198.) The base of each would cover one-fourth square inch. These columns, or long, square prisms, equal in volume one half-cube, the dimensions being $\frac{1}{2} \times \frac{1}{2} \times 2 = \frac{1}{2}$ inch. The half cube is $1 \times 1 \times \frac{1}{2} = \frac{1}{2}$ inch. In the oblong faces of the fourth and sixth gifts we approach the surface, while in the columns the line is anticipated.

The fifth gift emphasizes the number three, while the sixth brings out both the numbers three and six. Two layers form one-third of the gift. Four layers form two-thirds of the gift. One layer forms one-sixth of the gift.

ILLUSTRATION No. 201.

Two layers form two-sixths of the gift. Five layers form five-sixths of the gift. Two layers would equal each other, and each would equal one-fourth of the remainder of the gift. Two alternate layers together equal one-third of the gift. Two layers of bricks and one half-cube equal one-third of the gift. Six bricks and six half-cubes equal one-third of the gift. Six bricks and six columns equal one-third of the gift. Six bricks, three half-cubes and three

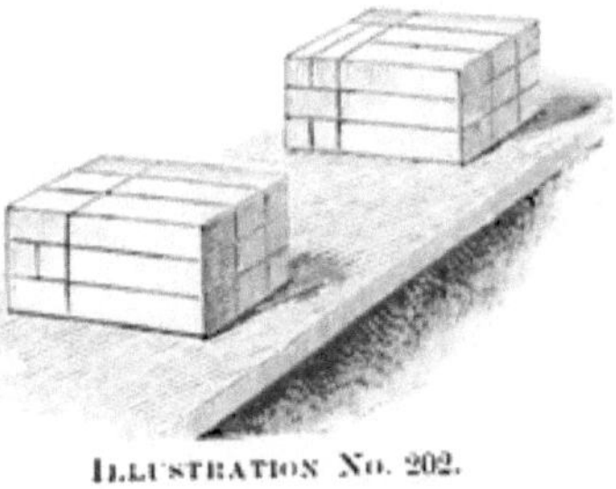

ILLUSTRATION No. 202.

columns equal one-third of the gift. Then the whole gift can be divided into thirds in three ways, viz: Front and back (illustration No. 199); right and left (illustration No. 200); taking two layers from the top (illustration No. 201.) It can be divided into halves in only one way. (Illustration No. 202). It can be laid in three groups, each group consisting of two layers, which would be one-third of the gift or two-sixths

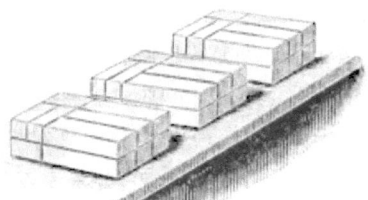

ILLUSTRATION No. 203.

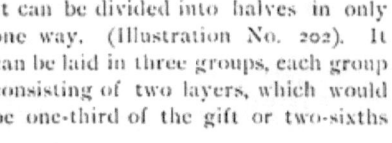

ILLUSTRATION No. 204.

of it. (Illustration No. 203.) Two of these groups could be joined to show one-third and two-thirds. (Illustration No. 204.)

FORMS OF COMPARISON.—The sixth gift allows of more forms of comparison than any of its predecessors. For instance, we have a comparison between short, square prisms and long, square prisms; between half and whole cubes; between half cubes and bricks; between bricks and cubes; between columns and bricks; between half-cubes and columns. We

ILLUSTRATION No. 205.

can show that two half-cubes equal one whole cube; we can show that two half-cubes equal one brick; therefore, one cube and one brick equal each other. One column equals one half brick. One column equals one half-cube.

Figures may differ in size and shape and yet be equal in volume. Thus, the sixth gift emphasizes the proportion of different parts in respect to size, and gives a clear idea of forms, their position and number.

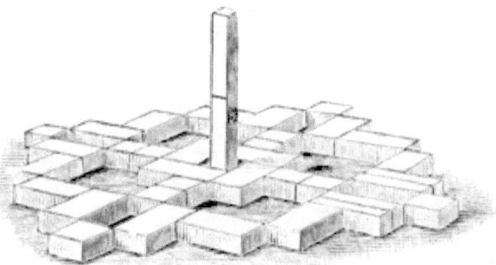

ILLUSTRATION No. 206.

FORMS OF BEAUTY.—The forms of beauty in the sixth gift are less diversi-

THE SIXTH GIFT.

fied than those of the fifth. For the square forms it is necessary to place two columns in the center, one above the other. A ground form is shown in the square and triangle with one pattern that may be derived from it. (Illustrations Nos. 205, 206, 207 and 208.) (For further work see Wiebe's *Paradise of Childhood*.)

FORMS OF LIFE.—The sixth gift admits of many forms of life and is especially valuable for building purposes, the structures bearing a close resemblance to Greek architecture.

ILLUSTRATION No. 207.

ILLUSTRATION No. 208.

(Illustration No. 209.*) This gift is introduced after the children have become acquainted with, but not tired of, the fifth gift. It is compared as a whole with its predecessor, the different ways for dividing both being pointed out. Then a brick is taken up for comparison, after that the columns, which are measured and named "square prisms," and the half-cubes in the same manner. The layers would naturally follow, each child having two laid on the table, one back of the other, at least three inches apart, the layer with half-cubes in front, to inculcate an orderly way of handling. These layers are divided into one-third and two-thirds and then the number of bricks, square prisms and half-cubes, is found.

Practice in building from two layers alone is given, and the structures are measured. The inventions and comparisons are almost endless.

"All Froebel's gifts are remarkable for the peculiar feature that they can be rendered exceedingly instructive by frequently introducing repetitions under varied conditions

ILLUSTRATION No. 209.

ILLUSTRATION No. 210.

---

* From Wiebe's *Paradise of Childhood*.

and forms, by which means we are sure to avoid that dry and fatiguing monotony which must needs result from repeating the same thing in the same manner and form. And still more, the child, thereby, becomes accustomed to recognize

ILLUSTRATION No. 211.

ILLUSTRATION No. 212.

like in unlike, similarity in dissimilarity, oneness in multiplicity, and connection in the apparently disconnected."

With the sixth gift we reach the end of the second series of development given by Froebel in the building blocks, the aim of this second series being to acquaint the child with the general qualities of the solid body by his own observation and occupation with the same.

ILLUSTRATION No. 213.

ILLUSTRATION No. 214.

SEQUENCE.—I.—Lay out the gift in layers, whole bricks with half-cubes for front layers, as in illustration No. 196.

II.—Notice the two layers at the right. From the front one take two

THE SIXTH GIFT.

bricks. Join them by their broad faces and place them on the table running front and back. From the back layer take two more bricks. Join the same as before and place in the same direction one inch to the right of the other two. Take two half-cubes from the front. Let them rest on their square faces on top of the center of the bricks right and left. On each of these place a column, long face front, exactly in the center. On top of each on its square face place a half-cube. Join two bricks by their ends and lay them across the top, right and left. This is a *small gateway*. (Illustration No. 210.) The laying out of the gift and the building of this one form may constitute a lesson. The gift is divided among three children.

III.—When the children are able, let each child have a whole gift. Build

three forms like the last illustration. Join them side and side, so the bricks on top just touch, which shows the *front of a building*. (Illustration No. 211.)

IV.—Notice the two parts which form the center of this building front.

Keep the right-hand part of this center in mind and place the extreme right-hand part of the whole front back of it, so that the base bricks of both touch by their ends. Do the same at the left. Repeat at the right and left. This gives a *bridge*. (Illustration No. 212.)

V.—Put the right-hand part of the front away at the right. Put the left away at the left. Do the same at the back. Turn the middle parts around until the bases run right and left and stand one inch apart. Place one of the right-hand parts directly in front of the middle parts, base bricks front and back, closing the opening at the base. The top brick will then run right and left and close the opening at the top. Place the other right-hand part in a similar position at the back of the structure. The center of the base is a one-inch hollow square, and at the top it is a two-inch square. There are now two parts left on the table. Take off the top bricks, all half-bricks and the columns. Roof the structure with four bricks resting on their broad faces. Lay a half-cube on its square face in the center of each half of the top. Stand a column on each of these, long face front, with a half-cube for a cap-stone. Two bricks are left. Join them by the ends and lay them right and left across the top. This represents a *spring-house*. (Illustration No. 213.)

VI.—These steps may all be retraced to the layers, or the gift may be built up direct from the spring-house.

It is always more interesting to the children when some story is connected with the sequence. The forms above given may illustrate a Summer day in a city park. For free play the children may be encouraged to invent other buildings or grottoes in the park. (Illustration No. 214.) Bird and flower songs would be appropriate, or the song, "Grasshopper Green,"* the subject of which might be found in some secluded spot. (See page 84.)

For further reading on the sixth gift see: *Paradise of Childhood*, by Edward Wiebe, and *Songs and Games for Little Ones*, by Misses Walker and Jenks.

EIGHTH PAPER.

THE SEVENTH GIFT.

In the seventh gift we study the first of the third and last set of Froebel's gifts. This set comprises the seventh, eighth, ninth and tenth gifts and is called the abstract set. The first set contains undivided solids; the second set divided solids; while now, commencing with the seventh gift, we proceed to analyze the boundaries of solids. From the solid the first step toward the abstract is the plane. From the plane Froebel passes to the line, and thence to the point.

ILLUSTRATION No. 215.

* *Songs and Games for Little Ones*, by Gertrude Walker and Harriet Jenks, published by The Oliver Ditson Company.

THE SEVENTH GIFT.

The seventh gift consists of thin polished planes, representing surfaces, made in the natural colors of light and dark woods. There are six forms: The circle, square, right-angled isosceles triangle, equilateral triangle, right-angled scalene triangle and the obtuse-angled triangle. (Illustration No 215.) These planes are called tablets. We advance now from the solid building gifts to the gift which deals only with surfaces.

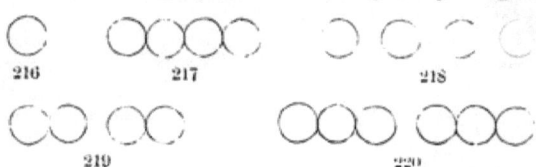
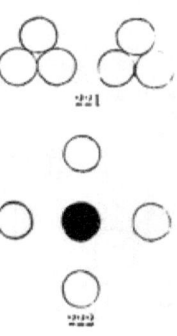

This gift combines elements into forms and thus begins with synthesis, while the building gifts began with analysis. The objects shown with the building gifts were real, concrete representations of buildings and had the three dimensions of length, breadth and thickness; but with the tablets of the seventh gift, the children cannot represent real objects, only pictures of them. To render the tablets tangible, they are given three dimensions, but we really deal with only two dimensions—length and breadth—for the third dimension is so small as to be left out of consideration.

The seventh gift is obtained by analyzing solids. As the Kindergarten solids may be reduced to the sphere, cube and cylinder, and these, in turn, to the sphere alone, the cube and cylinder being contained in the sphere, the seventh gift may be derived from the sphere. Bisecting the sphere in any way produces the circular plane. Within the circle the square may be drawn. The right-angled isosceles triangle follows from the square when divided from corner to corner. The equilateral triangle may be obtained from the hexagon drawn in the circle and divided into six triangles. Bisecting the equilateral triangle from apex to base gives the right-angled scalene triangle, or if the hexagon be drawn in the square face of the cube, the triangles left in the corners will be right-angled scalene triangles. Two right-angled scalene triangles joined by bases will give the obtuse-angled triangle, or by bisecting the equilateral triangle in each direction, the sides with the lines meeting at the center form three obtuse-angled triangles. This is easily demonstrated with a circle of paper.

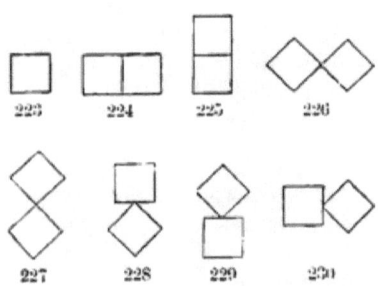

The seventh gift can be used to represent forms of life, but the results are crude and not so pleasing as those made with the building gifts. In artistic and mathematical possibilities, however, the seventh gift excels, the forms of beauty and geometrical forms being more extensive with this gift than with any of the others which come before it. The two colors combine to enhance the effect. Latent talent and originality in designing are soon disclosed by the use of the seventh gift, while many lessons are learned in form, angles and the direction of lines. The law of working by opposites is applied in the laying out of designs, as in the forms of beauty with the building gifts. This makes mathematical relations clearer and helps to awaken the fancy.

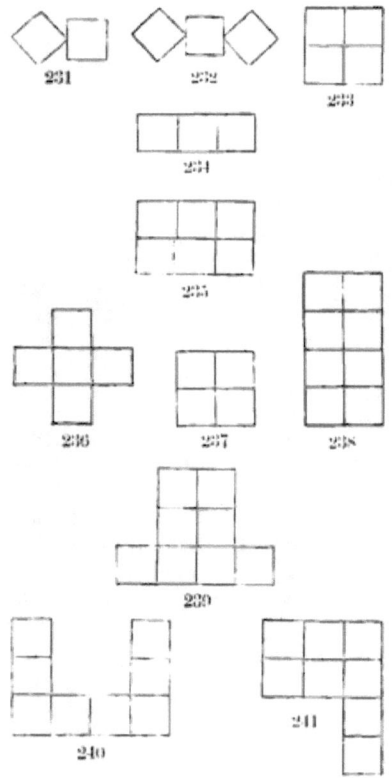

THE CIRCLE.—The first plane to be presented is the circle. (Illustration No. 216.) As it is derived from either ball or cylinder, it would naturally be given in connection with those solids. A clay cylinder may be made and thin slices cut from the ends to show that the tablet is really from it. The same result is attained when the sphere is bisected.

Lessons in direction and position may be given, the first arrangement being a row from right to left, either touching or apart. (Illustrations Nos. 217 and 218.) Other lessons would follow, consisting of groups of two or three tablets (Illustrations Nos. 219, 220 and 221), and from these symmetrical patterns may be laid either in central or border designs. (Illustration No. 222.) Many a childish game can be emphasized with circles, as they become in turn pictures of the plates for a tea-party, flower-beds on the lawn, closed seed-pods, or even the first snowballs of Winter. The circular tablet gives the simplest and easiest lesson in position and direction, and through his play the child is led to observe circular forms in the world about him.

THE SQUARE.—The next plane to be considered is the one-inch square. (Illustration No. 223.) This is the type of four-sided figures. With the square tablet the pupil becomes acquainted with the right angle and is taught to look for it in objects about him. He measures his tablet and finds that its sides are all alike, one inch long, and that its angles are all right angles. The square should be introduced in connection with a cube of the third gift, that the child may see that it is derived from it, that it represents its surface. The cube may be

THE SEVENTH GIFT.

called a table and the tablet a spread for it. It is named a square, and its edges are equal in whatever position placed. By experimenting it is shown that the corner of a small square covers the corner of a large square. Direction, front and back, right and left, up and down, has already been learned. It will not now be difficult to show that when a line running straight up and down meets one running right and left, the corner thus formed is a right angle. Fourteen tablets laid one above the other equal a one-inch cube. The same idea is illustrated by covering a cube with tablets.

By way of contrast two tablets may be joined into an oblong. This is measured as to sides and angles. It is not a square, because the sides are not equal, but the angles fulfil the conditions of right angles. The eye is thus trained to judge correctly of the right angle, which correctness is an important foundation for skilled workmanship in after life. A beginning is made in the Kindergarten for industrial work which, if carried into the school, will lead out into the arts and manufactures. As already mentioned in the paper on occupations, it is this same early training that has given the older countries their precedence in the industrial world.

From the opposite sides of the square the child gets the idea of parallel lines. Parallel lines joined to the right angle form the elements of architecture. The child is unconsciously pleased by this connection with the real things of life and begins to grasp the underlying unity.

With two tablets position is again introduced. They may join by edges (Illustrations Nos. 224 and 225), and run right and left or front and back; or, joined by corners, run the same way. (Illustrations Nos. 226 and 227.) Corner may touch middle of edge in front (Illustration No. 228), at back (Illustration No. 229) right or left, (Illustrations Nos. 230 and 231). The same designs may be repeated with three squares or they may alternate. (Illustration No. 232.)

Four tablets form a square similar to the top of the third gift. (Illustration No. 233.) Larger squares follow with more tablets. Oblongs of different lengths and widths would constitute another step. (Illustrations Nos. 234 and 235.) After these may come more difficult designs (Illustration No. 236), or a sequence, as in the forms of beauty with the third gift. A life sequence may be given with the third gift and afterward copied with the squares as follows :

	Car.	Wall.	Seats.	Sofa.
Illustration Nos.	237	238	239	240

Madame Kraus represents a flag (illustration No 241) by making an oblong of six square tablets, arranged from right to left, two by three inches, placing the two remaining squares below up and down, on the right or left hand side, to form the flag-staff, locating the staff according to the direction from which the child supposes the wind to blow. This suggests the song of the "hand and wrist game of the weather-vane," from Froebel's *Mutter und Koselieder:*

> Like the weather-vane I'm going,
> While the gusts of wind are blowing;
> I can turn my wrist and hand,
> As the best vane in our land.

The forms of life, however, are limited in comparison with the forms of beauty. Work with the squares lays an excellent preparation for weaving. In this first work with the seventh gift the Kindergartner must proceed carefully and in accordance with the development of the child, explaining and repeating the same idea under as many different circumstances as possible. The object is to acquaint the child with the created world in which he lives and make him in turn a creative being. Dr. Hailmann says that instead of giving the child a threefold nature—head, hand, heart—he would make the classification five-fold, viz., hand, head, heart, heart, hand—first the hand, to grasp and gain sense impressions, the head to know, the heart to feel; again, the heart for right-willing, and last, the hand a second time to execute.

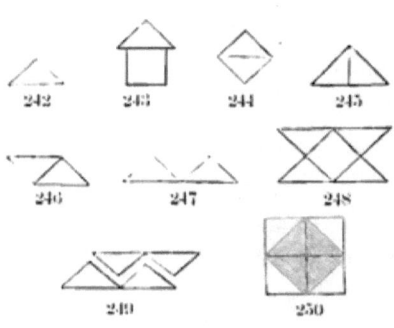

RIGHT-ANGLED ISOSCELES TRIANGLE.—The third plane is the right-angled isosceles triangle, called half-square for convenience, made by bisecting the square diagonally. (Illustration No. 242.) By this division a triangle is obtained with two edges, each one inch and one edge one and three-eighths inches long. One angle is a right angle, 90°, and each of the other angles measures 45°. The three angles of any triangle always equal two right angles. These two angles, 90° and 45°, are the first used by the draughtsman and designer.

As the square tablet is connected with the cube of the third gift, so the right-angled isosceles triangle follows after the half-cube of the fifth gift and should not be given until that gift is used. By introducing it after the fifth gift, the triangular face of the half-cube is emphasized. (Illustration No. 243.) Two tablets are joined to make a square. One is drawn away and the new form is thus disclosed. A half-cube is placed over it, showing that the tablet is like the cube's triangular face. When two triangles form a square it is found that a slanting line divides them. This line is called a diagonal and it is longer than the sides of the square. The square had four sides and four angles, but this new figure has but three sides and three angles. Figures of three sides and three angles are called triangles. The half square has one right angle and two sharp angles. The sharp angles are called acute angles. Two of them will make a

THE SEVENTH GIFT.

right angle. What is opposite the right angle? The line called the base of the triangle. This line has been shown to be longer than the sides and the right angle to be larger than either of the two others. We may then give the fact that the longest side is opposite the widest angle. After forming the square from two tablets (illustration No. 244) a large triangle is obtained by joining right angles at center of base, the long sides extending out right and left. (Illustration No. 245.) How long is the base, or longest edge, of this new triangle, and what is the angle at the top or apex? This triangle is a larger half square, for two more added to it would form a square. More half squares may be given out to make into larger triangles and, all being joined by acute angles, placed with the right angle at the back and the longest line running right and left in front, a neat border pattern will be made.

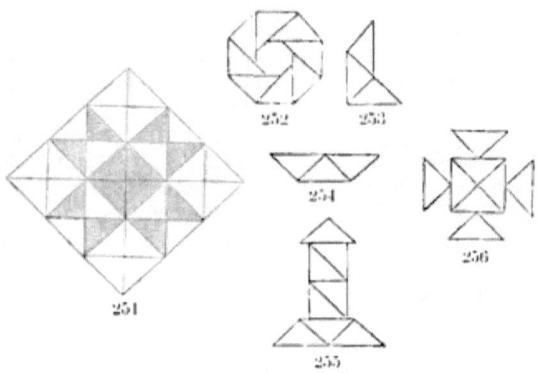

Two half squares will form a rhomboid having two acute and two obtuse angles. (Illustration No. 246.) Exercises may be given in placing the half square according to dictation, as in the one mentioned above with the triangles made of two half squares (illustration No. 247), or in making two rows, the row in front touching by acute angles, long lines in front running right and left, the second row back of the front row, the right angles of both touching and the long lines at the back extending right and left. (Illustration No. 248.)

Another pattern has the same row in front, the back row being moved so as to have the right angle merely touch the right angle made by the opening between the front angles. (Illustration No. 249.) For more difficult work join four black half squares together to form a square, having a corner front. Add white half squares around this, touching by their long edges and with their right angles out. Thus you have a white square enclosing a black one. (Illustration No. 250.) Adding more tablets enlarges and elaborates the design. (Illustration No. 251.) Join eight half squares into a hollow octagon. (Illustration No. 252.) Three half squares make either a shoe or boat trapezoid. (Illustrations Nos. 253 and 254.) Four will make a boat trapezoid, a square, an oblong and a large triangle. Five form a shoe, a boat trapezoid or an irregular pentagon.

The forms of both life and beauty follow those of the fifth gift. (Illustrations Nos. 255 and 256.) These are merely the simplest combinations, as an attempt to exhaust the forms derivable from the half square would require a book in itself. Dictated work shows the child the possibilities of his material and gives him a foundation for future invention and free play. The two should be judiciously mingled. "Nothing comes of nothing," and the child cannot invent until he has first learned to observe.

EQUILATERAL TRIANGLE.—The equilateral triangle (illustration No. 257) follows the right-angled isosceles or half square. It is the simplest of all triangles, because all its edges are equal and all its angles are equal. Each edge is one inch long and each angle is of 60°. It stands as the type of three-sided figures. Previous to this tablet the right angle has been more prominent than the acute angle, but with the equilateral triangle the acute angle stands alone. If compared with the former tablet, the right-angled isosceles, we find that both have three edges and three angles. The right-angled isosceles triangle has two edges of one inch each; the equilateral has all three of one inch. The equilateral triangle has no right angle, but three acute angles. The right-angled isosceles triangle has two acute angles, but they are sharper than those of the equilateral. If the equilateral triangle is laid upon the right-angled isosceles triangle, these facts will be demonstrated. Either angle of the equilateral triangle may be the apex and either side the base. The triangle is deeper from apex to base than the isosceles. Its name is derived from its equal sides and its equal angles are the result of its equal edges. With two triangles we can neither make a square, a triangle or form a right angle. The only figure produced is the rhombus. (Illustration No. 258.) This is a new figure, for while the rhomboid has opposite sides equal and parallel and opposite angles equal, the rhombus has also all its sides equal.

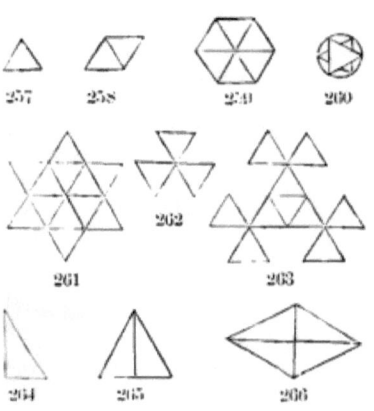

The rhomboid has two acute angles of 45°, two obtuse angles (this name is not to be given the children yet) of 135°. The rhombus, however, has two acute angles of 60°, and two obtuse angles of 120°, twice the size of the first. A number of rhombi may be made and laid together to show a border pattern. Six equilateral triangles united to form a solid center give the hexagon. (Illustration No. 259.) The rhombus and the hexagon are the two most important figures to be obtained from the equilateral triangle. Count the edges of the hexagon and observe which sides are parallel. The angles are twice the angles of the equilateral of which the figure is made, or 120°. It combines three rhombi. Lay the hexagon on paper and draw a circle around it, and also develop it from a circular folding paper, by dividing the paper into halves and then into thirds and folding lines to connect the radii. Placing one equilateral triangle over another to represent a six-pointed star and drawing a line around it touching the points illustrates the circle in another

THE SEVENTH GIFT.

way. (Illustration No. 260.) Three equilateral triangles construct a boat trapezoid; four, a rhomboid or a two-inch equilateral triangle; twelve, a six-pointed star (illustration No. 261); three, a clover design. (Illustration No. 262.)

The forms of life are fewer than with the right-angled isosceles triangle and the forms of beauty are usually three or six sided figures. (Illustration No. 263.)

RIGHT-ANGLED SCALENE TRIANGLE.—The right-angled scalene triangle (illustration No. 264) is obtained by dividing the equilateral triangle from apex to base. The size in common use for the Kindergarten has one edge one inch long, another one and three-fourths inch, or, as we tell the child, "not quite two inches," and the third, or hypothenuse, two inches long. It has one right and two acute angles. The first acute angle is $60°$, and the second one-half of $60°$, or $30°$. The right-angled scalene triangle is another tablet used by the draughtsman in connection with the right-angled isosceles triangle and the T square. These two triangles contain the standard angles, viz.: $90°$, $60°$, $45°$ and $30°$. The child in the Kindergarten becomes familiar with these angles through play and lays the foundation for the geometric work of the school. Froebel believed that much valuable time was lost by the old methods of teaching, and advocated giving the child the beginnings of all things in his play.

When the right-angled scalene triangle is introduced, call attention first to the angles. They should be recognized as one right and two acute angles. One of the acute angles is twice the size of the other. To prove this, join two tablets by their acute angles of $30°$ and place this acute angle formed of two of $30°$ over the angle of $60°$ of a third tablet. They will exactly coincide. (Illustration No. 265.)

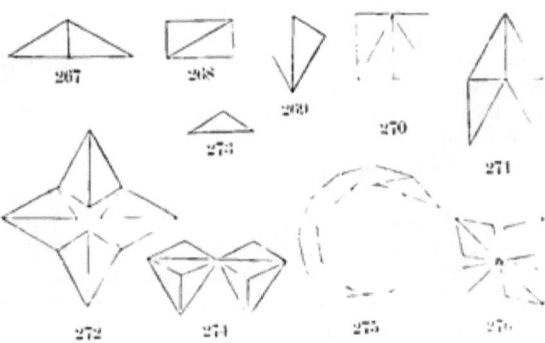

Make an equilateral triangle of right-angled scalene triangles. If two more are made and joined by their bases, the rhomb is formed. (Illustration No. 266.) The obtuse-angled triangle appears when two tablets are joined by their angles of $60°$. (Illustration No. 267.) Joining the longest sides of two tablets so that an angle of $60°$ and one of $30°$ come together gives an oblong (illustration No. 268), but if the longest sides are put together with two angles of $60°$ touching and two of $30°$, the kite trapezium appears. (Illustration No. 269.) Thus two tablets will show an equilateral triangle, an obtuse-angled triangle, two rhomboids, a kite trapezium and an oblong. Three form a shoe trapezoid in three ways, an irregular pentagon, and a large right-angled scalene triangle. Four give an irregular pentagon, a rhombus, two rhomboids and an oblong. Five will afford a shoe trapezoid in two ways, an irregular hexagon and irregular pentagon. (Illustration No. 270). Twelve tablets or six trapeziums form a hexagon. As the sides and angles of the right-angled scalene triangle are all unlike, it allows of greater variety and ingenuity in arrangement than any of the other tablets, while the forms of knowledge demonstrate the important fact that though shape may differ comparative size is the same.

The right-angled scalene triangle may be used to some extent in making forms of life, and some of the forms of knowledge may be used as such. (Illustration No. 271.) The forms of beauty are many and varied. (Illustration No. 272.)

OBTUSE-ANGLED TRIANGLE.—The last plane of the seventh gift is the obtuse-angled triangle. (Illustration No. 273.) This may be formed by joining two right-angled scalene triangles by their short edges, right angles touching and also those of 60°. The angle at the apex is 120° and those at the base are 30° each. Two edges are each one inch long and the base line is one inch and three-fourths long. One angle is obtuse, two are acute. The obtuse-angle is four times the width of the acute angles. The two acute angles together equal one angle of the equilateral triangle and the obtuse angle is twice one angle of the equilateral. If three obtuse-angled triangles are joined with their obtuse angles in the center, they make an equilateral triangle. Two obtuse-angled triangles joined by bases give a rhombus equal and similar to the rhombus made from the equilateral triangle. But if two tablets are joined by equal edges, acute angle meeting obtuse angle, the rhomboid appears. How does this differ from the rhombus? The older children will note the distinction after having repeatedly made the forms and learned the names. Experiment to find how many acute angles will form the right angle and how much larger the obtuse angle is than the right angle. Combine two tablets to make an arrow-head and give it the name trapezium. Place a number of these in a row on the table, with their points in front and their acute angles touching. Lay another row of single tablets back of the first, with their base lines in front. This forms a pleasing border design. (Illustration No. 274.) Twelve tablets may be arranged to approximate a circle. To do this, lay short edge to base, as shown in illustration No. 275. From these twelve tablets make six rhombs and combine these into a six-rayed star.

With each of the tablets it has only been possible to show the fundamental combinations. After these have been mastered, especially the forms of knowledge, almost innumerable designs may be constructed. But as all the after work is based upon the way two or three tablets may be combined, the various arrangements should be first practiced. The *forms of beauty*, as shown in illustration No. 276, lead out from the forms of knowledge.

A sequence may be derived from almost any form of beauty by simply following the rule, mentioned before, of working by opposites. A change at the right demands a similar one at the left. A child accustomed to follow this rule will readily finish a pattern of which one-half is given.

After each tablet with its combinations has been considered, several or all of the six forms should be used to construct one design. For instance, combine squares and half-squares; squares, half-squares and equilaterals; squares, half-squares, rhomboids and scalene triangles and obtuse-angled triangles. The imagination thus becomes stimulated and the outcome in design from these simple materials is almost as varied as the results obtained from stone, brick and mortar.

In some few Kindergarten books it will be found that the tablets differ in dimensions from those here given, but we have chosen the sizes most generally accepted in America. The right-angled scalene triangle here used is one-half the equilateral, thus bringing the angles of all the tablets into symmetry and making them the draughtsman's standard, *i. e.*, 90°, 60°, 45° and 30°. The right-angled scalene triangle sometimes used in Germany is one-half an oblong, with a length twice its width. This makes its angles fractional and destroys the relationship of the tablets. Another improvement is the adoption of neutral colors for the tablets. In this way the figures are laid in light and shade. Then, that the forms may be made permanent, papers, called parquetry papers, are manufactured in the standard colors. When desirable work has been done with the tablets, the design is pasted with these papers upon ruled mounting sheets. Care is taken to give harmonizing colors, thus educating the taste in that direction. The lines on the mounting sheets afford the same guide in the parquetry pasting that the lines on the tables do for laying tablets. The child is pleased with the tangible result and a permanent application of principles is secured.

"All this work tends to increase the power of production, to give exercise in plastic formation and comparison, to so fix the attention on an object that it shall be quickly perceived in its totality as well as in its parts, to train the eye to note relations of size and proportion, to quicken the sense for symmetry and beauty, to give mathematical ideas in preparation for arithmetic and to train the hand. The constant seeking for opposites and their connection leads to clear understanding, and by the orderly succession of things throughout, the foundation for logic is laid, and that by seeing and doing rather than by the abstract formulæ which the school usually inflicts upon the child."

NINTH PAPER.

THE EIGHTH, NINTH AND TENTH GIFTS.

The eighth Kindergarten gift consists of wire rings and half and quarter rings, in three different sizes. (Illustration No. 277.) Froebel chose steel for this gift, as being more practical and keeping its form better than wood. This gift belongs to the third set, because, while it is in itself a whole thing, and is, therefore, concrete, it is used to represent an outline of a surface, and is in that sense abstract. The large rings are usually two inches in diameter, the small ones one inch, and the medium-sized between the two. The seventh gift represented surfaces—the circle and square and the triangular forms derived from them—while the eighth gift shows the boundaries of surfaces. The sphere was the first solid given to the child, and the circle the first surface; therefore, the first boundary must be the curved line or ring. It is suggested by passing the finger around either the ball or the curved surface of the cylinder. In no case should the rings be called circles, for a circle is a surface, as, for instance, the flat face of the cylinder, while the rings are only the boundaries of circles.

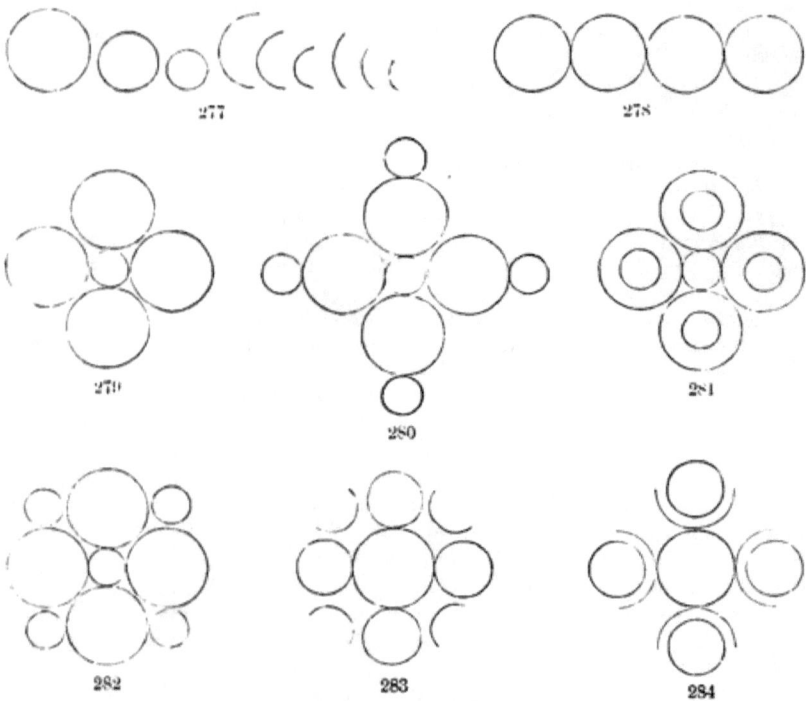

While the eighth gift belongs to the abstract, we do not wait till the child has finished with the building set, but commence giving him the ring, it being a familiar form, even with the first gift. That is, we make each week a whole, and give lessons that follow Froebel's law of progress from the concrete to the abstract.

Begin the lesson on this gift by showing a piece of iron ore, some nails, a knife blade or scissors, a magnet, a small garden-rake, wire and other common objects made of iron. Tell the children that all these things are made of iron, and that iron is dug out of the ground where the Heavenly Father placed it

THE EIGHTH, NINTH AND TENTH GIFTS.

for our use. The place where iron is found in large quantities is called a mine, and the man who goes down into the ground and digs it out is a miner. Iron ore is the name for the pieces as they are dug from the ground. Describe the way the iron-ore is put into furnaces and melted, telling how the other sub-

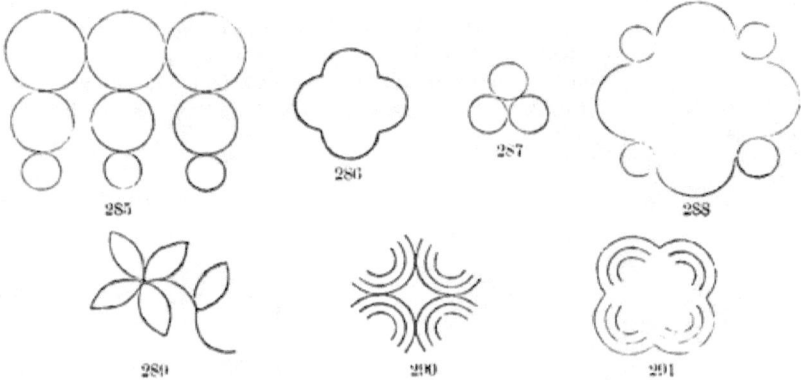

stances mixed with it are taken away when it is very hot, so as to leave it pure. Then give the moulding process and the name pig-iron for the bars of iron when ready to be made up into useful articles. Certain ways of working the iron and of blowing air into the red-hot liquid change it into what is called steel, which

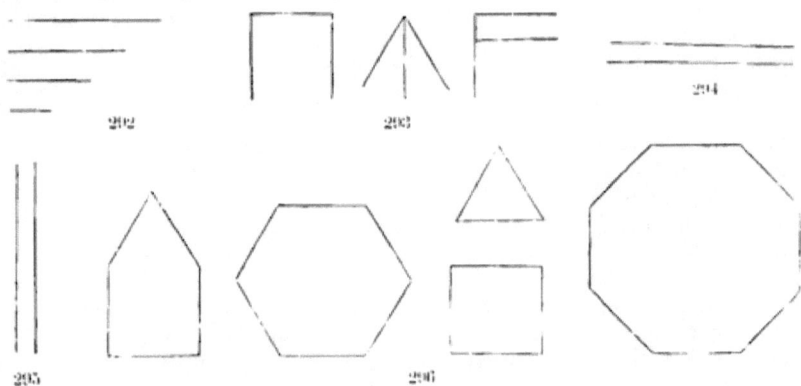

is especially valuable for all cutting utensils, because it can be given a hard, sharp edge. Mention the qualities of iron, as, hard, dark, cold, heavy, ringing, malleable and ductile. This should include rust and the care of iron, its use as a medicine, etc. A description of mines, with the shaft, carts and railways, galleries, miner's lamp, dangers of the miner's life, how the mules are taken up and down, the fact that some of the mules never see the light, respect for the miner, and, above all, the Divine love and wisdom of the Heavenly Father in giving so much iron for our use, may all be touched upon. Make a list of the things made of iron and steel; collect pictures of these articles and of mines and miners for a scrap book. Other gifts and occupations may be brought in to make the miner's cottage, the wagon for the iron ore or the railway track down into the mine, and thus the children will really enter into the life and work of the miner, the uses of iron, and learn lessons never to be forgotten. The more the Kindergartner or mother knows of all the processes involved, the more vivid her representation will be and consequently the more interest the children will manifest.

In many similar ways the Kindergarten cultivates the child's feelings along with his intellect. The schools have trained the intellect to the exclusion of the heart, which neglect shows in the social troubles of the day, the universal brotherhood of man not being recognized. Froebel believed that man must be trained to live in unity with God, with Nature and with his fellow-man. His system begins with the young child and seeks to develop

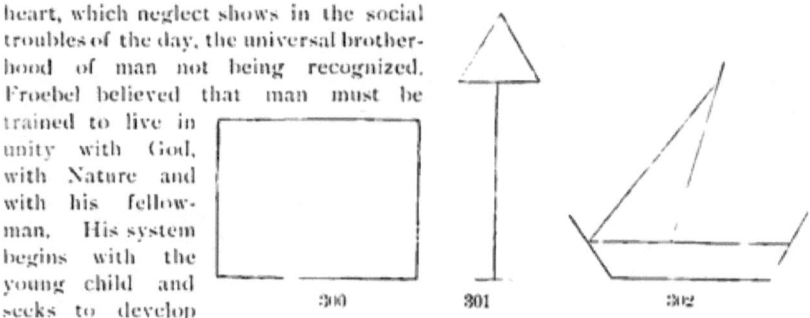

him simultaneously on all the planes of his being, physical, mental and moral.

Present the largest ring first, and call attention to round objects. Consider some of the properties of the ring itself—that it is round, bright, smooth, hard. Place it on the table so that a crossing-place is in the middle of it. Then give an exercise in placing several in a row. (Illustration No. 278.) Remove all but one ring in an orderly way, and let the children spin this and find the "silver ball." Clothe the work with a story to render it more pleasing, and let both the distribution and the gathering up be orderly. Sufficient time should be allowed for this part of the lesson, to avoid hurry and confusion.

Then symmetrical patterns may be developed, using different sizes together

THE EIGHTH, NINTH AND TENTH GIFTS.

to emphasize front and back, right and left. (Illustrations Nos. 279 and 280.) Circular parallel lines would constitute a lesson, also designs bringing out the "slanting opposite." (Illustrations Nos. 281 and 282.) Sequences, involving both the whole and half rings, may be evolved from a single design. (Illustrations Nos. 283 and 284.) Call attention to border patterns in wall decorations. Place three of the largest rings in a horizontal line, touching. Place a similar row of the next size in front of the first row and touching, and again the smallest ones in front. (Illustration No. 285.) Or, they may be placed within each

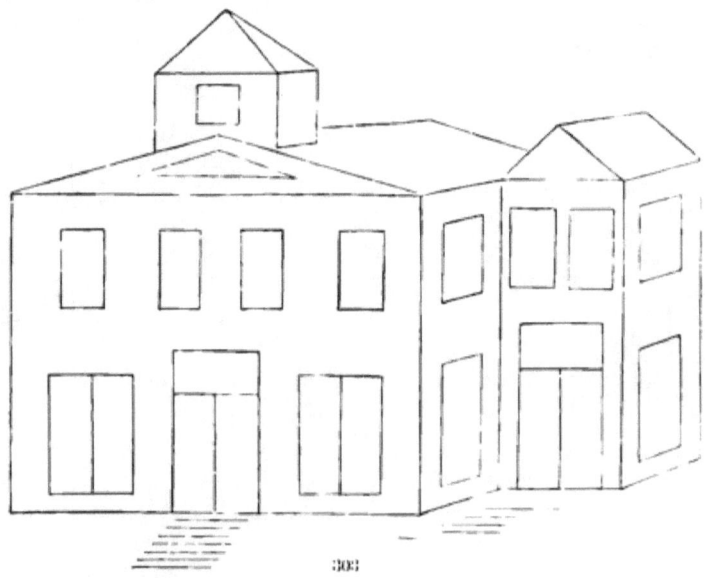

other, all having the same center. By varying this in several ways a sequence can be shown, or, again, the children might be asked to suggest other changes.

Arrange a group of three. (Illustration No. 286.) Several groups placed short distances apart give a pretty border pattern which might afterwards have various embellishments. Half rings are arranged to form a center; this is afterwards added to, or each child is given the same quantity of material, after the center is made, and asked to lay a design at pleasure. (Illustration Nos. 287 and 288.) Forms of life, especially in flower designs, are developed with the quarter rings (illustration No. 289), while illustrations Nos. 290 and 291 show a sequence in half rings. Forms of life in the eighth gift are necessarily limited, and the forms of knowledge are mostly contained in the forms of beauty. As the curved line is the line of beauty, all the forms—even the simplest combinations of a small number of rings or half rings—are forms of beauty and appeal to the child's ideas of the beautiful to a greater degree than anything made from the other gifts. Looking at the beautiful in either art or nature cultivates an appreciation of the good, the true, the sublime; it also fills the mind with right thoughts and leads through material things to the spiritual. Give the child positive education and the negative will take care of itself. A great preacher says: "To fill the mind with beautiful images is the best mode of culture for the very young. Make sure of the imagination and you secure the character." Order, cleanliness and harmony are the prerequisites of beauty.

THE NINTH GIFT.—Wooden sticks in five lengths—one, two, three, four and five inches long—and in the form of square prisms compose the ninth gift. (Illustration No. 292.) They might be of any length and very thin, but are, in fact, made about the thickness of a match to prevent breaking and to be the

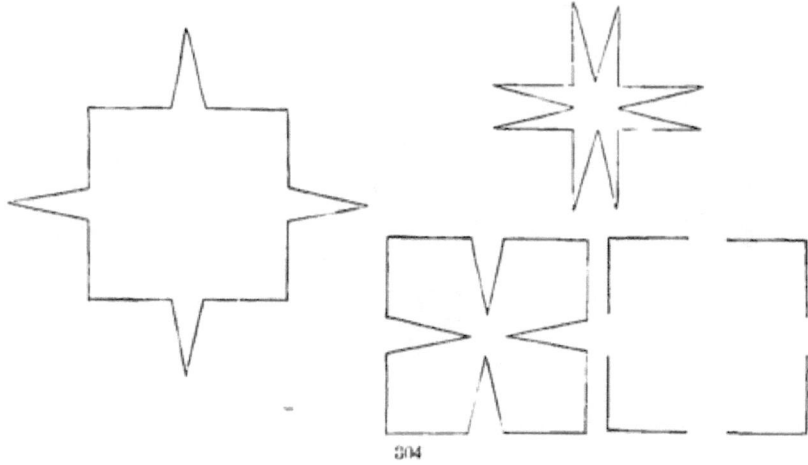

more easily retained in position. They may be obtained in the natural wood colors or in the six colors of the spectrum. The colored sticks are especially pleasing to the children and may be used where color is a point to emphasize, or to represent certain familiar objects, as growing grass or the national flag.

This gift, with the seventh and eighth, belongs to the third or abstract set. It is used to teach the line, and lines teach both direction and enclosure of space. In the stick we have the beginning of outline drawing, including perspective. It embodies the edges of the cube, the limitations of surface.

The first line to be taught is the vertical. This is a most important line. We use terms derived from the vertical line to represent moral qualities, for instance "uprightness," and "erectness," suggesting manliness. The vertical line also has its use in art, for when the artist paints a picture he groups all his figures about a vertical line. When teaching the child the vertical line, tell him that it is derived by dropping a line from the highest point in the sky, called the zenith, to the earth.

THE EIGHTH, NINTH AND TENTH GIFTS.

The next line taught is the horizontal, of which the horizon is the perfection. Connecting the vertical and horizontal lines, we have the slanting line. The ninth gift is used indirectly to teach number, with the elements of addition, subtraction, multiplication and division.

In giving the lessons commence with a two-inch stick. This corresponds to the edge of the second gift cube. Carry the child back to the tree from which the stick came. Gradually, as would be natural, bring out the different kinds of trees he knows and the uses of wood, then the benefits the trees confer in the way of shade, fruit, the gathering of moisture and as affording places for birds to build their nests. Tell about Arbor Day and why it was instituted, thus instilling a love for trees and a desire to take proper care of them. Plant a

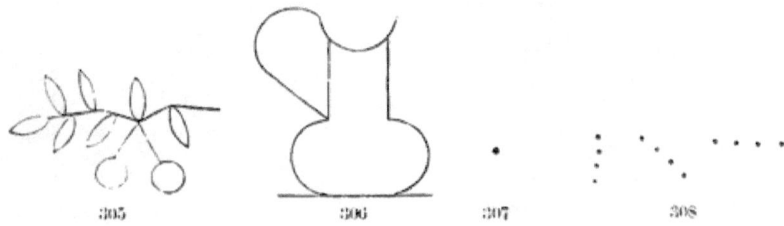

maple seed or an acorn and let the children see it germinate. Teach them how the shoot grows and finally becomes a tree, registering its age by each year adding a ring to its circumference. Give an account of the process necessary to prepare the stick for use, mentioning more or less of the particulars, according to the age and intelligence of the children. Call attention to articles made of wood,

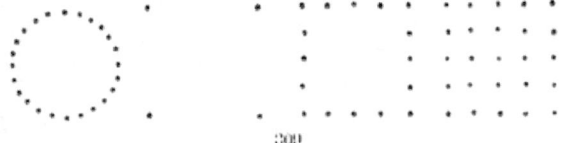

making a list of them. Follow this by exercises in placing a stick, front and back, right and left, and slantwise. To keep in the play spirit and cultivate the imagination, arrange a short sequence in forms of life, using three sticks to make a doorway, an umbrella, a flag. (Illustration No. 293.) Parallel lines, right and left, and front and back, follow. (Illustrations Nos. 294 and 295.) After the lesson has been given with the sticks allow the child to draw what he has made, either on paper or blackboard. Sewing cards are also useful in this connection. Let the various simple forms be sewed, commencing with long vertical, horizontal and slanting lines, with the holes far apart. This occupation will apply the lesson taught by the gift.

The first geometrical figure to be outlined is the square, following the square tablet of the seventh gift and the face of the second gift cube. After the fifth gift has been thus given and the triangle of the seventh gift, use the sticks to lay triangles, pentagons, hexagons, octagons, oblongs, and squares of five different sizes, one within the other. This last would approximate the face of the cube. (Illustrations Nos. 296, 299 and 300.)

Begin to talk about angles in connection with the use of the sticks. Place a piece of folding paper on the table and frame it with two inch sticks. Take up the paper and note that four square corners have thus been made. A square

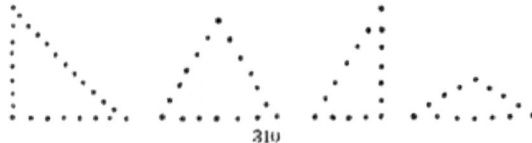

corner is a right angle. Look about the room for right angles and, if necessary, test the angles by seeing if the corner of the paper will fit into them. Follow the right angle by angles larger and smaller than it is. (Illustration No. 297.) Border patterns are pleasing. One may be given alone and afterwards changed, or added to according to fancy to constitute a sequence. Enhance the interest by the use of a story with this lesson. (Illustration No. 298.)

The ninth gift may be used to show an endless variety in forms of life and to some extent in the forms of beauty. These last are more or less geometric patterns, which also contain the forms of knowledge. Illustrations Nos. 301, 302 and 303 show a shovel, a boat and a house, simple examples of forms of life.

Illustration No. 304 is a sequence derived from the square. This would

come under the head of forms of beauty. Forms of beauty made with the third, fourth, fifth, sixth and seventh gifts can also be outlined with the sticks, omitting the perspective.

Sticks and rings are often combined, especially in forms of life, and, being more concrete, are much liked by the youngest children. The example here given is a bunch of cherries and a water pitcher, using both sticks and rings. (Illustrations Nos. 305 and 306.)

THE TENTH GIFT.—Any small seed that may be easily handled singly and that will remain in place will do for the tenth gift. (Illustration No. 307). Most Kindergartners select lentils, which belong to the bean family, as being well adapted to the purpose. As the point has neither length, breadth nor thickness we indicate it by a dot. Tell the child what the seed is. He will have a curiosity to know and this curiosity should be satisfied. Then plant some of the seeds that he may see them grow. It is also well for the Kindergartner to make a collection of seeds.

THE EIGHTH, NINTH AND TENTH GIFTS.

The tenth is the last Kindergarten gift, and, with the seventh, eighth and ninth, constitutes the third or abstract set. In the gifts we begin with solids, undivided for the first two, divided for the next four, with the seventh introducing surfaces, the boundaries of the solid. Then the eighth and ninth gifts emphasized lines, the limits of surfaces, while in the tenth, points, the limitations of the line, are indicated. As a line is a succession of points, the tenth gift is used to represent the line. Anything that can be indicated with the line can be shown with points. The tenth gift may represent the line or the ends of the line, giving at the same time direction. (Illustration No. 308.) It may represent a surface, outline a surface, or indicate a surface. (Illustration No. 309.) By this means the forms or faces of the preceding gifts are emphasized with the particular character of each. The same plan is also carried out to indicate the planes of the seventh gift. (Illustration No. 310.)

312 313

The particular use of the tenth gift, however, is to emphasize the point in itself and in its relation to lines, surfaces and solids. In the cube, for instance, it shows where three lines meet and is a corner. The seed should be introduced to represent the point in connection with sticks. Give each child a two-inch stick and also some seeds. Place the stick front and back, and let two seeds be placed in a similar position at one side to indicate the ends. Then add more seeds until a line is made of points. Afterwards make horizontal and slanting lines in the same way. Many of the lessons given with sticks can afterwards be rehearsed with seeds. A border pattern is shown in illustration No. 312; forms of life, like the rake and umbrella in illustration No. 311; leaves, flowers and animal forms are also represented, or a story may be carried out. (Illustration No. 313.) Use the rings of the eighth gift for a border to the child's flower-garden. Put seeds in the rings to represent the planting of flower-seeds. This especially delights the child. (Illustration No. 314.) The seeds are also used in the mass to make pictures of streams, houses, animals or trees. (Illustration No. 315.)

SUMMARY.—Summing up the gifts, we find them classified as follows:

FIRST SET.—Nursery gifts, symbolic, containing undivided solids and teaching color and form. The first gift consists of six soft worsted balls in prismatic colors. The second gift consists of the wooden ball, cube and cylinder.

SECOND SET.—Building gifts, analytic and synthetic, containing divided solids. The third gift consists of a two-inch wooden cube divided into eight one-inch cubes. The fourth gift consists of a two-inch wooden cube divided into eight bricks, each 2 x 1 x ½ inches in size. The fifth gift is a three-inch wooden cube divided into twenty-seven one-inch cubes. Three of these are divided by a diagonal cut into half-cubes and three by two diagonal cuts into quarter-cubes. The sixth gift is a three-inch wooden cube divided into twenty-seven bricks of the same dimensions as the fourth gift. Three of these bricks are divided by a lengthwise cut into halves and three breadthwise into halves.

THIRD SET.—The abstract set is synthetic, showing surfaces, boundaries of surfaces, limitations of boundaries. The seventh gift consists of thin pieces of wood in six forms, viz : circle, square, half-square, equilateral triangle, right-angled scalene triangle, obtuse-angled triangle, to represent surfaces, all being derived from the circle. The eighth gift consists of wire rings, half and quarter rings in three sizes, and shows the boundary of a ball. The ninth gift consists of sticks of different lengths to show lines, the boundaries of surfaces. The tenth gift consists of seeds for the point, element of lines, limitation of boundaries.

THE FOUR APPLE TREES.*—Many years ago there was a man who wanted to have a beautiful orchard. So he sent for some young trees, knowing that he

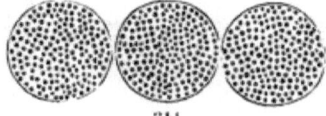
314

315

should not have to wait so long for his orchard if he planted trees which had already had a good start in growing. Unfortunately, however, the trees arrived just at the time when the man was obliged to leave home for several days. He was afraid the trees would not live unless they were planted very soon, and yet he could not stay to attend to them. Just then a man came along who wanted work.

"Do you know how to set out fruit trees?" asked the owner.

"Yes, indeed," said the other man.

"Then you may stay and set out these young apple-trees. I am going to have an orchard, and I have marked the places for the trees with stones."

By-and-by the owner of the trees came back and went to look at his orchard. He had been gone four days.

"How is this?" he asked, "only four trees set out?"

"That is all I had time for," answered the other man. "I dug great holes, so that the roots might be spread out to the farthest tip ; I hauled rich earth from the woods, so that the trees might have the best of food ; I set the trees straight and filled the holes with care. This took all the time, but these four trees are well planted."

* From *In the Child's World*, by Emile Poulsson.

"That is too slow a way for me," said the owner. "I can plant the whole orchard in one day."

So he went to work and planted the other trees in his own way. He did not dig the holes large enough or deep enough, and, therefore, many of the little root mouths were broken off when he set the trees into the holes. He did not take pains to get soft, rich earth to fill the holes, and so the trees could not have as good food as they needed. The poor little trees lived for a while, but they were never very strong, never bore very good apples, and at last were cut down. Finally all that was left of the orchard was the four trees which had been planted with such faithfulness and care. These four trees are now older than an old man, and have been bearing delicious great apples.

TENTH PAPER.

THE OCCUPATIONS.

THE New Education is designed to produce spontaneous action and a creative, inventive spirit by encouraging the child to embody in some form the ideas he gets from inanimate things. The "occupations" of the Kindergarten secure this result, because they apply the principles learned from the gifts and give permanence to their various transformations.

Froebel chose the sphere, cube and cylinder as typifying the forms of Nature. When the gifts are presented in the Kindergarten, they are analyzed as to their properties, their activities, and their resemblance to the forms of the heavenly bodies, of minerals and of life. But we constantly find these forms or their parts combined in Nature, not only in the works of the Creator, but also in those of His creatures. Thus the ant lays out her opposite lines with mathematical precision, and forms a surface which is to her a "habitation and a home"; the bird weaves her straw and threads into a spherical form to afford shelter for her young. Man, too, finds himself in a world of ever-varying wants, and he must study how to meet them. He is a "creative being," but he does not really create anything. He only combines what a loving Father, who created the world and "saw that it was good," has placed at his disposal. These combinations of man we call his occupations.

The savage found it necessary to provide himself with food, clothing and protection from the weather, so he constructed rude mills for grinding grain, knives for destroying game and shaping garments of skin, and chisels, hammers, and other tools for building purposes; and the ingenuity of man has ever since been devoted to meeting these same needs. New possibilities open, he draws ever nearer to the beautiful, and so there comes an improved and extended mental condition. The spread of wants takes a direction other than the material. New duties arise, and new agencies are found to perform them. Thus we speak of our food processes, our applied science, the arts of war and of design, all to satisfy the needs of advancing civilization.

So has the development of the human race gone steadily on. "Cursed is the ground for thy sake," and "In the sweat of thy face shalt thou eat bread," says the old dispensation, to provide man a means of regeneration. Froebel, who had carefully watched childish instincts manifested through play, declared that

ILLUSTRATION No. 316.

ILLUSTRATION No. 317.

ILLUSTRATION No. 318.

"the child develops as the race has done," and improvised the occupations of the Kindergarten (epitomized industries of the human race) as aids to the orderly development or true education of the child.

In this work of development the hand plays an important part. The occupations or manual exercises of the Kindergarten train the hand, and with it the eye, and so the whole intelligent being. Dr. Murray, in his *Handbook of Psychology*, says: "The hand shows the superiority of man over the lower animals, and

ILLUSTRATION No. 319.

ILLUSTRATION No. 320.

there seems to be a proportion between the development of general intelligence and the development of touch in the animal kingdom."

For the best results the hand must be trained while the muscles are flexible and before the fingers have become set and stiff. There will be no limit to manual dexterity if training is commenced early and carried on gradually and systematically. As we grow older, things that could easily have been learned in childhood are acquired more slowly and only with the greatest pains. Besides, the child is not generally conscious of himself; he wants to do new things and strives to imitate what he sees going on around him. This is the striving of his creative power.

Early training is a great help toward skilled labor. European nations have long since recognized this fact, and have established technical schools to train the hand in various industrial pursuits, the gratifying results of which clearly appear in their manufactories. Here in the United States it has been acknowledged that children who have had the Kindergarten training are able to take up trades earlier and to do better work than those who have not. President

THE OCCUPATIONS.

Hunter, of the Normal College of New York City, says: "Comparing children who have had the benefits of the Kindergarten and those who have not, it has been proved that the Kindergarten children are brighter, quicker and more intelligent; and especially afterwards, in all such work as writing and drawing, requiring muscular power and flexibility in the wrist and fingers, they preëminently excel." How could it be otherwise?

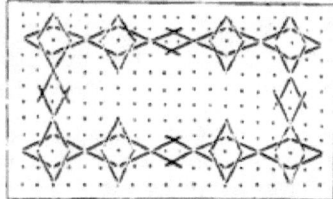
ILLUSTRATION No. 321.

Trainers of animals always commence with their dumb pupils when very young, a lion-tamer taking his dangerous subject while only a few months old. It was recently announced in a well-known journal that a Kindergarten for colts had been established in California. These valuable babies are there taken into a special room for a short time each day and taught confidence in their trainer and to use properly and economically their powers in running and trotting.

"For every talent in man, means of development are offered in the Kindergarten." Formerly it was thought not necessary to give a child certain trainings unless he was to be a specialist, but Froebel declares that he has a right to be developed on all sides first, in order that he may attain roundness of character and be fully prepared for life. Moreover, some talents do not show themselves spontaneously, except in the few cases where they are so strongly marked that they must find expression.

The Kindergarten occupations not only improve all talents, but if carried into the school, often indicate special fitness for certain pursuits. This is one of the most distinctive advantages of the Kindergarten, as is shown by the fact

ILLUSTRATION No. 322.

ILLUSTRATION No. 323.

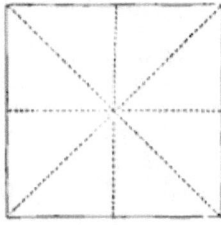
ILLUSTRATION No. 324.

that many a scholar who has not had such preliminary training leaves school without knowing what particular calling he would enjoy or is fitted for. He allows the choice of his field of labor to be governed by chance or circumstances, and too often realizes afterward that he has "mistaken his vocation." It must not be forgotten that these occupations are a means, not only of physical, but also of intellectual, social and spiritual development, and so are well fitted to produce roundness of character; for "the mere scholar and the mere hand-laborer are both incomplete human beings."

The more muscles that are brought into play, the better will be the physical development and health. "Two or three repetitions of an impression are sometimes enough to produce a habit in a baby," and thus awkward and unnecessary movements may be easily overcome and the continued growth of muscles used in after life insured, while a decided help is given in all sports and games that require correctness of eye and quickness of hand. The child trained on Froebel's gifts and occupations will acquire a skilful use of his hands and a habit of accurate measurement with the eye which will be his possession for life.

A child is often called restless and naughty, when the fault lies in the fact that he has no suitable outlet for his activity. A normally constituted child likes to really work and is always asking or seeking to "do something." Refer-

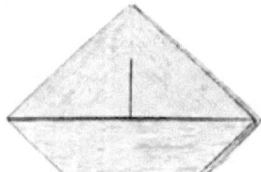

ILLUSTRATION No. 325.

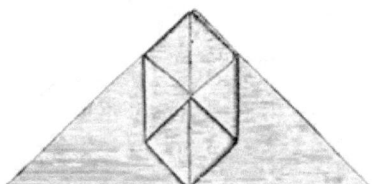

ILLUSTRATION No. 326.

ring to this general quality of childhood, a well-known writer says: "The exceptions should be carefully watched as probably indicating some morbid condition of the brain or the physical indolence which, in childhood, means delicate health." If no proper sphere of action is given, this activity becomes destructive. The child breaks his toy apart because he wants to work upon it and is irritated and disgusted at the result.

As urged above, many intellectual and moral qualities are brought into play by the occupations. The child must observe and execute accurately; he must have patience and perseverance to complete the work, and these two qualities help to control his temper and make him forbearing with his companions. He respects himself because he can do something well, learns to respect labor, and a love of the beautiful is cultivated, leading to the Giver of all that is good.

Poverty and crime are often the result of a lack of training to do any work well. Prisons and reformatory schools are conducting Kindergartens of manual training, because so many of their inmates are incompetent to perform skilled labor. Why not establish Kindergartens and technical schools instead of paying taxes to maintain prisons and reformatories?

The most common Kindergarten occupations are sewing, weaving, paper folding, cutting and pasting, peas-work, clay-modelling, parquetry, drawing, pricking, stringing balls, cubes and cylinders, stringing straws and colored papers, making paper chains, and the intelligent use of the peg-board.

THE OCCUPATIONS.

SEWING.—The materials for this occupation are easily found and the directions are simple. Bristol cards about four inches square come in packages of one hundred, and upon them circles, designs in circles and outlines of utensils, fruits and flowers may be pricked. Lay the cards on felt or a cushion, and make the holes with a Kindergarten pricking needle or a hat-pin. Do not make the holes too close together, as fine work is hurtful, and use appropriate colors.

ILLUSTRATION No. 327.

ILLUSTRATION No. 328.

Cards are also sold already pricked in squares for vertical, horizontal and oblique lines and their combinations; larger cards bear pictures of animals, trades, houses, etc., the outlines being marked for the holes to be pricked. For older children there are sequences in natural history and botany.

Sometimes this occupation is overdone because it is easy, the child being allowed to work at it too long. Sewing helps to an exact perception of colors and their shades, and it also requires neatness, precision, economy and obedience. (Illustrations Nos. 316 to 321.)

WEAVING.—In weaving, the cultivation of the æsthetic sense should always be kept in mind, and good forms and combinations of colors should, therefore, be used; moreover, after-utility should be considered. Leather mats and

ILLUSTRATION No. 329.   ILLUSTRATION No. 330.   ILLUSTRATION No. 331.

wooden strips are sometimes used in the beginning to teach the use of the fingers and the principle of over and under, and then under and over. Mothers can cut mats out of stiff paper for this first use. The same principle underlies the Kindergarten weaving as that which governs the manufacture of fabrics. A single strand is weak in itself, but a combination of strands is strong. "Union is strength," is an axiom at the foundation of church, home and state. In the mat, the strips and the needle we have the warp, woof and shuttle.

Commencing with the simple, one over, one under, which one child told his mother was "just like darning stockings," other combinations are formed which lead to the most intricate designs. (Illustrations Nos. 322 and 323).

Weaving cultivates an appreciation of numbers, requires lightness and strength, because of the delicate materials combined to make a firm surface, exemplifies the connection of opposites, gives perception of color, and increases self-control and patience.

A torn or wrinkled mat cannot be mended to look as good as new, and so the child must take the *consequences* of his own wrong-doing. Have the child do as much of the work as possible in pushing up the strips, cutting and pasting.

The mats and strips are sold together in packages. The strips have a narrow margin, and it is better for the child to cut or tear them off one at a time. The needle commonly used and several designs are illustrated in the "Christmas Work."

PAPER FOLDING.—The material for this purpose consists of squares, triangles and circles of paper. A ground form is the starting-point, and from

ILLUSTRATION No. 332.

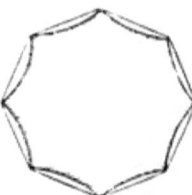

ILLUSTRATION No. 333.

ILLUSTRATION No. 334.

this by slight changes a variety of figures are made. Sequences are thus emphasized and the relationship that mathematics bear to artistic production is indicated.

The *first ground form* in the square paper consists of the diameters and diagonals, or, as the child calls them, two books and two shawls. (Illustrations Nos. 324 to 326.)

The *second ground form* in the square paper is as follows: Fold the first, then fold the corners in the center, reverse, and fold the corners again to the center. When open, this will show quite prominently a square in the center with a diagonal line running out from each corner of the square. Crease the diagonal lines and the paper will look like a stiff table-cloth. This is called the table-cloth ground form or fundamental, and from it follow many of the forms given. (Illustrations Nos. 327 to 331.)

In the triangle the designs follow from the corners folded into the center, and in the circle from the diameter. (Illustration No. 332.)

By means of these simple pieces of paper are illustrated geometrical figures, forms of crystals, and objects of life, such as houses, tools, etc. Only the simpler forms are given to young children, but the occupation joined with drawing follows on into the school. (Illustration No. 333.)

Paper-folding requires careful handling, as well as correct sight for laying the papers straight and making the patterns regular. It brings out in another form lessons learned from the gifts, testing what has been acquired and fixing it more thoroughly.

THE OCCUPATIONS.

PAPER-CUTTING AND PASTING.—A square of paper is folded by a certain rule and cut on certain lines, and the pieces thus cut are then pasted in symmetrical forms on sheets of paper. For simple designs the folds are the two diameters, and then folding to make a square one-fourth the size of the original one. Directions and illustrations will be given in the next paper, that on "Christmas Work." Other papers can be bought already lined on one triangular fold. The cuts that can be made are innumerable, while the work proves most fascinating to the bright and ingenious child and leads to conventional designing. (Illustration Nos. 334 and 335.)

Paper-cutting inculcates political economy, because each piece that is cut must be saved and made use of in the design formed, as otherwise the proportion would be spoiled. It also teaches that everything is good if in its rightful place, shows the relation of parts and whole, and cultivates a perception of harmony of form and color. It also leads away from destructiveness by providing a proper use for the scissors on suitable material. Use round-pointed scissors.

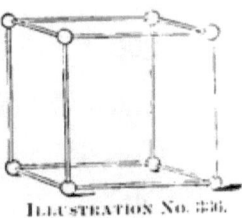

ILLUSTRATION No. 335.

ILLUSTRATION No. 336.

Free-hand cutting commences with figures which have both sides alike, such as vases, etc., and leads gradually out into more intricate designs. It is used in the school with drawing. A young child may commence by cutting out pictures having broad outlines. Give short cuts at first.

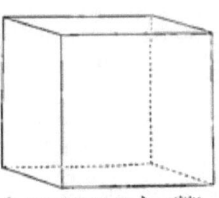

ILLUSTRATION No. 337.

ILLUSTRATION No. 338.

ILLUSTRATION No. 339.

PEAS-WORK.—This occupation consists of reproducing mathematical forms, forms of crystals, and common objects by means of sticks and peas. These make the skeletons of the forms or objects, and the chief use of the work is the help it gives in analysis and preparation for perspective drawing. (Illustration No. 336.)

CLAY-MODELLING.—Froebel said, "What children universally love to do must have in it some educational value," and so he gave to the little ones the gratification of working in plastic substances. Commencing with the ball, cube and cylinder, the child is led out into the world of industry and art around him. (Illustrations Nos. 337 to 339.) He learns to express himself, to embody the sense of form he has received from the gifts and other Kindergarten work. This occupation increases the natural disposition toward art in one child and shows whether another possesses any such tendency. It leads directly to casting, modelling, pottery, sculpture and architectural ornamentation. It trains both hands, counteracts the tendency to destroy fragile objects, and also insures neatness, since good work cannot be done with muddy fingers. A small child must necessarily be allowed to roll and pat his clay, but an older one should learn as soon as possible to use thumb and fingers only.

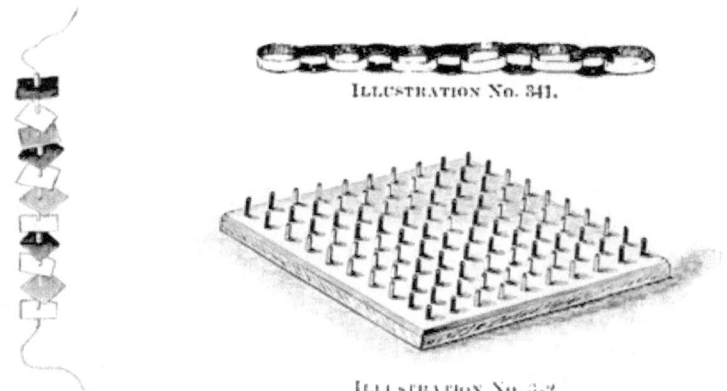

ILLUSTRATION No. 341.

ILLUSTRATION No. 342.

ILLUSTRATION No. 340.

PARQUETRY.—This is the pasting of small squares, triangles and circles into designs, and will be given in connection with the seventh gift.

DRAWING.—The drawing of the Kindergarten can only lay the foundation for future artistic work. The Froebel drawing consisted of lines and designs on netted paper, but most Kindergartens now teach free-hand drawing by letting the child draw the ball or cube as he sees it, and also reproduce patterns he has laid with the sticks or parquetry. Dotted paper and slates are also used for practice in drawing lines. Outline drawing consists of laying down pasteboard patterns of geometrical forms, flowers, leaves or animals, and drawing around them. Some finishing touches may be afterward put in. After a pattern has been used many times, the figure may be drawn without it.

PRICKING.—On account of injury to the eyes resulting from fine work, and the danger of wounding the fingers with the needle, this occupation has been discarded in many Kindergartens.

CHRISTMAS WORK.

The *stringing of balls, cubes and cylinders* was mentioned in connection with the second gift. The same work may be done by alternating short straws and small colored circles. When the materials are made at home, wet the straws before cutting. (Illustration No. 340.)

Small *strips of paper* may be pasted together to represent a *chain*. (Illustration No. 341.)

THE PEG-BOARD.—This is used to teach position and numbers. It is a smooth board measuring 6 x 6 inches, checkered with half-inch squares, and with holes at the corners of these squares to receive pegs. (Illustration No. 342.)

Preserve the child's work in some form—either in a scrap-book or in the shape of presents to friends.

The intention of all the occupations is to lead the child to know and express himself. Much care is necessary to adapt them to the child and to connect them properly with the gifts.

ELEVENTH PAPER.

CHRISTMAS WORK.

"Oh, clap, clap the hands,
And sing out with glee,
For Christmas is coming,
And merry are we!"

THE Christmas work in the Kindergarten follows naturally from the occupations just described in the preceding paper, hence a description will here be given of the articles that may be made in the occupation work and given away to their friends by the children at Christmas time.

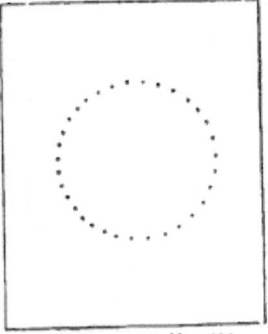

ILLUSTRATION NO. 343.

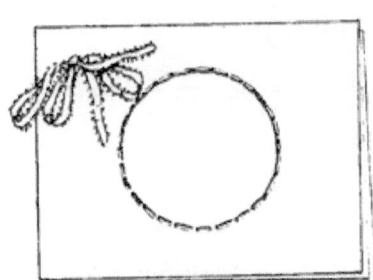

ILLUSTRATION NO. 344.

In the Kindergarten celebration of Christmas the pleasure of giving is emphasized, while the idea that presents are to be received is kept in the background. Each child works with enthusiasm, for is he not to give mama the joy of having something made by her darling's own little hands? And though the sewing knots and the weaving goes wrong with nearly every strand, he patiently rectifies the faults and perseveres to the end. Appropriate songs are

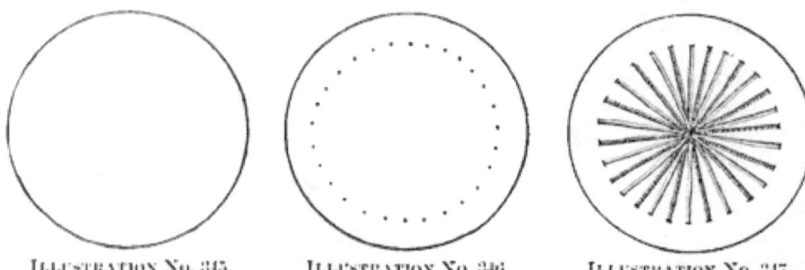

ILLUSTRATION No. 345.   ILLUSTRATION No. 346.   ILLUSTRATION No. 347.

learned, stories of the Christ child are told, and the very atmosphere seems filled with the message, "It is more blessed to give than to receive." Thus, while the eye and hand are being trained, the love of the beautiful developed and ingenuity fostered, the whole moral nature is being unconsciously elevated.

Mrs. Alice H. Putnam says in one of her lectures: "The whole matter of moral training seems so tremendous, it seems so hard a thing to get at the individual conscience of each child, that every earnest person must at one time

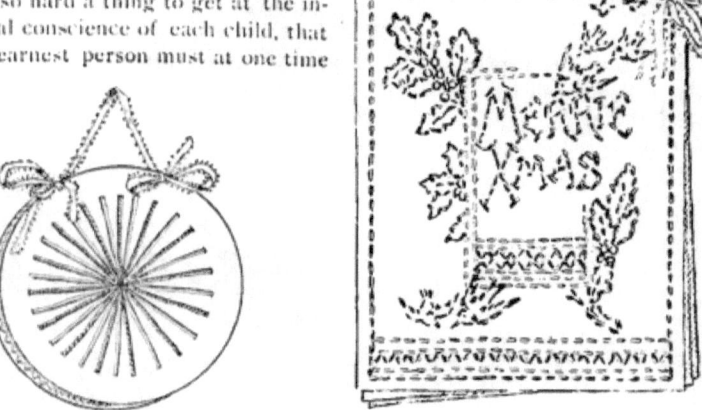

ILLUSTRATION No. 348.   ILLUSTRATION No. 349.

or another ask, 'Who is sufficient for these things?' What if the answer should be as of old, that they are hid from the wise and prudent and revealed unto babes? Is it too much to believe that certain lines of work in which we know children are always interested might be so managed as to embody some of these great lessons? Is it claiming too much for the element of color, for instance, to say that a right use of colors—not merely a power to recognize the colors of

CHRISTMAS WORK.

the prism, but such a use as will bring the child into the very closest contact with harmonized tints and shades, will have a refining tendency? Will it not help to soften that which is harsh, to modify coarse tastes, and will it not begin to fill the heart as it does the eye? Will not the actual making of symmetrical forms at least make the child more conscious of that which is out of proportion, and if he knows the law by which he can gain the result which has pleased him, will he not be apt to follow it occasionally, at least? If he once feels the delight which comes

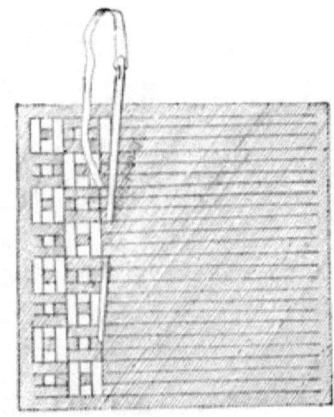

ILLUSTRATION No. 350.   ILLUSTRATION No. 351.   ILLUSTRATION No. 352.

from giving that which he has himself created to another, will he not be the more ready to bring the same happiness again and again?"

One of the easiest occupations for Christmas work is that of sewing, and even its simplest products may be offered as gifts. The four-inch square of white

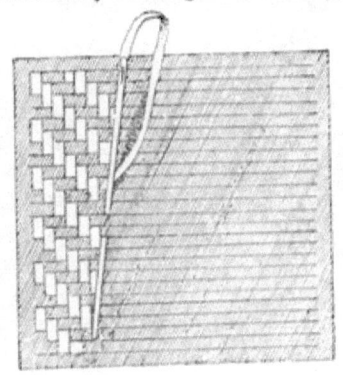

ILLUSTRATION No. 353.   ILLUSTRATION No. 354.

paper upon which the little three-year-old's fingers have sewed a circle in red is not thrown away; two squares of blotting-paper are placed at the back, the three are fastened together at one corner by a ribbon bow, and the result is a gift, which, though exceedingly simple, may express as much love and require as much effort by the child as many a larger and more costly one. (Illustrations Nos. 343 and 344.)

A trifle more skill may be required in the making of a needle-case. Cut two circular sections of stiff Bristol-board, prick a hole at the center of each and

ILLUSTRATION No. 355.

corresponding holes near their edges, and sew with two colors alternately, producing a wheel effect. Cover the wrong sides with colored paper cut the same size and paste on. For the needles, provide two pieces of flannel, either white or in a delicate shade of pink or blue; pink the edges, place them between the cardboards, and fasten all together in two places with ribbon bows. Geometrical designs, and outline pictures of fruit, flowers and animals may be used in similar ways, and large and beautiful patterns, already stamped for pricking, can be purchased at Kindergarten supply stores. (Illustrations Nos. 345 to 349.)

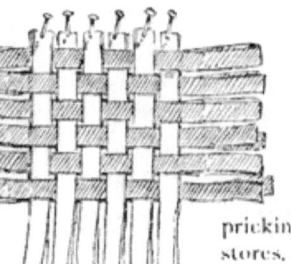

ILLUSTRATION No. 356.

ILLUSTRATION No. 357.

ILLUSTRATION No. 358.

Weaving also yields many pretty articles for presents. One of the first that comes to mind is the calendar, for which mats of any size may be used. The

CHRISTMAS WORK.

ones illustrated are seven inches square, with one-eighth inch strips. A spring needle is made for the weaving. (Illustration No. 350.) The colors here used are maroon and green, purple and yellow, and a reddish-brown and yellow. The pattern for the calendar is as follows:

Over 3, under 3, for the first strand.
" 1, " 1, " " second "
" 3, " 3, " " third "

This completes a square, and the order should then be reversed, thus:

Under 3, over 3, for the fourth strand.
" 1, " 1, " " fifth "
" 3, " 3, " " sixth "

ILLUSTRATION NO. 350.

Then work as at first, and so alternate to the end. When the mat is finished and the edges pasted, fasten a small calendar in the center by means of brads, and tie the mat to a piece of stiff cardboard by two bows of ribbon, leaving a loop for hanging. (Illustrations Nos. 351 and 352.)

 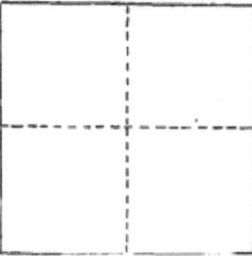 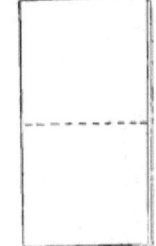

ILLUSTRATION NO. 360.   ILLUSTRATION NO. 361.   ILLUSTRATION NO. 362.

Woven mats make pretty sachet-holders. Weave a design of two and two in steps, as follows:

Over 2, under 2.
Under 1, over 2, under 2.
Under 2, over 2, under 2, to the left.
Over 1, under 2.
Over 2, under 2.

Repeat the above, paste neatly, fill with cotton sprinkled with sachet powder and tie with ribbon. Or, use the pattern,

Over 2, under 1.
Under 2, over 1.

and paste together like a roller; put inside a sheet of tissue paper slashed at the ends and extending beyond the mat, and fill with powdered cotton. Tie ribbon about the ends, and arrange a loop for suspension. (Illustrations Nos. 353 to 355.)

Half-inch strips of pretty papers are sold for free-hand weaving. These may be braided into mats for lamps, and their ends may be cut into narrower strips and curled. (Illustration No. 356.) The two colors used for illustration

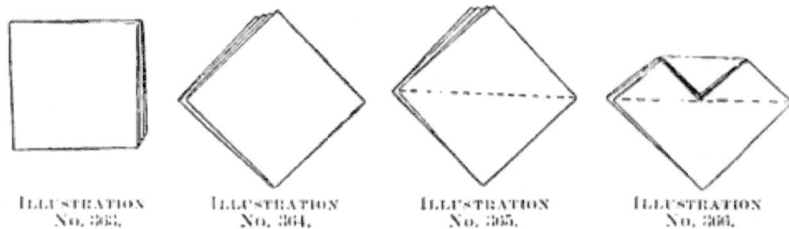

ILLUSTRATION No. 363. ILLUSTRATION No. 364. ILLUSTRATION No. 365. ILLUSTRATION No. 366.

are red and white. Double the red strips and pin them close together to a large pad or cushion, with the closed and open ends in alternation. To make the cushion or pad, pin a towel tightly about a large, flat book. Commence

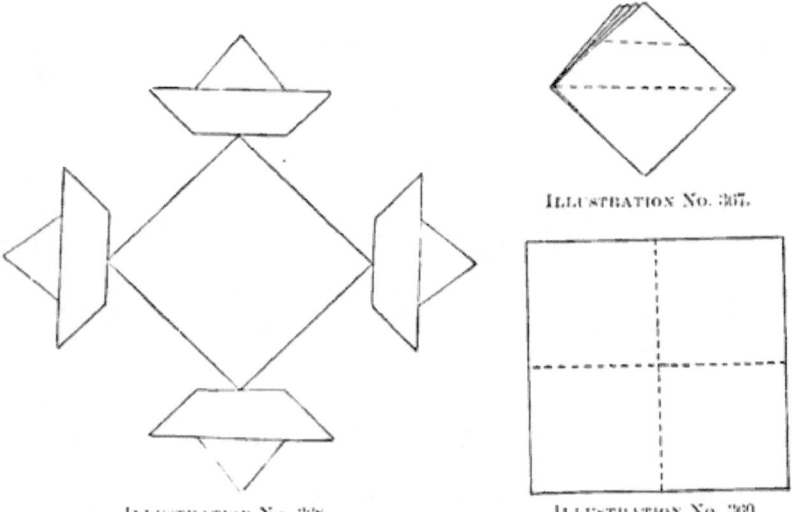

ILLUSTRATION No. 367.

ILLUSTRATION No. 368. ILLUSTRATION No. 369.

with one of the other strips at the right, and put it first over and then between those pinned to the cushion. Then begin at the left and weave similarly toward the right. (Illustration No. 357.)

The handkerchief case shown at illustrations Nos. 358 and 359 has twelve strips each way. Ends are slipped in on the inside, and pasted near the edge

CHRISTMAS WORK.

of the mat. Two mats of the same size are made and are interlaced together with ribbon at one side, a bow being formed at each end, and one corner is turned back and fastened with a bow. The case is then complete.

An oblong mat may be woven and fastened tightly about a small drinking glass, and the ends may be arranged in small loops at the top and may be cut

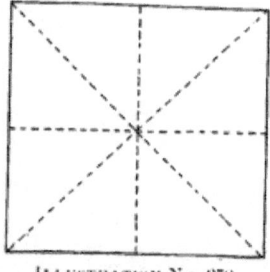

ILLUSTRATION No. 370.

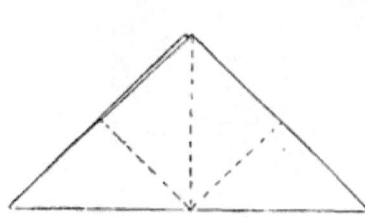

ILLUSTRATION No. 371.

and curled at the bottom. Red and black dress braid will make convenient strips for a child to practise with.

Paper-cutting furnishes a great deal of training and amusement for little folks, and the designs may be used in various ways. The Kindergarten papers for this purpose are four inches square. (Illustration No. 360.) For simple

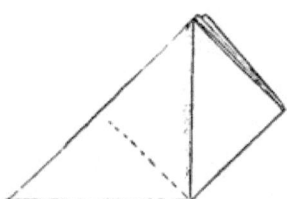

ILLUSTRATION No. 372.

ILLUSTRATION No. 373.

ILLUSTRATION No. 374.

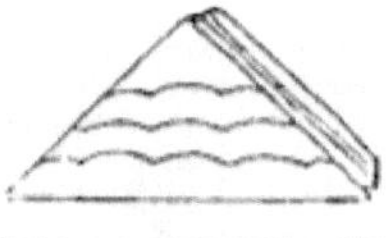

ILLUSTRATION No. 375.

designs, fold a paper twice at the center (illustration No. 361), making four squares, or "windows" as the children sometimes call them. Fold together first (illustration No. 362), and then this half together (illustration No. 363). Illustration No. 364 shows a closed corner; hold this closed corner down, and draw a line from corner to corner, right and left (illustration No. 365). Fold the upper point down to the line (illustration No. 366), cut on these lines (illustration No. 367), and make the design (illustration No. 368). Any number of designs will follow from the different cuts on the small square. More difficult ones may be readily devised. Fold the paper into halves both ways (illustration No. 369), and then diagonally both ways (illustration No. 370). Place the paper in diagonal folds longest line down (illustration No. 371). Fold both ends up to top or apex (illustrations Nos. 372 and 373). Turn with base down (illustration No. 374). Draw the part circles as shown at illustration No. 375, cut on these lines, and arrange and paste the pattern. Place tissue paper at the back to be used for shaving, fasten with ribbon, (illustration No. 376), and form a loop for hanging. This gift the children like to make for their fathers.

ILLUSTRATION No. 376.

A great variety of articles may be constructed in parquetry work, which is derived from the planes of the seventh gift. Papers in different colors may be purchased, cut in small circles, squares, half-squares, equilateral triangles, obtuse-angled triangles, right-angled scalene triangles and rhomboids. These will form many pleasing designs, and may be used to decorate match-holders, photograph-frames, boxes, etc. To make a pretty little match-holder, first cut from stiff Bristol-board an equilateral triangle measuring ten

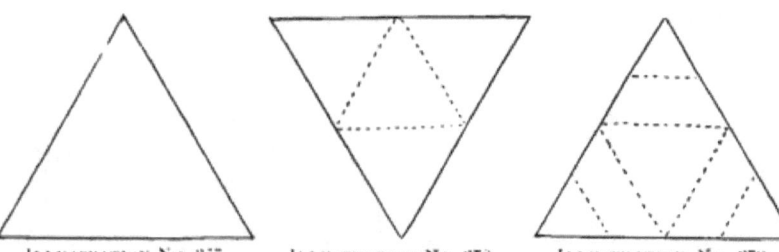

ILLUSTRATION No. 377.   ILLUSTRATION No. 378.   ILLUSTRATION No. 379.

inches at each side. (Illustration No. 377.) Find the center of each side, and draw lines between these points, thus forming an equilateral triangle with five-inch sides inside the large triangle (illustration No. 378). The inner triangle will form the bottom of the ornament, and the side triangles the sides. Now, to leave an opening at the top, fold the points almost down to the bottom (illustration No. 379). Tie together with a bow of ribbon at each corner, form a suspension loop, and decorate the sides with a contrasting color. As a whole, this is an excellent problem in inventional geometry. An artistic match-holder may be made of pale pink Bristol-board with dark triangles. (Illustration No. 380.)

ILLUSTRATION No. 380.

TWELFTH PAPER.

THE GAMES.

THE games are the organized plays of the Kindergarten, the dramatic personification of what the child sees in the life of the world about him. Play, or the play spirit, is the basis here as in all Kindergarten work. Play is universal. We find pictures on the old Egyptian monuments of children playing. In all countries and all ages not merely children but grown persons as well, find play, or some form of recreation, necessary to health and happiness. Journals of hygiene advise open air sports as the best gymnastics, because they contain the interest and stimulus of play. Even animals are not exempt from the universal desire to play, as witness the kitten going round and round after its tail, the dog frisking before his master, or the horse galloping over the field when freed from the harness. There are times, as on a bright June morning, when Mother Earth herself, freshly clad in blossoms and verdure, appears to be glad to be alive and having a grand play spell.

A GLIMPSE OF FROEBEL.—The Baroness Von Marenholtz-Bülow, who has done much for the dissemination of Froebel's Kindergarten principles, was first attracted toward the cause by seeing Froebel himself conduct the games with a group of village children in the town where she was stopping. "In the year 1849, at the end of May," she writes, "I arrived at the baths of Liebenstein, in Thuringia, and took up my abode in the same house as in the preceding year. After the usual salutations, my landlady, in answer to my inquiry as to what was happening in the place, told me that a few weeks before there had settled on a small farm near the springs a man who played and sang with the village children and, therefore, went by the name of 'the old fool.' Some days after I met in my walks this so-called 'old fool.' A tall, spare man with long grey hair was leading a troop of village children between the ages of three and eight, most of them barefooted and scantily clothed, who marched two and two up a hill, where, having marshalled them for a play, he practiced them upon a song belonging to it. The loving patience with which he did this, the whole bearing of the man while the children played various games under his direction, were so moving that tears came into my companion's eyes as well as my own, and I said to her: 'This man is called an old fool by these people, but, perhaps, he is one of those men who are ridiculed or stoned by contemporaries and to whom future generations build monuments.'" Seeking an acquaintance with Froebel, she made a deep study of the system and was from that time on a most earnest and interested Kindergarten worker.

How to make the most and best use of Kindergarten games is now engaging the attention of all earnest teachers of children. In a recent number of the *Kindergarten Magazine* it is reported that calls for help and inspiration in this direction are coming from all parts of the country. In the musical world, too, during the Winter of 1894-5, interest was turned toward the history of children's songs and games, showing how these songs and the incidents that gave rise to them mirror the character, education and customs of the people. Among the songs considered in that connection were the familiar "Sally in our Alley," "Little Sally Waters" and "Here we go Round the Mulberry Bush." A series of articles on this interesting subject appeared in the *New York Tribune*, written by Mr. Krehbiel, the accomplished musical critic of that newspaper.

PLAY THE BUSINESS OF CHILDHOOD.—Philosophers, noting this tireless play instinct in the young child, began early to inquire into its use. Professor Hailmann, in one of his pedagogical translations, reviews the opinions of past educators as follows: "Plato thinks that 'the plays of children have the mightiest influence on the maintenance or non-maintenance of laws;' that during the first three years the 'soul of the nursling' should be made 'cheerful and kind' by keeping away from him 'sorrow and fears and pain' and by soothing him with song, the sound of the pipe and rhythmic movement; that at the next period of life, when the children 'almost invent' their games, they ought to come together at the temples and play under the supervision of nurses who are to take cognizance of their behavior. 'From the first years,' he says, 'the plays of children ought to be subject to laws, for if these plays and those who take part in them are arbitrary and lawless, how can children ever become virtuous men, abiding by and obedient to law? If, on the contrary, children are trained to submit to laws in their plays, the love for law enters their souls with the music accompanying the games, never leaves them, and helps in their development.' Aristotle advises the need 'of entertaining employment' for children. Luther thinks that 'to restrain the natural gayety of childhood serves only to spoil the temper both of body and mind; this gamesome humor, which is wisely adapted by Nature to their age and temper, should be encouraged to keep up their spirits and improve their health and strength; the chief art is to make all that they have to do sport and play.' Richter says: 'Activity alone can bring and hold serenity and happiness. Unlike our games, the plays of children are the expressions of serious activity, although in light, airy dress.'"

"What gives pleasure to children generally and at all times, serves for their development in some way; therefore, physical development is the unconscious aim of all activity in early childhood."

Play is the natural and universal activity of the child, the business of childhood, the means by which he is to become acquainted with life about him and his own powers. It is the work suited to his state of growth. Each period of life—babyhood, childhood, youth, manhood—has the means supplied by Nature for its full development, and through the experiences of each stage comes preparation for the stage beyond. In the *Education of Man* Froebel says, speaking of the plays of infancy and childhood: "Play is the highest stage of the child's development, of man's development at that period, for it is the spontaneous utterance of the inner life flowing from an inner necessity and impulse. Play is the purest and most spiritual product of man's activity at this period, and is at once the type and image of human life in its entire range, of the secret life that flows through mankind and Nature; hence it gives birth to joy, freedom, contentment, tranquility and peace with the world. In it are the springs of all good; the child that plays sturdily and with quiet energy, holding out to the point of bodily fatigue, will surely become a sturdy, quiet and steadfast man, promoting with self-sacrifice his own and others' welfare. Is not the playing child the most beautiful sight at this period of life—the child fully absorbed in his play and falling asleep while thus absorbed? Play, as above indicated, is at this period no mere sport; it is deeply serious and significant. Cherish and nourish it, you who are mothers; protect and guard it, you fathers! The penetrating eye of one thoroughly acquainted with human nature plainly discerns in the spontaneously chosen play of the child his future inner history. The plays of this period are the germs of the entire future life, for in them the whole nature of the child is expanding and showing his finest traits, his inmost soul. In this period lie the springs of the entire course of human life, and upon the proper conduct of life now will it depend whether the future is to be clear or clouded, gentle or boisterous, calm or agitated, industrious or idle, gloomy and morbid or bright and productive, obtuse or keenly receptive, creative or destructive—whether it is to bring concord and peace or discord and war. On play, too, depend likewise, in keeping with the peculiar natural constitution of the child, his relations to father and mother, brothers and sisters, to the community and the race, to Nature and to God. For as yet the life of the child in its various aspects, individual and social, natural and religious, is a life of undivided unity and simplicity; he scarcely knows which is dearest to him, the flowers themselves, his own joy in them, the joy his mother feels when he brings them to show her, or the dim sense of the kind Giver. Who would analyze the joys in which childhood is so rich? If the child is injured during these tender years, if the germs of his future life are enfeebled, then he can grow to the strength of manhood only with the greatest toil and exertion, and only with the greatest difficulty can he save himself, during the intervening development and education, from becoming crippled, or at least one-sided."

Froebel was the first to organize and utilize play as a factor in education, thus guiding and directing the surplus energy of the child until it merges into the work of the school and of life. In play it is the exercising of the child's activity that gives pleasure. In work the pleasure follows from the result or end attained by activity. Froebel believed that the child's play can be utilized to awaken his perceptions, and that in imitating the life about him he is developing the possibilities of a complete human being. This is Froebel's idea of the directed Kindergarten game.

PHYSICAL AND ETHICAL.—The games gather the experiences derived from the gifts and occupations and give an opportunity to live out what has been previously observed. Thus the games form another factor in educating the *whole* child. First the physical being is brought into active exercise, but not in the sense of gymnastics as such. The child stands straight, keeping in position on the circle because that is one requirement of the play. Being actively interested in the singing, the deep, full breath and proper expansion of the chest naturally follow. Then, if a boy is a blacksmith hammering new horse-shoes, a carpenter sawing or lifting boards, or joins with others to represent a little stream flowing between stones and under bridges, or is one of a flock of birds flying over the fields or hopping in the dewy grass, he is constantly exercising different sets of muscles until all parts of the body have been brought into active play. The physical training, while most important, is thus incidental and holds the interest of the child as no set exercises could do. In this connection it may be well to say that in games requiring violent movements the accompanying song is best given by those not taking an active part, the children being told that some may be a chorus and sing the song for those who show the play. All are then engaged and the action does not interfere with the natural breathing required for the song.

The mind of the child is also employed, his creative powers being awakened. His imagination is likewise exercised by entering into and acting out the life he wishes to represent, and each new experience brings him into a higher plane of being. If he represents a bird, a fish or a frolicsome colt, his intellect is trained, helping him to understand and enter into the life of what he is representing and, for the time being, to really be that thing.

Ethical teaching is also included in the Kindergarten game. Through this life and movement in which the child rejoices and his delight in representing Nature, there comes to him a spiritual truth which leads him to trace all life back to its source, making true religion possible. The game is the child's introduction to the necessary adjustments of the larger social life of the world. "Two cannot play together except they be agreed." Thus the community spirit is fostered, and the child finds himself one of many, each exercised in self-control and self-sacrifice and doing his part to make himself and others happy. It is also an aid in self-government, the child's will being strengthened and guided, for he finds that obedience to law gives the truest freedom, both on the material and spiritual plane. He discovers this when he is excluded from the games because he disturbs the unity. He soon learns to submit his will to the general good, not from the oppression of the law or fear of punishment, but from the love of right. The family life is emphasized, the shelter and peace of the home, the care of the stronger for the weaker, the celebration of family festivals, departure and separation and the joy of reunion and homecoming.

The child plays the part of the baker, the joiner, the grass-mower, the sailor, and thus learns respect for bodily labor and notes the patience, perseverance and skill required on the part of these workers. He observes the interdependence of all people, and through this study of how individuals and nations help each other, he gains his first idea of the universal brotherhood of man. In such games as the "Weather-vane" and the "Trees swaying in the wind," are pictured the unseen forces of Nature.

Generally speaking, physical training and ethical teaching are the predominating objects of the Kindergarten games. There are other important lessons

THE GAMES.

to each of which an entire paper might be devoted, but these will be merely mentioned in the summary of a good Kindergarten game. No one will gainsay the value of the physical training, and as to the ethical teaching, Dr. Parkhurst in a recent article "On the Training of a Child," says: "A child's training should be ethical rather than intellectual. It is easier to make a person bright than sound. Intellectual training may be gained from books, but morality cannot be printed."

MANAGEMENT OF THE GAMES.—As to the general management of the Kindergarten games, when the period for this exercise arrives, usually about the middle of the forenoon, the children form in marching line, singing some such simple melody as this:

"We'll march and march and march around,
And marching, gaily sing,
Then hand in hand so quietly,
We'll quickly form a ring.
Tra, la, la, la, tra, la, la, la,
Tra, la, la, la, la, la, tra, la, la, la,
Tra, la, la, la, la, la!"

All joining hands, sing:

"Merrily, merrily, let us form a ring,
Joyfully, joyfully, let us dance and sing!
Tra, la, la, la, la, la, la, tra, la, la, la, la, la, la!
Merrily, merrily let us form a ring!"

Then follows another short song:

"Now the time has come for play,
Tra, la, la, la, la, la, (clapping hands)
Let our leader show the way,
Tra, la, la, tra, la, la!
Heads erect and join your hands,
Each beside the other stands,
Tra, la, la, la, la, la, la, la, la, la, la!"

The Kindergartner, who supervises the games, advances into the center of the ring, when all sing:

"Let us look at Miss ———,
So happy and gay;
Let us look at Miss ———,
What does she now play?"

the center, the last-named song is sung as a salutation as he makes known his game.

This illustrates one way of opening the games. That it should be exactly like the above is neither necessary nor desirable, for the stereotyped game is contrary to Froebel's principles, the idea of the game being to dramatize the thought brought before the child for the day or the week. In games representing Nature the children should be encouraged to interpret what they feel to be the characteristic life of the thing represented. For all to be constrained to make the same gesture, at the same time and in the same direction, is to render the play stiff and unnatural. In trade games a more strict imitation is necessary. But in all cases the child should first be prepared through talks and pictures until he has a vivid conception of the subject, and can make definite his reproduction. One Kindergartner explains her own methods thus: "We let children try to play out their crude and unformed ideas, and then suggest to them each time additions or changes until these ideas become educational, and at the same time are in a certain sense free, spontaneous play directed." Sometimes the children themselves make the suggestions and thus help each other to get clear and definite ideas. In all cases keep within the experiences of the children, what they have seen, felt and thought! Another important rule is to keep the child simple and unconscious by making the thing he does and not the child prominent.

In *The Kindergarten* for April, 1892, Mrs. Walter Ward, a prominent London worker, gives the following valuable suggestions for insuring a good Kindergarten game:

"I.—Take care to select for each season of the year an appropriate series of games.

"II.—Reflect carefully on the respective duties of the head teacher, the pianist, the assistant teachers.

"III.—Classify the peculiarities of individual children, physical, mental, musical, linguistic.

"IV.—Make up your mind what to do about tired children, and who should look after them.

"V.—Consider the various physical exercises that may be introduced in connection with the games; it will be a useful exercise to classify the games by their physical aspect alone.

"VI.—The musical side must not be neglected.

"VII.—The intellectual teaching is important, as it is the necessary factor in securing the interest of the children and thus maintaining order in the games.

"Finally, a true Kindergarten game affords opportunity for: (a) intellectual training, (b) ethical teaching, (c) physical exercise, (d) dramatic action, (e) musical and rhythmical training, (f) concise, simple and accurate language."

We give the "Blacksmith"* as a representative trade game and one much in favor with the children:

---

* From *Songs and Games for Little Ones*, by Gertrude Walker and Harriet S. Jenks, published by the Oliver Ditson Co., New York.

THE GAMES.

THE BLACKSMITH.

For further reading in regard to the games see:—

The Kindergarten and School, by Four Active Workers.

Education of Man, Hailmann's translation.

On the Training of a Child, Dr. Parkhurst, in *The Ladies' Home Journal* for August '93.

Kindergarten Magazine, For April, 1892.

Songs and Games for Little Ones, by Misses Walker and Jenks.

THIRTEENTH PAPER.

after *The Education of Man* was written. *The Education of Man* may be said to embody Froebel's theory, while the *Mother-play* applies the results or experience of his seventeen years of active work at Rudolstadt, Jena and Blankenburg.

Froebel had spent much time observing his countrywomen, especially such as might be called artist-mothers, in play with their children. Selecting such songs as were common to the race and handed down by tradition, he freed them from all that was coarse, uneducational and unchildlike, tested them in the families of his friends and developed this book " to raise the mother's *instinct* into *insight*, that she might by conscious aims and methods aid the growth of her child's limbs and senses, and awaken its moral and spiritual emotions." Here we have given universal and ideal experiences of child life. The child of six years, as he turns the pages of the book, finds it a record of his life up to that time. Froebel says his object is to " reveal the process of development of the inner, instinctive life of childhood and convert the intuitive, purposeless action of mothers into an intelligent plan," in a way never before attempted. So, upon these productions of instinct in the everyday home life he saw about him, he brought to bear his own insight into nature and life and revised and adapted them to suit his purpose.

ADVERSE CRITICISM.—The book has met with much adverse criticism, the verses and music being pronounced poor, and the pictures—the work of a sign-painter—crude, even ridiculous, by some. Froebel did not have the power of expressing himself easily and his thoughts are often clothed in language that is obscure. He himself says of the book : " I have here laid down the fundamental ideas of my educational theory ; whoever has grasped the pivotal idea of this book understands what I am aiming at." Again : " If only mothers and teachers would follow its guidance, they would at last see, in spite of all opposition, that I am right."

The Baroness Marenholtz-Bülow, who was the first person in Europe to undertake the dissemination of the principles laid down in the *Mother-play*, declared that in no other way was so much opposition to Froebel's system excited as in any endeavor to circulate this book and yet, on the other hand, there was no book that gave so much pleasure to mothers when once it was understood. The Baroness zealously defended the *Mother-play*, a defense taken up and continued by Frau Henriette Schrader, a great-niece of Froebel and a member of his last training class. Frau Schrader is now Director of the *Pestalozzi-Froebel Haus* in Berlin, where all her work, both with the Kindergarten children and with the pupils of her training class, shows a beautiful application of the principles embodied in the *Mother-play*.

It is generally conceded that the most profound student of the *Mother-play* in the United States is Miss Susan E. Blow, who first introduced its study into the schools of St. Louis some ten or fifteen years ago. Miss Blow has lately made a new free translation of the book, which, as she is an accomplished German scholar, promises to throw new light upon Froebel's thought. *Merry Songs and Games*, by the late Mrs. Clara B. Hubbard, of St. Louis, was the first American song-book to set parts of the *Mother-play* to new and better music. In England a well-known translation was made by Frances and Emily Lord. The quotations used in this paper are from the translation published by Lee & Shepard, of Boston.

Froebel himself used the *Mother-play* as the basis of all his lectures to mothers and Kindergartners, and to-day it is fast becoming an important study in training-schools and mothers' clubs for all who wish to train little children according to Froebel's principles and methods. As the care and training of children naturally devolves upon women, it is hoped that coming years will find Froebel's book not only put into the hands of teachers and mothers, for which last it was especially intended, but that its study will also be made a part of every girl's education as a preparation for possible motherhood.

In studying the *Mother-play* certain principles, which appear throughout Froebel's teachings, are to be kept in mind. The first of these, in the words of the Baroness, is that "the keynote of the book is the analogy between the development of humanity and that of the individual." The second principle is the importance and opportunities of infancy, or the germ stage. A third relates to the symbolism of material things. This was especially brought out in the explanation of the second gift. A fourth thought concerns unity, or the child's relations to God, Nature and his fellow-man. This last includes the necessity of developing harmoniously this threefold relation and the desirability of having this threefoldness illustrated in each play as physical, mental and moral training.

MISS BROOKS' CLASSIFICATION.—The following classification of the *Mother-play*, is the one used by the Kindergarten Department of the Teacher's College, New York City. Permission to use it was kindly granted by its originator, Miss Angeline Brooks :

"The first Classification is According to the Development of the Child, as follows : I. To Grass Mowing ; II. To Children at the Tower ; III. To Light Songs ; IV. To Songs of Knights ; V. The Remainder of the Book.

"The next classification is based on unity and makes this division of the book :

"I.—The Child in Unity with Self and the External World : Play of the Limbs ; Falling ; Weather-vane ; All's Gone ; Taste; Smell ; Tick-tack; Little Gardener.

"II.—Unity in Home and Family Life: Thumbs and Fingers ; This is the Mother ; Go to Sleep ; Grandmother and Mother ; Flower Basket (father's birthday) ; This little Thumb is one ; Hide and Seek (literal separation); The Coo-coo, (spiritual separation and reunion).

"III.—The Child in Sympathetic Relations (unity) with the Lower Animals : Beckon to Chickens ; Beckon to Pigeons ; Fishes ; Rabbit ; Bird's Nest ; Pigeon House ; The Barnyard Gate.

"IV.—The Child in Unity with Self and Others (through the industries) : Grass Mowing ; Charcoal Burner ; Baker ; Wheelwright ; Joiner ; Carpenter ; Toy-man and Target (unity through commerce).

"V.—The Child in Unity with Others because of Right Doing : Knights and Good Child ; Knights and Bad Child ; Hide Thee, Child ; Children at the Tower.

"VI.—The Inneruniting life ; Light Bird ; Little Window ; Rabbit on the Wall ; Boy and Moon ; Girl and Stars ; Little Child Drawing ; Church-door and Window over it."

FIRST GROUP.—The first group in Miss Brooks' second classification of the *Mother-play* relates to the child in unity with self and the external world, and it begins with the mother at her child's birth.

Froebel was not satisfied with his teaching until he had conceived the Kindergarten and back of that again declared that the child's development, to be one continuous, unbroken whole, must start with the baby in its mother's arms. His teachings continually, and upon deeply-conceived principle, carry us back to the beginnings of all things. "The hand that rocks the cradle is the hand that rules the world."

For at least the first three months of the child's life, it should be kept as quiet as possible, handled by few people, its mother being the best caretaker, and not kissed, tossed in play or carried into noisy places. During this time it is one with the mother, being visibly affected by both her physical condition and her states of mind.

PLAY OF THE LIMBS.—When the child commences to make the first vague movements with its arms and legs, then Froebel would commence the nursery play. This is his motto for the mother :

> When first the child delights to try
> What strength within his limbs may lie,
> The mother's nursery-play begins.
> It is a hint from Heaven,
> Unto the mother given,
> Through outward, inner life to waken ;
> Through play and thoughtful sport to quicken
> The sense that feeling, foresight brings.

His song for the child is :

> How the little limbs fly out.
> Tossing, rollicking all about !
> Thus will they gain life and strength,—
> Stamp the flax-seed out at length,
> That feeds the pretty lamp all night,
> Where mother's love burns still and clear,
> While watching o'er her child so dear.

The picture given with song and motto is divided into three parts. The first represents the child on a blanket spread over a table, kicking and cooing after its morning bath. The child instinctively wants to join in the nurturing care and service going on around him, as thus he tests his strength to prepare for action in life. To meet this desire the mother plays with him and when he pushes out hand or foot, allows it to come against her hand or breast and gently pushes it back again. The child takes pleasure in this exertion and repeats the act over and over again, each time making the motion a little more definite. He also begins to realize that his mother has a personality separate from his own and it awakens a bond of sympathy between them. Whatever the mother is, that she imparts to her child, therefore the first aim of the mother must be to make herself right. "You cannot train up a child in the way he should go, unless you happen to be going that way yourself."

On the front cover of his book Froebel has the words: "Mother-love, mother-play, mother song." So the mother plays, sings and talks to her baby. The play develops him physically, the song appeals to his emotions, and her words give mental training. His gestures and cries are his first language. As the play gives purpose to his motions, so the words and song give him an idea of the definiteness of language. The spiritual side of the child develops with the physical and is reached through it. The spiritual union or oneness with the mother leads to God, of whose love earthly ties and affections are intended to serve as types and symbols.

Every mother should rejoice in a strong, kicking, crowing child. He may be harder to hold, but physical vigor bespeaks mental and moral power. Former ages disregarded and neglected the body, but this age traces the connection between sound bodies and sound minds, the relation between grace of physique and grace of spirit.

Each obstacle overcome, however small, gives greater strength. The body grows and holds its own through physical exercise, while intellectual power and strength of character are gained by overcoming obstacles. We hear a great deal nowadays about atrophied faculties, faculties that die from want of use. "Possibilities are inherent, but their development depends upon exercise." By her joyous play with her child the mother encourages him to delight in effort, and thus lays the foundation of a sturdy independence in after life. By making the exertion a little more difficult each time, she gives the child the idea of continued and increased perseverance and that she encourages and opposes him for his own good and growth. If his efforts are crowned with success, he enjoys the struggle and is filled with the hope of achievement. All tasks should be graduated to the child's strength and environment, otherwise the impetus toward effort is lost, and discouragement and despair will take the place of faith and hope.

The burning lamp in the picture suggests the mother's love. An adjoining picture shows the poppy plant from which the oil is stamped and the mill for stamping it. This indicates the labor of both the mother and others in the care of the child, and with the words of the song about the child's own limbs growing strong enough to finally stamp out the oil himself, contains the first presentment of his answering gratitude to his mother and future duty and responsibility toward her.

In a third picture there is shown a woman climbing a steep hill with a heavy burden on her back. The mother, who has brought her older children to play in the stream which turns the mill near by, points this woman out as another mother providing for her child. The children themselves are in their play showing the mother that each has a separate individuality. One child has a practical turn of mind and utilizes the water's force to turn his small wheel. Another boy sits thoughtfully by and watches this operation. He will be philosophical and spend his time studying out the "why and wherefore" of life. The little girl, taking off her shoes and stockings, wades fearlessly into the stream. She goes direct to her purpose. Each child will work out his life in his own peculiar way, and the mother, as she watches them, finds food for thought, both for the daily training of each character and for the choosing of a vocation for each. This wise mother will not allow a false standard of appearances to influence the child's calling, and Johnny, who has a mechanical genius, will never be forced to become an unwilling merchant.

THE FALLING GAME.—The next play in this group is entitled, "Ah! there falls my baby down." This game is the familiar one of allowing the child to fall a short distance to a soft pillow, by taking the supporting hand away from his back, tossing him up in the air and catching him as he descends, or encouraging a jump from shelf or table. The child's system thus receives a slight shock, and he is impressed with the idea that danger might come from a real fall. "The Play of the Limbs" indicates conscious life expressing itself through activity, while "The Falling Game" denotes these activities directed toward self-preservation, one of the basal instincts of humanity. Control of the movements of the body leads to self-control on a higher plane. A marked indefiniteness of movement on the part of an adult is a sure sign of deficient mentality.

If the child falls through carelessness, he must learn to pay more heed to the motions of his feet and body. If he drops a delicate article and it breaks, he discovers that increased possessions demand added responsibility and negligence must take the consequences of its own acts. Through this play the child gets presentment of law governing the Universe and that obedience to law gives the greatest liberty. Nature never changes her laws. If the child falls, he must pick himself up and make a better adjustment to circumstances next time. If he touches fire, it burns him and burns serenely on. If he indulges a capricious appetite, pain is the reminder that he has disobeyed.

The child will have many falls through life, some through carelessness and heedlessness, others through untruthfulness and disobedience. His mother can never guard him so carefully but that he will have both physical and spiritual falls. She can only strengthen him and show him how to adapt himself to natural laws and his environments and be a law unto himself. To pick up a child when he falls and soothe and cry over him, to be too anxious about his welfare, to be foolishly fond of him, to live *for* and not *with* him and to shield him from every temptation, is to deaden the germs of self-control, judgment and caution. In "The Falling Game" Froebel intends that the mother shall begin early to cultivate the germ of "standing alone." He would have her decide in every act whether she is giving a capricious command or enunciating a universal law, and then, if in ordinary circumstances and according to his strength, the child falls, he must take the consequences. This is not cruelty but love, for if the mother shields him, she is obeying the law for him and not he, and she only weakens him for contact with the world where she cannot shield him. Universal law a child sees and accepts as reasonable.

"It is not necessary," says Dr. Parkhurst, "that authority should be put before the child in a manner calculated to irritate and offend. Authority is as strong a friend if yielded to, as it is bitter as an enemy when resisted. Everything in nature obeys. Everything in art obeys. Only man mutinies, and his mutiny is his misery—always has been since the first Adam mutinied and always will be till the last Adam ceases to mutiny. In whatever direction we look and whatever improvement in existing conditions we seek to effect, we come back to it again and again, that the end is determined by the beginning and that the foundations of all public betterment have to be laid in the children."

This play also typifies spiritual union with father and mother, and through them with God. The father stands for law, the mother for love. Law, order and harmony must prevail in the home, otherwise the child's first standard is broken. When the child plays at falling, he laughs and is full of glee, for he has a feeling of trust that his mother will guard him from danger. In the same way, in spite of discouragements, the human being can never fall if he trust in God and obey His laws. Back of all and through all is love, which recognizes each effort the child makes in right doing and, if he falls, encourages him to rise and be stronger next time. "Nothing is fatal but discouragement."

> "When first the child begins to imitate,
> Do not the little effort underrate;
> Do thou the same—it will the more delight him,
> And even to renewed attempts invite him."

THE WEATHER-VANE.—Physically imitating the movement of the weather-vane gives excellent training to the hand and arm. Any play that will develop a self-reliant use of his limbs is of benefit to the child. But the main thought of the play is to early bring the child into sympathetic relations with one of the great forces of nature.

> "Who can see the wind?
> Neither you nor I;
> But when the leaves hang trembling,
> The wind is passing by."

The child looks upon the vane moving and asks why it moves. He is told that it is the wind and that God made the wind. Having seen the effect he is gratified to know the cause, and his thought is led to God, the first great Cause. Then he sees that the wind blows his kite, makes the leaves tremble and the trees bow their heads. It waves the grass and moves the clouds and sail-boats. The child first sees the world as chaos. The diversity created by the force of the wind he finds to be the result of one cause and so he discovers unity. What the child imitates he is trying to understand. He wants to "test the force by which things go." The play of "The Weather-vane" is a type of all the unseen causes which produce a visible effect in our lives. Other examples may be found in gravitation, solar and magnetic forces, the growth of the plant from the seed, of the chicken from the egg, or the motion of a river. Here is Froebel's use of the symbolism of material things. The law of life is from within, invisible, and so the child's desire to know natural causes is turned to a desire to know spiritual truths.

"ALL'S GONE."—After the child has had his supper, he looks down and is surprised to find that his bowl is empty. Then his mother says:—

>Gone, gone, my child, all gone—
>The supper now is gone;
>
>Baby is not now without it;
>Little mouth knows all about it,
>Little tongue hath in it dipped,
>Down the little throat it slipped.
>
>Now it makes my baby gay
>Full of frolic, full of play;
>Now with health my child shall beam,
>Red and white like rose and cream.

"The Weather-vane" illustrates the visible effect of an invisible cause, while "All's Gone" shows the invisible effect of a visible cause. It teaches the thought of a resurrection:

>"There is no death,
>What seems so is transition."

Nothing in Nature is lost; it only disappears to reappear again in new form. Decay on one plane ministers to life on another. Every stage of development involves death or sacrifice in the preceding. The child looks into the bird's nest to count the eggs and lo, the nest is empty! "But," says the mother, "the eggs are not destroyed. Look at yonder birds! See, how fast and free they fly! Did not their songs of praise waken you this morning?" In the Autumn the leaves die and fall to the ground and the earth seems barren and covered with rubbish, but in the Spring these things are purified into new life, and leaves and flowers take the place of dry branches. "'I wonder what becomes of the frog when he climbs up out of this world, and disappears, so we do not see even his shadow, till plop! he is among us again when we least expect him. Does anybody know where he goes to? Tell me somebody, pray!' Thus chattered the grub of a Dragon-fly as he darted in and out among the plants at the bottom of the water." *

Nothing is lost except through neglect. Neglected opportunities are real losses; apparent losses are often blessings in disguise. Every step of development represents an apparent loss. Froebel teaches a sense of responsibility in this play. The little girl finds her bird cage empty because she neglected to close the door. Her little plant is forgotten and, therefore, droops and dies. Care

---

* Mrs. Gatty's *Parables from Nature.*

and perseverance are needed. Possessions too easily obtained are often not appreciated. In the "Little Gardener," Froebel says in this connection to the mother, advising the care of plants and pets for children:—

> "Would'st thou the mind of the child for the cares of life untold?
> Let him observe the life-cares here enrolled.
> Would'st thou for cares of inward life prepare him?
> Make sweet to him the life-cares that are near him."

In the songs relating to smell and taste Froebel shows the importance of the cultivation of the senses as organs of the mind and not as ministers for the gratification of the body. Every part of the human organism is intended to serve a good and lawful purpose, and it should be the mother's object to assist her child toward a right use of his powers and thus convert every energy to good. The child's clothing may be such as to hinder his growth and spoil his temper. If he never shares his food with others, if it is made too pleasant to the palate and too much attention is paid to eating, the seeds of gluttony are planted. Irregularity in eating and sleeping prevents self-control and punctuality. A bed too soft induces indolence and does not beget a hardy endurance. Everything about the child either helps or hinders its development. There can be no mean.

Notice the connection between taste as a physical sense and taste as a sense of beauty! Elizabeth Harrison's *Study of Child Nature* has excellent and practical thoughts on the senses of taste and smell.

"TICK-TACK."—The "Tick-Tack" song is the last one belonging to the first group:

> "Who would find the prosperous way,
> The laws of order must obey;
> Who would win a happy fate,
> Must learn his time to regulate.
> He whom this practice shall annoy,
> Will be bereft of many a joy.
> Then teach the child to value order, time,
> For these are priceless gifts in every clime."

We shall not have space to take up this play in detail. It embodies many of the thoughts contained in former plays. It shows rhythm as the basis of order and harmony on the earth and in life. This seeking for rhythm is an early manifestation of the child which the mother meets when she rocks him and sings to him. Rhythm is the basis of the solar system and the sub-divisions of time. Pendulum beats are the rhythmic measurements of time. These measurements depend upon mathematical laws, which are equally fundamental in the works of God and the labors of man. To understand the clock the child must learn to count. Truth, exactness and order are necessary to character.

THE SECOND GROUP.—The second group in Miss Brooks' classification based upon unity relates to unity in home and family life, and is illustrated by these plays:

Thumbs and Fingers.
This little Thumb is one.
This is the Mother.
This little Thumb.
Grandmother and Mother.
Brothers and Sisters.
Finger Piano.
Flower Basket (father's birthday).
Hide and Seek (literal separation).
The Coo-coo (spiritual separation and reunion).

These plays meet the child's awakening sense of his relationship to the mother and the home family. They contain the duties of parents to children, of children to parents, the relations of grandparents, the connection of the home with society at large, and presuppose, as a foundation, the right formation of the home. The first relationship begins with the mother, and from her leads out to father, brothers and sisters, grandparents and into the world beyond.

The mother, by a wise love and sympathy, makes herself the center of her child's life. To her he comes with his joys and sorrows, sure of her never-failing interest.

"'The Lord cannot be everywhere, so He made mothers.' This statement, attributed to a Jewish rabbi, although it be poetic rather than scientific in terms, conveys to us the scope of the mother's calling. She stands in very truth the handmaid of the Lord, called to His holy of holies, to work out His law of creation."

If the mother, as her child grows older, finds that she no longer possesses his confidence and he reveals himself to others instead of seeking her advice and commendation, she must look for the cause back to early childhood, when she hushed his eager prattle because she was "too busy to be bothered." Common politeness compels us to listen to an older person, but we allow personal convenience to rule with the child, thereby wounding his feelings and lessening his respect. Children are excellent judges of character and are quick to determine whether the motive back of an answer be a good or a selfish one. The normal child is predisposed to be grateful, reverent and confiding, but whether these qualities will grow or be perverted greatly depends upon early training and the ideals presented for his imitation. It is life itself and his effort to adjust himself to its increasing power that is the cause of his ceaseless questionings. The child has a right to be answered. Though it be a trying task to answer a thousand questions a day, have patience and the reward will come in due time—indeed, it is even then present. If the mother possesses her child's confidence, he cannot go far astray and in this close life of mother and child an immortal soul is being developed.

* Now stiffen your chubby round legs, dear,
  And stand up straight in my lap ;
  I hold you now—ere many moons
  You'll stand alone, mayhap.

---

* From Miss Blow's *Mottoes and Commentaries*.

> But your life will still lean on mine, dear,
>   For a mother and child must be
> Drawn together through all their lives,
>   As the constant moon draws the sea.
>
> Drawn together though long miles should part,
>   Together, even as now,
> While I fold you close to my loving heart,
>   And press a kiss on your brow.

The first plays of this second group teach the naming and counting of the fingers. Froebel says of "This Little Thumb":

> Teach the child about his fingers,
>   How to name them one by one.
> Above all teach him how to use them;
>   Thus are many pleasures won.

Besides naming the fingers, we have comparisons as to their relative uses and strength. The picture accompanying the motto has three divisions. The largest one symbolizes the hands, the right one being considered as masculine, the left as feminine. The interpretation is, strength in union, harmony in the home circle, society and state. It also shows each act in the individual to be the result of thought and feeling; hence the necessity of cultivating the heart as well as the head. In the last two lines of the song, Froebel says:

> And though these little gifts have each a part to fill,
> They're all together bound and governed by one will.

A smaller cut depicts the mother holding her youngest child on her arm and teaching it this little game. Two other children sit near by, each busily at work. Calling the little one's attention to these older children, the mother tells him that he, too, may learn to use his fingers as well as they. A third picture shows a boy climbing a tree, one girl planting a flower and another one bringing water for its care. Here is increased strength, added power for action and usefulness.

This play, together with "This Little Thumb is One," includes the whole subject of industry as a necessary factor in a happy life and the need of cultivating the hand, man's most useful servant, in early childhood. For further explanation of this subject, the reader is referred to the paper on the occupations on page 101.

PURITY BASED UPON KNOWLEDGE.—The fundamental thought of "Thumbs and Fingers" relates to delicate and indelicate action touching the mysteries of life. The first steps of sin are oftenest taken in ignorance. The remedy is positive, not negative, teaching healthful occupation and a realization of the true principle of life, showing this to the child as much as possible in the varied aspects of Nature. Parents should answer their children's questions truthfully and be themselves the first to put a right construction upon all necessary information, not allowing it to come to the child through less careful sources. Here the necessity of a mother's possessing her child's confidence is most clearly seen. Mothers would do well to co-operate in suppressing sensational advertising pictures. As an emblem of life in its utmost purity, the lily is taken. Without this beautiful flower, says Froebel, no garden is complete.

In the "Grandmother and Mother," "This is the Mother," and "Brothers and Sisters," we—

> Behold the good family, great and small,
> Who with thoughtful care and one in will,
> Work well and true joy's cup to fill.

When teaching the child about the family as a whole through these finger plays we are laying the best foundation for unity in the child's future life. "A house divided against itself cannot stand." Unity in the home is the surest preparation for unity in church and state. If there be discord in the child's first social community, what standards for social relations has he to fall back upon in later life? The family life is the first step in the solution of all social problems. The Salvation Army, the Social Settlements and Young Women's Christian Associations are all working for a loftier home ideal, while the Kindergartens and schools are asking for co-operation. In the higher walks of life thoughtlessness and indulgence are the main factors to be considered.

The race's long period of infancy led to the foundation of the family. Upon the child's right relations in the family and the impressions of life there imprinted are his future estimates of social and religious institutions founded. Love of humanity and of God springs from love of kindred, and "it is only the sacred fire on the altar of home that can kindle this holy flame in the child's heart."

In these plays the child's imagination is stirred by pictures of love, gratitude and service, and he gets his ideas of ideal childhood and of his own duties in the home. The sacredness of the home is portrayed by showing the various families in Nature. In the picture of the "Grandmother and Mother" we have first the human family, and grouped about it, earth, air and water families. The child sees himself mirrored in the relations of his parents to his grandparents, while the parents see their own relation to their child in the relations of grandparents to them. This number, five, seen in the two grandparents, the two parents and the child, Froebel considers of some significance and looks for it in five-petaled flowers and the seed kernels of certain fruits.

"Brothers and Sisters," denotes repose and the watchful care of the mother and of God.

The "Finger Piano" refers to the value of counting and numbers, and in this case especially to the controlling of time and the foundation of music. Froebel would have us commence early to cultivate singing and train the ear to fine distinctions of time. He points to this as one of the elements of inner harmony, and says: "How important it is early to plant the germ of both inner and outward harmony in every child! Learning to hear it within, the child will strive to give it outer form and expression; even if in such effort he is only partially successful, he will gain thereby the power to appreciate the more successful efforts of others. Thus enriching his own life by the life of others, he solves the problem of development." Another thought is, the importance of the present hour and the impossibility of thoroughly repairing lost opportunities.

In the "Flower-basket," the child is represented as gathering flowers for his father's birthday. The cementing of family relationships is the basal idea of this play. Love expressing itself in action grows with the doing. In his motto to the mother, Froebel says:

> Keep the loving interest warm,
> Before the mind forgets.

It is a very poor love that does not express itself through self-sacrifice and helpful acts to the one beloved, and every act, instead of decreasing the store, increases the capacity for loving. It is the parable of the talents over again, for the one who buries his talent loses "that which he hath," just as the heart which does not express itself in loving deeds grows hard, cold and selfish. The mother says: "This is your father's birthday. We will do all we can to make the day pleasant for him, because we love him and he does so many kind things for us." So the children hasten to gather flowers and make themselves clean and sweet to celebrate the anniversary. When the father sees their happy faces as they cluster around him, he says: "We will thank the Heavenly Father for this pleasant home and loving mother and children."

The next play, "Hide and Seek," is Froebel's version of the universal play of "Peek-a-boo," the inner meaning of which is, separation for the joy of reunion and the arousing of personality. By this separation the child realizes his dependence upon his mother, through contrast, that important factor in all education, but if she does not show joy upon his return or allows him to remain so long hidden that the dependence is broken and he learns to love hiding for its own sake, confidence is broken and he is taking the first steps in falsehood and deceit.

> The aim, the goal, is union sweet;
> We separate, only again to meet.
> Learn, mother, to apply this law so true;
> Child-tending then will Heaven's joy bring to you.

Other games involving separation and return are "Falling, falling," and the "Pigeon House." The answer to developing consciousness is the need met in this play. Developing consciousness is the basis of desire for change, travel and adventure. It also lies at the foundation of the child's assertion of his own will and his idea of freedom. It is a critical time for the mother when the child is first conscious of a fault, for then his conscience is awakened. If she possesses his confidence, he will not think of hiding from her. But she must be careful to do justice in the matter of correction, always impressing the inevitableness of punishment. As far as possible let it be the same as his elders suffer, the natural consequence of his own deeds.

The child's attention to his mother's call, thus strengthening the call of conscience by obeying it, Froebel exemplifies in the "Coo-coo" game. This song is a development of "Hide and Seek." The child hides, and while hidden calls out "Coo-coo!" to his mother who is searching for him. There may be separation and still union, while in union there is also individual character, each answering to his own call of conscience. Says Miss Blow: "Though visible presence be removed, there is constant communication. The cry of the heart has become articulate and the child learns with glad surprise that the unseen need not be the unknown, unheard or unfelt. All life is transition. Froebel has traced the baby's progress from the moment when, through the typical experience illustrated in the 'Falling' game, he learns his physical distinctness from his mother, to the day when in the cuckoo call he gives sign of his presentiment of spiritual identity." *

If the mother has accustomed her child to be obedient to her call, if she does not require tasks too great for him, or such as violate his own peculiar individuality, he will learn to love the call of conscience, and later in life, when his personality is necessarily separate from his mother's, he will be able to obey the voice of reason instead of yielding to personal inclination.

THE THIRD GROUP.—The third group in Miss Brooks' classification shows the child in sympathetic relations with the lower animals and is exemplified in these plays:

    Beckon to Chickens.   Bird's Nest.
    Beckon to Pigeons.   Pigeon House.
    Fishes.   Barnyard Gate.

It is said that the play "Beckon to Chickens" was the origin of the *Mother-play*. One day when walking in the country Froebel met a young woman carrying a child in her arms. Coming to a poultry yard, the mother told her child to "beckon to the chickens." Froebel was impressed with the significance of the game, and, upon reaching home, wrote out this play and tried it in a family of his acquaintance. From this grew the collection we now have.

Every vigorous, healthy child is attracted by the life of Nature about him, for in it he sees his own life mirrored. Through these plays the child is making the beginning of a sympathetic understanding of Nature. They form the best possible preparation for the future care of plants and pet animals. The care of plants and animals teaches toleration, kindliness and responsibility. Interest is developed and a foundation is laid for systematic observation and scientific study. The child comes to realize the beauty and order of the Universe, each thing in its right place and doing its appointed work. Through this wonderful order harmony reigns. This knowledge is a hint for inner peace and right living with fellow-men.

In recognizing the dependence of animal and plant upon him, the answering love the animal shows and the growth and blossom of the plant as a reward for his effort, the child gains his first perception of the meaning of gratitude. We only know what we have experienced. The child cannot experience gratitude from merely telling him that he ought to be grateful. He must first have

---

* From *Knighthood a Symbol of Moral Power*.

the care of some living thing and feel what that care involves. In protecting his pet animal, the child imbibes a feeling of good will toward all helpless and defenseless things, which engenders kindliness toward human beings less fortunate than himself and a toleration for human failings. Through his home life and his care of animals and plants, the child is early placed in relationship with his superiors, his equals and with persons and things beneath him. These are all the relationships of life. They contain the duties of man. Froebel would have us place the child in these relationships and make his duties, "definite and inexorable."

The "Bird's Nest" play is a type of home, of unselfish devotion and parental love. It also shows God's watchful care and wisdom. Who taught each kind of bird to build its nest away from danger and near to its own special kind of food? Why are the little ones hatched in the Spring? They stay comfortably and quietly in the nest when both the father and the mother bird are away in search of food, for the Heavenly Father keeps them and His sunlight warms the nest. So the child must learn not to fret when his mother is away, for she keeps him in her thoughts wherever she may be.

The "Pigeon House" is another phase of separation. It portrays the desire to go out into the world and the joy of reunion because of loving welcome home. Every individual needs a home and country to which he is bound by bonds of love, and also needs to go away from them in order to learn to appreciate the strength of these ties. Outside experience is required to cultivate self-reliance and independence. Within the limits of right and wrong the child must be allowed scope for his free choice, otherwise individuality cannot be developed. By relying too much upon the assistance and prudence of others he falls into danger when left to depend upon himself, because he is confused and undecided. To the mother Froebel says:

> What to the child gives inward joy,
> He loves to represent in play.
> The dove flies away from his little home;
> The child through the green fields loves to roam.
> The little dove comes back at night;
> The child, too, keeps his home in sight.
> Then all the life and all the play
> That filled the long and happy day,
> All he has found, all he has seen,
> He loves at home to tell again;
> And all these joys, together bound,
> Now in a varied wreath are wound.

Another interesting song in this group is the "Fishes." No one who has watched a child peer into a globe of gold fishes or gaze from a bridge into the brook below will doubt the potency of the attraction he feels. Froebel says that birds and fishes attract children because of the purity of their native environment and the ease and freedom with which they move in it. "Clearness and freedom, purity and unhindered self-activity, these," he says, "are the conditions of life in which the child is happy and in which he is strengthened and developed. Let the child find this delight in the pure and free early and thus lay the foundation of his moral development."

The child tries to grasp the fish because he wants to make its freedom his own. In like manner older people are attracted to persons who possess the qualities they wish to emulate. There is also a lesson of individuality to be learned from the fish. If caught, its free and graceful motion is lost. Out of its element it is not itself and then no longer attracts the child. Each one is doing his noblest when he is doing his own peculiar work. Every individual, even the humblest, has a work which no one but himself can do. Let no man be ashamed of his work! If well done, the highest is no more worthy of honor.

There is also a moral lesson in the straight and crooked movements of the fishes. This is shown, in the picture illustrating the song, in the movements of the fishes themselves, the winding of the brook, the straight and gnarled branches of the trees and the coil of the serpent. We may trace the analysis in straight and crooked lines, straight and crooked motions, straight and crooked deeds. One writer says: "Words stand for physical facts which find parallels on spiritual planes. The fish may be more beautiful when its motion is crooked than when it is straight, but crooked and straight applied to deeds have a fixed and unvarying significance, and the child can learn that 'crooked deeds' are never beautiful, 'crooked thoughts' never true. Early in life he can find the symbol in the fact and learn to transfer from the realm of things to the realm of thought the experiences he has gathered."

THE FOURTH GROUP.—The fourth group, showing the child in unity with self and others through the industries, embodies these plays:

> Grass Mowing.
> Charcoal Burner.
> Baker.
> Wheelwright.
> Joiner.
> Carpenter.
> Target.

Through commerce:

> Toyman.

These are called the labor plays. Their burden is unity, interchange of labor, interdependence and gratitude. The child sees himself as a part of humanity and is inspired to do his share in the service of life. Selfishness is counteracted by seeing all people about him doing something for others.

> Hasten to the meadow, Peter!
> Mow the grass—what can be sweeter?
> Bring us home the fragrant fodder
> For the cow, for milk and butter.
> Cow is in the barnyard straying;
> Milk her now without delaying.
> Cow the good rich milk is giving—
> Milk and bread are baby's living.

Let us grateful be for labors,
Bringing us so many favors.

Hasten to the meadow, Peter!
Mow the grass—what can be sweeter!
Thank thee, Peter, for the mowing!
Thank thee, cow, the milk bestowing!
For the milking, thank our Molly;
Baker, for the rolls so jolly;
For the supper, thank mamma—
So no thanks forgotten are.

When the child has his supper and, perhaps, plays first the game of "All's Gone," the mother tells him of how Molly milked the cow, Peter mowed the grass for the cow to eat, the farmer sowed the seed and the Heavenly Father's sun and rain made the grass grow—all that Baby might have milk for his supper to change into good rich blood and help him to become strong and healthy. Here the child sees cause and effect, one phase of the law of unity. This linking together of connected events in a related chain is the basis of many pleasing stories for children. A familiar illustration is "The House that Jack Built." The moral and spiritual value of the play lies in the idea of dependence upon other people and upon the Heavenly Father. Froebel wishes to foster this idea of giving and taking services as a means of showing the child his loving relationship to everything about him and to help him realize the universal brotherhood of man. A child's apparent lack of gratitude is often due to the fact that he does not know the sacrifice and trouble back of the things which come to him so easily. Many an older person is apt to forget that there is anything wonderful in the common blessings of everyday life until aroused by some untoward event which breaks the chain of necessary co-operation. When visiting food markets or house-furnishing shops, interest the child in the number of hands that have been at work and in the states and countries represented. Outside of the moral lesson, this would awaken a zest for the study of geography. Do not emulate a mother who in a recent visit to one of the large stores replied to her child's inquiry as to the use of the overhead mechanism for making payments and change: "I don't know what it is for unless it is to make little boys ask questions."

It is also a wise plan to allow each child to take some definite share in the household affairs. These plays give the key to a better adjustment of social problems. The strife between labor and capital is largely a matter of false standards and lack of brotherly love. Manual and mental labor are no longer distinct but are growing more and more each to need the other. Industrial pursuits demand intellectual training and science needs the hand to execute its bidding. The perfectly healthy person is he who exercises body, mind and spirit. Says the Baroness Marenholtz: "One of the most effectual means of calling the ideal side of human nature into play is early artistic culture."

Again, children should not acquire the idea from their daily surroundings that worldly gain and prosperity are the end and aim of existence, but be led to see that added wealth should mean added culture, responsibility and morality. High position involves a greater circle of influence and, therefore, the example set should be worthy of emulation, instead of showing, as it too often does, weakness, indulgence and loose morality.

Froebel's "Charcoal Burner" teaches that even the roughest work, if faithfully performed, commands respect.

In the "Baker," the nursery "Pat-a-cake," we have another illustration of cause and effect, unity. The admonition to the child to bring his cake before the oven gets cold, inculcates punctuality and readiness in each doing his part.

The "Carpenter" again teaches unity, the seemingly unrelated things brought together to make a useful whole, a sheltering home for the child.

The "Wheelwright" repeats the impression of the benefits of skilled labor as shown in the wheel and its important use in our present civilization. The pictures accompanying the song show the wheel from the child's plaything up to the chariots of the gods.

The "Target" relates to form, size and number, the qualities of objects and "points to the intellectual mastery of all objects in time and space."

The "Toyman" pictures commerce and introduces the child to his relationships with others through trade. The toyshops show the products of human toil provided to meet human needs. What the child chooses may be an indication of his tastes, what he desires to imitate. What a child imitates he is trying to understand. His imitations are keys to his inclinations. Of the "Toyman" the Baroness says: "It is a bad plan to encourage children to expect that whenever they are taken into a shop something will be bought for them; greed of possession is apt to be awakened in them in this manner. They should be allowed to look around and admire all the various products of human art and industry, and, if anything falls to their share, there should be pointed out to them in reference to it how many different pairs of hands and what a variety of industrial machinery must have been called into play for its production, and how all human labors fit into each other and combine to produce the requisites of material existence. Every object which calls forth their admiration may be made the occasion of representing the different labors of human beings one for another as so many signs of mutual love. This, at any rate, is the ideal side of commerce. With this idea is associated the duty of preparing the child to take, one day, its own share in the common work."

THE FIFTH GROUP—The fifth group, showing the child in unity with others because of right doing, is exemplified in these plays:

> Children at the tower.
> Knights and good child.
> Knights and bad child.
> Hide thee, child!

With these plays we come to a more advanced stage of development. The lessons conveyed in the former plays have been mainly accidental. The child has pictured them to himself, but now the "ought" and "must" are plainly discerned. Here is direct moral training in the appeal to good motives and the mastery of the will. Moral training is necessarily a training of the will to choose the right. The earlier plays are based on the child's desire to investigate the life around him, but this group and the one following it are founded upon an expression of the inner life.

The "Children at the Tower" is a review of all the other plays, and is to the child a history of himself. Here two families are represented as visiting each other, and while the elders are chatting together the little ones are playing the games already learned. Here the hint to the child is his own mental and moral growth.

Of the next play, "The Knights come to see the Good Child," the song says :

> Five knights I see riding at a rapid pace,
> Within the court their steps I trace.
> "What would ye now, fair knights, with me?"
> "We wish thy precious child to see ;
> They say he is like the dove so good,
> And like the lamb of merry mood ;
> Then wilt thou kindly let us meet him,
> That tenderly our hearts may greet him?"
> "Now the precious child behold !"
> "Well he merits love untold.
> Child, we give thee greetings rare,
> This will sweeten mother's care,
> Worth much love the good child is ;
> Peace and joy are ever his.
> Now will we no longer tarry,
> Joy unto our homes we'll carry."

This play is the symbol of right and wrong. The good is made attractive and the child is loved for what he is or may become and not for what he seems to be. It is a matter of character and not of reputation. The knights stand for goodness on the side of what is right and true. In early times knights were pure and noble. They promised helpfulness and love, were brave, courteous, obedient, ready to serve those weaker and smaller than themselves and were sworn to protect women and children. Those who entered the service were trained to it from early childhood.

If the child will be worthy of the knights' good opinion, he must choose between the good and evil. Beauty and position are not to be considered. Only real worth can win their praises. Outward appearance solely, as a standard of living, is the origin of much folly and crime. "The whole problem of the development of humanity consists in passing from semblance to reality."

This is the verse for the knights and the ill-humored child :

> Five knights I see riding at a rapid pace,
> Within the courtyard their steps I trace.
> "What would ye now, fair knights, with me?"
> "We wish thy precious child to see."
> "Ah, friendly knights, I grieve to say

> I cannot bring him to you to-day.
> He cries, is so morose and cross,
> That all too small we find the house."
> "Oh, such tidings give us pain.
> No longer we sing a joyful strain ;
> We'll ride away, we'll ride afar,
> Where all the good little children are."

In this play the mother is sorrowful, but allows her child to endure the consequences of right and wrong as shown through the approval and disapproval of the knights. The knights love the good and turn away from the wrong. The child becomes conscious that if he is ill humored he will no longer be sought by the knights—for the good affiliate with their own kind—and must suffer separation from them.

In the third play the child is again good and now the mother, knights and child all play together.

THE SIXTH GROUP.—The sixth group shows the inner-uniting life, and is illustrated by these plays:

> Light bird,
> Little window.
> Rabbit on the wall.
> Wolf songs.
> Boy and Moon.
> Girl and stars.
> Little child drawing.
> Church door and window over it.

This last group of *Mother-play* songs deals with shadow pictures and the transforming power of light to symbolize the inner or spiritual life. Everything is made use of to convey to the child a sense of the union of all things and thus lead from the visible to the invisible world and the Divine Power ruling all. The aim of the light songs is to cultivate all that is high and noble in the child and to show him that the purest joys of life are in things higher than the material world.

"The Little Boy and the Moon" has its lesson for the mother. In telling the child about the heavenly bodies, suit the explanation to his understanding, but make it a truthful one. Through his interest and wonder in natural phenomena we may lead him to an apprehension of God.

The "Light Bird" symbolizes truth. Deeds done in the light are deeds of goodness and love, but those done under the cover of darkness are evil and wicked. It also teaches that we cannot always obtain possession of all that pleases us. We may spend our lives in pursuing illusive pleasures without gaining anything soul-satisfying. If we want true draughts of happiness, we must go to the never-failing fountain. Discrimination is necessary to distinguish between gold and dross. Froebel here points to the eye as connected with spiritual insight. The Bible tells us: "If thine eye be single, the whole body is full of light."

The thought of the "Rabbit" is the sun's light bringing color and form out of darkness as the inner life and peace beautify the countenance. Our darkest experience will work for good, or make us better able to help others, if we but accept the lesson intended and keep the light of God shining in our hearts. Only darkness within can produce darkness without.

The "Wolf songs" say : "Keep the imagination pure."

The "Window songs" picture the influx of light, increasing as the spiritual eye is able to bear the full blaze of truth.

"The aim of the 'Shadow Plays,'" says Miss Blow's free translation, "is to suggest how we may avoid awakening the child's lower instincts." Of the child who has broken a pane of glass it says : "Sometimes we are like this little boy ; we do something which keeps light from getting into our hearts. Then what a sad time we have in the dark and how much trouble we have to take before we can get the light again !"

"Like the child in the picture," continues the translation, "who has opened the door into the dark cellar, open all the doors and windows of your heart to the dear light ! Then everything within will be clear, and everything without will be fair. The world will be all beautiful to you, as it is to the little boy who stands in his mother's lap watching for the coming of the sun.

"As symbolic of the soul's progress these songs move from perception of the light to aspiration towards it. This aspiration deepens into a conviction of relationship, and relationship completes itself in inward identification. Indwelling light then manifests itself in outward act, and life becomes luminous and transparent."

IN CONCLUSION.—At a first reading the *Mother-play* may seem trifling and absurd, but to the student who really tries to get at its meaning it offers valuable information in child training. Froebel begins at the beginning and intends that the mother shall really and intelligently commence to train her child as soon as it is born. The reason he lays so much stress on this is because impressions begin at and even before birth. We cannot say how or when these impressions begin, but that impressions are there is proved by the fact that every human being, even the baby of six months, is the result of his past experience. The little baby has no capacity for giving out but a great capacity for absorbing the atmosphere in which it lives. Therefore, it is of the utmost importance that his surroundings shall in every way be pure and helpful to his development. His physical conditions of proper food, exercise, rest and bodily care should be such as will conduce to healthy growth. In doing this a happy medium must be maintained between over exercise and insufficient development. His moral nature is also influenced by the character of his surroundings. Equally with an older person, is he made happy by a bright, clean, orderly room and the companionship of joyous, wholesome people, or depressed by uncomfortable, dingy surroundings and dejected by sad, morbid or ill-natured persons. He responds to the kindly tones, the friendly touch, the smiles and the affection as certainly as he does to the unrest and anger of those who handle him.

In the beginning the child cries because he is uncomfortable, but under wrong training this may gradually lead out into self-will until he becomes the autocrat of the household, ruling his elders with despotic sway. Here, too, Froebel's philosophy gives us the key. His teaching is that if you have reason to believe that the child is physically comfortable, leave him alone. He is simply crying to command attention. It is not advisable to handle the child and pass him from one to another every moment of his waking hours. He should be accustomed to kick and coo and play by himself. Constant change, which seems to be the order of the present age, lays the foundation for superficiality in character.

The foundation of a religious life is laid in infancy. In this, too, Froebel's *Mother-play* tells us how to proceed. We are not to give direct teachings and doctrines to the child. Dry precepts have no meaning to him and are worse than useless. We are to impress him through the religious atmosphere of the home and the ideals there presented to him with the beauty of goodness. The mother's prayer by her child's bed, the peace and serenity filling her heart, the family commendations or criticisms of neighbors, all have their influence and help to form the child's standards of life. The spiritual nature develops with the physical and moral and the full development of the physical nature helps to a fuller growth of the moral and spiritual. We do not know when the child begins to understand God, but that he has an instinctive yearning after God is manifested in his questionings about the source of all things.

The child shows his development to be analogous to that of the human race. Primitive natures feel the need of something higher than themselves to rest upon, so they worship the forces of Nature or set up graven images. Froebel follows the teachings of the Saviour and uses the symbolism of Nature to impart spiritual truths. Of Christ it is said : " Without a parable spake he not unto them."

Finally, Froebel would have us give the child wholesome surroundings, knit the bond of sympathy with mother and the family, teach him to express love by activity, to carry the right standards into the larger world of brothers and sisters in mutual helpfulness and right living, to find the unity in Nature and so through gradual and at last complete influx of light, to be one with God. To the mother he gives this motto :—

> Believe that by the good that's in thy mind,
> Thy child to good will early be inclined ;
> By every noble thought with which thy heart is fired,
> Thy child's young soul will surely be inspired
> And canst thou any better gift bestow,
> Than union with the Eternal One to know?

Although in each song may be found illustrations of the principles set down in the preceding paper on the study of the *Mother-play*, we may say that the first group meets the child's early manifestations of motion and his observation of the unseen forces of Nature. The second group deals with the home life, the expression of love in activity, and the importance of separation and reunion. The third group teaches love for the lower animals, develops spiritual and moral lessons, inculcates responsibility and uses observation as the basis of scientific study. The labor songs inculcate independence and a fitting standard for right social relationships. The songs of the knights set forth the beauty of goodness and the necessity of right motives. The "Light songs" use light as the symbol of God, the source of all life and movement. The transforming power of God's love on the human heart leads to union with Him.

For further reading on *Die Mutter und Koselieder* see:

Kindergarten and Child Culture Papers,	by Henry Barnard, L.L. D.
Mother-play and Nursery Songs,	Josephine Jarvis' translation.
Mottoes and Commentaries on Mother-play,	by Susan E. Blow.
Symbolic Education,	by Susan E. Blow.
Parables from Nature,	by Mrs. Gatty.
Kindergarten Magazine,	Volumes 7 and 8.
Kindergarten News,	for 1894–1895.
Knighthood a Symbol of Moral Power,	by Susan E. Blow, in the *Kindergarten Magazine,* for April and May, 1895.

FOURTEENTH PAPER.

A DAY IN THE KINDERGARTEN.

HAVING considered the occupations and gifts in full, it may be well to show how they are combined for a day's work in the Kindergarten.

First of all, the room itself should be as large, light and airy as it is possible to make it. It should have several windows, one or more of which admit full sunlight and are provided with suitable shades. These shades are best in yellow. There should be growing plants in the windows and shallow pans of earth may be brought in when seeds are to be planted. An aquarium is always an object of interest, but if it is a globe, it must have a large exposed surface of water and great care must be exercised or the fish will be likely to die. Bunches of wheat, other grains and grasses, shells, minerals and birds' nests are kept in cases where the children may handle them and thus learn to know and appreciate them. "That which one loves as a child will probably interest him when he becomes a man. If, then, we would make naturalists or scientists of our children, how can we better begin than by familiarizing them with natural playthings, such as those that God has given them?"

Let the colors of the walls and hangings be neutral. Gray, shades of brown, blue-gray or terra-cotta will prove satisfactory. Denim makes a suitable material for hangings, is inexpensive and either side of it can be used.

PICTURES FOR THE SCHOOL-ROOM.—As to pictures for the walls, choose none but the best, excluding everything crude in coloring and design. If it is not possible to buy many at first, select one of a mother and child—Raphael's "Madonna of the Chair" will answer admirably. Gradually add pictures of animals and birds in their correct colors, pictures of trades, such as a blacksmith or carpenter at work, copies of such pictures as Landseer's "Cattle," Rosa Bonheur's " Horse Fair," Sir Joshua Reynolds' " Angels' Heads," Murillo's " St. Anthony of Padua ; " and portraits of heroes, poets and other noted people, among the first being that of Frederick Froebel.

One of the best authorities on the interior of the school-room says : " In selecting subjects for school-room decorations, besides those of architecture and natural scenery, those illustrating peace, heroism and religion are desirable, and that which most faithfully reflects the true and simple, the strong and courageous. The serious in art never becomes wearisome—it appeals constantly to the human soul. The saddest picture in the Art Palace of the World's Fair was daily surrounded by crowds of people representing all conditions and degrees of culture."

Each Kindergartner will necessarily make her arrangement of tables and ring according to her room. A long room has advantages over a square one, because the black circle painted on the floor for the morning ring and to mark where the children stand for the games can be in the center, with the tables placed at the ends. It insures better order if the tables can have a permanent place and the ring is left entirely free for the morning talk and the games. If, however, limited space renders it necessary to move the tables, let the older children sit at the tables, as they will not feel the disturbance as much as the little ones. One of the most common and probably the best arrangement of the tables is in the form of three sides of a square, the children sitting with their backs to the windows, the light falling over their shoulders upon the work.

Always make the children comfortable physically before attempting to give them a lesson or engage their attention. If any child is so small that its feet do not touch the floor, do not let them dangle, but provide an ottoman. Sometimes a drink of cold water or the simple bathing of the child's face and hands, which gives a slight shock to the system, will do much toward calming its restlessness.

HOURS.—The usual hours for the Kindergarten are from 9 A. M. to 12 M. in public or mission schools, while in private Kindergartens the time varies from two to three hours. Dr. G. Stanley Hall advocates a short recess in the middle of the session to prevent overstraining the attention and to allow the children relaxation. Sometimes a lunch is brought and served before the games. Where this is done a recess is not necessary, the lunch-time allowing of sufficient relaxation. When neither lunch nor recess is considered advisable, if a child is tired (though care must be taken not to cultivate a disposition to complain), he may be excused from the games and sit quietly at one side for five or ten minutes.

If the session is from 9 A. M. to 12 M., the following division of the time is suggested :

        9.00 to   9.35—Morning talk.
        9.35 to   9.40—Gymnastics.
        9.40 to   9.50—Marching.

A DAY IN THE KINDERGARTEN.

9.50 to 10.20—Gift lesson.
10.20 to 11.30—Marching.
10.30 to 11.10—Games.
11.10 to 11.15—Gymnastics.
11.15 to 11.50—Occupation.
11.50 to 12.00—Good-bye songs and dismissal.

BEGINNING THE DAY.—At the time for opening the Kindergarten the leader or one of her assistants seats herself at the piano and begins to play some quiet selection. Great care must be taken to select none but the best music and that suited to children, in order to cultivate a correct ear and good taste. With this opening music the children seat themselves in the chairs which have been previously placed on the circle. The circle is the symbol of unity, and so the Kindergarten day is opened by the children being seated in a circle, acting together as a unit, a whole, a larger family of which the Kindergartner is the head. To enable each one to share in the responsibility, a quiet child is placed next one inclined to be boisterous, and an older one is given charge of one smaller and weaker. Each feels a part of the whole and takes an interest in helping; a larger family life is introduced, and the social life of the world is commenced.

While the children are taking their seats (illustration No. 381) the music changes to march time, played softly. To this the Kindergartner begins to clap her hands in time, the children joining. The healthful exercise and united action, conveying a sense of time and rhythm, soon have their intended effect.

When the room is quiet, a chord is struck and all rise and stand erect, singing a song about the clock and moving first one hand and arm and then the

ILLUSTRATION No. 381.—THE CHILDREN TAKE THEIR SEATS.

other, or both together, to represent the swinging of the pendulum. There are many songs for this purpose. One was given in the Second Paper, quoted from *Songs and Games for Little Ones*. Another is :

Tick, tack, tick, tack, steadily the clock goes on,
Tick, tack, tick, tack, marking seconds one by one,

> Tick, tack, tick, tack, caring not for rain or sun,
> Tick, tack, tick, tack, still the clock goes on.

The clock song brings to the minds of the children the idea of order, regularity, and a fixed time for certain things—in this case the opening hour of the Kindergarten. The mystery surrounding the mechanism of the clock, its simulation of life, together with the rhythm of its beat, makes it an object of interest to the child. Froebel lays special stress on the teaching of order and time and its manifestation in Nature in his "Tick, Tack Song," given in the *Mutter und Koselieder*, which teaching will be emphasized in another paper.

"GOOD MORNING" SONGS.—Following this a "Good Morning" song is sung, which not only embodies greeting and courtesy to each other, but also calls attention again to the time for the Kindergarten.

> Good morning, good morning, good morning to all!
> The clock points the hour, and we come at its call;
> We're happy at work and we're happy at play,
> Then hurrah, hurrah for each happy day!

This song, with slight change of words, occurs in several of the Kindergarten song books. The day is named, the kind of day and some record is kept of the weather, the children themselves describing the sky, the Kindergartner in every case drawing out from the children what they know and not putting into them her knowledge. A calendar is kept in a convenient way on the blackboard or a cardboard, parquetry papers in colors being pasted on to mark the days, separate colors being used to distinguish Kindergarten days from other week days, with an additional color for holidays.

Another "Good Morning Song" greets the sun as the center about which the Solar System moves, the source of light and heat. If the day be cloudy, the children play that they are birds and fly above the clouds where the sun is always shining.

> Good morning, merry sunshine,
>   How did you wake so soon?
> You've scared the little stars away,
>   And shined away the moon.
> I saw you go to sleep last night,
>   Before I ceased my playing;
> How did you get way over there,
>   And where have you been staying?
>
> I never go to sleep, dear child,
>   I'm shining all the night;
> But as your world keeps turning round,
>   It takes you from my sight;
> And when it brings you back again,
>   You'll find I still am here,
> To shine a bright good morning,
>   Down upon the children dear.

The Kindergarten Magazine for February, 1892, suggests that the following two stanzas be used instead of the last one above quoted:

A DAY IN THE KINDERGARTEN.

I never go to sleep, dear child,
  I'm always shining bright,
But as your world goes turning round,
  It takes you from my light;
And then I shine upon the moon,
  And she shines back to you,
So that my light you often see,
  When hidden from my view.

And as your world goes turning round,
  It whirls you into night,
But brings round other boys and girls,
  Into my shining light.
And so I shine, forever shine,
  While you both sleep and wake,
And now you've rolled around again,
  My kind "Good-morning" take!

From this idea of the sun as a center is developed the spiritual or religious idea of a central and ever-prevailing Providence. Thus, without reference to creed or denomination, the child is impressed with the thought of gratitude and reverence.

Another "Good Morning Song" much liked by the children is found in

Songs and Games for Little Ones, published by the Oliver Ditson Company. It is given above.

THE MORNING TALK.—Talk over each song point by point with the children, to be certain that they understand the words. The friendly greeting of playmates, the joy of entering upon a new day, the recollection of all the helping hands that have been engaged in making ready the bath, the breakfast, and other intermediate steps before coming to the Kindergarten, when properly called to his attention help to show the child the social interdependence of men and he naturally desires to thank the loving Father who planned so wisely for

MORNING HYMN.

Rebecca J. Weston.   *D. Batchellor.*

1. Father, we thank Thee for the night, And for the pleasant morning light, For rest and food and loving care, And all that makes the day so fair.

2. Help us to do the things we should,
To be to others kind and good;
In all we do in work or play
To grow more loving every day.

From "Voice for the Music Course," by per. F. B. Ginn.

His creatures. Normal children are essentially religious and are made unhappy if they are not led back to the first great cause.

Other lessons in connection with the sun allude to light as the source of color. The prism showing sunlight broken into its colors may be introduced, as may also Milton Bradley's color wheel and his color tops, the last named being put into the hands of each child to observe for himself. Dress materials and the shades and tints of flowers and leaves may be matched. The numerous combinations of color are thus studied in an experimental and interesting way, until the children become accurate judges of how much of each color is needed for any shade, tint or hue. This is accomplished in a truly reverential spirit, for if a gay flower is matched, does it not show how many colors the sun used to paint the brilliant petals? In fact, all the work of the Kindergarten gives practical direction to the moral and religious nature of the child, because in the games, the plays, the gifts and occupation work, and in the songs he puts into play-practice his relationship to Nature, family, society, country and Creator. A "Morning Hymn" admirably in line with this thought is given above.

The morning talk may be said to be the keynote of the Kindergarten day, for by it the Kindergartner seeks to establish the unity of the day by bringing the children into loving relationship with herself, with each other, with society through interdependence, and, in all and above all, to recognize God through

His works as the Creator and as the Center of the Universe, the Source of all power, knowledge, love and blessing.

SUBJECTS.—The morning talk must necessarily vary from day to day, no two days being alike. It may concern the playing of finger games, the seasons, animal or plant life, an example of bravery or unselfishness or the choosing of familiar songs by the children themselves. For this no stereotyped programme can be given. Whatever it may relate to, the morning talk is with, and not at, the children. The wise Kindergartner studies her children, their needs, age and condition in life, and, using the common yet wonderful things of Nature and the experience of daily life, seeks to develop character by presenting the ideal to the children in such a way as shall lead them to adopt and cherish it. In the words of Miss Poulsson: "Here, indeed, is serious, responsible, holy work for the teacher. No normal training, no school of science, can outline her course. Only by continual, earnest thought and study and unremitting seeking can the Kindergartner find out how to make all things serve as tools with which to draw such pictures of goodness and truth that the childish hearts may be attracted by their surpassing beauty and won to loving and devoted allegiance. Everything in the Universe has its inner meaning, which will help to delineate the beauty of goodness. Let the Kindergartner's intent, therefore, be to seek the moral germ (if it may be so called) which is in all things and ever hold the underlying purpose of the morning talk to be the awakening of the child's higher nature."

LESSONS IN DISCIPLINE.—At the close of the morning talk a chord is struck on the piano. The children rise and take their chairs to the tables. Then some simple gymnastics are given to relax the body and relieve the tension of sitting. Following this the children form in line and march for about ten or fifteen minutes. This marching is not only good as a physical exercise, the rhythm exerting a quieting and order-inspiring influence and giving a firm, graceful carriage of the body, but it contributes moral training as well, since the rights of others must be respected, individuality submerged for the time being, and a spirit of obedience and self-control cultivated, it being necessary for all to follow the leader.

> "Theirs not to make reply,
> Theirs not to reason why."

Then comes the gift lesson. (Illustration No. 382.) During this the children are seated at the tables, there being several groups according to the intellectual development of the children, those of about the same advancement sitting together. As each gift has been described in detail, we will only say that the gift lesson gives both intellectual discipline and manual training. The child, while handling his gift with dexterity and delicacy, learns to recognize, compare, criticise and invent. The morning talk may be illustrated by the gift lesson, the gift being used to picture the subject to the child, while the facts about the gift itself are developed simply and naturally through its use. From half an hour to forty minutes is the usual time allotted to the gift lesson. This includes both distribution and collection, the children themselves doing the work and thus cultivating habits of order and neatness.

ILLUSTRATION NO. 382.—THE GIFT LESSON.

At a given signal the children again march, this time, perhaps, singing patriotic songs or, with opened windows, take several turns around the rooms at a good running pace.

GAMES.—Then, forming a ring, they stand on the circle and play the games. (Illustration No. 383.) As the games have been described in detail in the Twelfth Paper, we will only give a general outline of them here. A leader is chosen who indicates by some gesture the game he would like to play. If it be a special game, he chooses those to take part; if a general one, all join in playing it. Then this leader chooses another child to select a second play. Choice is generally made of those who show the greatest desire to add to the general enjoyment. As it is not possible to allow all to choose a game, the method of choosing affords excellent moral training, especially to the *only* child, or the spoiled child who has been accustomed to be placed first as a matter of right. The games close with another march, some simple gymnastics or finger plays, the Kindergartner always clothing the old in a new dress.

THE OCCUPATION.—Then the children return to the tables for the occupation. The occupation applies the principles contained in the gift lesson. Here the child with unrelated materials constructs a tangible object, which result of his labor may be carried home as a present to some one he loves, thus fostering generous and kindly impulses, or, if left in the Kindergarten, other like objects may be added to it from day to day until all are finally collected in book

A DAY IN THE KINDERGARTEN.

form at the close of the year. During the occupation the children are allowed to chat quietly among themselves, helping each other and making suggestions. But each child must persevere to the end, for no unfinished work is permitted without adequate reason. All are encouraged, and good work—that is, the child's best effort—is always recognized and commended.

ILLUSTRATION NO. 383.—READY FOR THE GAME.

When the time for closing arrives the children march to the circle and sing this "Good-bye" song:

> Now our work is over, over is our play,
> Let us to each other say, "Good-bye" to-day.
> When the morning sunbeams wake us from our sleep,
> We'll return in gladness, fresh and clean and sweet.

Thus it will be seen that the Kindergarten day rightly conducted is a unit, a complete whole. The morning talk gives the keynote, the gift lesson takes up and illustrates the predominating thought, the games impersonate it and the occupation applies the gift lesson. The child is thus developed on all sides of his being in a simple, natural way through his divinely-appointed instinct of play. "Play," says the great and wise Plato, "is the business of childhood." Well-directed play is, therefore, for children the best preparation for the work which they will be called upon to perform later in life.

A WEEK OF KINDERGARTEN WORK.—The following is offered as a suggestion of a programme for the first week of Kindergarten work:

MORNING TALK :—Connect the home life of the children with the Kindergarten, and draw out their Summer experiences.

FINGER PLAYS :—Ball for Baby, Counting Lesson and Merry Men.

PRAYER :—First Stanza.

SONGS :—Greetings, "Good Morning, Merry Sunshine," "Tick, Tack," Bird Song, Baker, Finger Song for Family, Shoemaker and "Good-bye."

GAMES :—Songs for forming the circle, Wandering game (to get the children acquainted), Blacksmith, Carpenter, Squirrel, "Come, Take a Little Partner!"

MONDAY GIFT LESSON :—Red ball of the first gift—motion, texture.
MONDAY OCCUPATION :—Stringing red Hailmann bead balls.
TUESDAY GIFT LESSON :—Seventh-gift circles, simple border pattern.
TUESDAY OCCUPATION :—Paste the same design in parquetry papers on mounting sheets.
WEDNESDAY GIFT LESSON :—Red ball and another of a different color from the first gift ; show flowers and materials of the same colors.
WEDNESDAY OCCUPATION :—Sorting different materials in the colors of the gift lesson.
THURSDAY GIFT LESSON :—Large ring of the eighth gift.
THURSDAY OCCUPATION :—Sewing (in the circle).
FRIDAY GIFT LESSON :—Second gift balls compared and rolling game.
FRIDAY OCCUPATION :—Making a clay ball.
For further suggestions see :
The Kindergarten Magazine for February, 1892 ; *Songs and Games for Little Ones*, by Misses Walker and Jenks.

FIFTEENTH PAPER.

THE HOME KINDERGARTEN.

WHILE it is hardly possible to conduct the conventional Kindergarten in the home, still there is much the mother can do if she has the Kindergarten spirit. Everything that helps the child to a better physical growth, everything that cultivates obedience, truthfulness, self-reliance, everything that trains in punctuality and observation, is in reality Kindergarten training. The Kindergarten supplies what the home is sometimes unable to supply, either from lack of play room, the multiplied duties of the mother or the want of associates of the child's own age.

There are many things to be said for and some against the Kindergarten. I am a firm believer in it, but when it develops self-consciousness, tends to a restless desire for constant change of amusement or is in charge of a Kindergartner who is not both naturally fitted and thoroughly trained for the work, then the Kindergarten does more harm than good. Mothers who were formerly well-known Kindergartners do not always send their children to the outside Kindergarten, but often prefer to gather the children of a few friends about them and give the work in their own home nursery.

On the other hand, the outside Kindergarten is often a better preparation for the school life which follows, as it provides a more gradual transition from the free home life to the strict discipline of the primary school. Then, too, mothers cannot devote all their time to their children. They must be companionable to their husbands ; they must attend to household, social and religious duties and give some attention to mental and spiritual cultivation. Besides, to do the other duties well, they must have time for relaxation, rest and recreation.

The wife and mother must not think of her husband and children for to-day alone; she must do everything she can to be fresh and companionable for them and herself ten or more years ahead. The only way to accomplish this is to decide between essentials and non-essentials. Every mother must decide for herself how much of these things she is able to do. In cities it is generally wise to send children to the Kindergarten, but in small towns which are without a Kindergarten and in the country my advice would be to the mothers to make their children's lives as wholesome and healthy as possible and leave the rest to Providence. If there comes an opening for Kindergarten work, take advantage of it.

Now as to things to work with, it is not absolutely necessary to have the exact Kindergarten material in order to develop the child according to the Kindergarten method. To understand this it may be well to restate some Kindergarten principles. The Kindergarten gifts and occupations are only a means to an end, the tools used suited to the child's age and strength, for the development of character. Character should be the aim of all education—a fitting, as said so many times before, of the human being to live rightly with God, Nature and his fellow-man. It goes without saying that for this right living the individual succeeds best who is sound physically, mentally and morally. Then, as we cannot divide life into distinct periods and tell just when and how each development begins, Froebel would have us begin at the beginning. So, as all early development comes through the senses, he arranged material which he personally proved, if rightly used, would meet these requirements and allow the child to educate himself by his own activity—at the child's age called "play." The Kindergartner and mother watch his development by his manifestations and supply new and more difficult material to meet, direct and stimulate his increasing growth. They stand to the child as the careful gardener stands to the plant, ever ready to water, to prune, to give sun, shade or any condition necessary to induce this particular plant to reach its highest perfection of growth, flower and fruit. Sometimes the gardener with the simplest contrivances is able to accomplish as much and more than the man with every convenience at hand. In like manner we often see mothers in the humblest homes, bringing up children who are worthy of the honor and esteem of all who know them, because the mothers have been able to make the most and best use of every-day things and to find beauty and goodness in all.

FRAU SCHRADER'S WORK.—Froebel himself would have been able to conduct a Kindergarten in a desert, for even there he would still have had the sand and sky. This use of every-day material is one great point that Frau Schrader, Director of the Pestalozzi-Froebel Haus, Berlin, is said to insist upon to her training class. In Germany many Kindergartners take service as governesses, and I believe the training classes there require their graduates to do one year's work in a family before beginning as teachers in the schools.

Mrs. Susan S. Harriman, in a paper read before the Educational Association last Summer, tells what she saw of this simple home work when visiting

Frau Schrader's establishment. The school, as is usual in all schools, is divided into classes according to age and development. At stated periods a child is taken from each of these classes to help form a group the members of which are of different ages, this group corresponding to the home circle. Some young woman is put in charge of this group whose business it is to keep the children busy and happy, mentally helpful to each other, and to use some simple home duty or occupation as a means of educational training. The group Mrs. Harriman describes was engaged with an ordinary home work-basket and through it occupation was found for each of the group. One child wound and fastened the spools; another sorted and arranged the needles; a third used the emery; one girl made a dress for her doll from a piece of silk found in the basket; another did some mending; an older boy was given a pencil and paper on which to write a letter or do a bit of drawing. Mrs. Harriman, in commenting upon this method, says: "The value of this work as a means of developing the power of adaptability, of enabling a girl to turn everything to use and make it serve her purpose, cannot be overestimated. 'Eyes and they see not, ears and hear not,' describes the condition of most of us. We are looking for more favorable circumstances and better materials to work with when every day finds us surrounded with a wealth of opportunity that we overlook because it is so near at hand. Making the most and best of opportunities that are near by has been the foundation of many a successful career."

Mrs. Harriman, speaking of the practical work of Frau Schrader's school, says that though situated in the heart of a great city, it has beautiful flower and vegetable gardens. In the care of these the children help as much as they are able, removing dead leaves, planting seed and picking flowers and fruit. Many of the German schools have valuable gardens where the pupils have practical work in horticulture and forestry combined with the ordinary school studies. Mrs. Harriman describes a small class at Frau Schrader's school, the members of which picked currants, stemmed them, pressed out the juice and made it into jelly for their own use at luncheon and to carry to sick friends.

A mother of my acquaintance who believes in interesting her children in household occupations often places a chair by her baking table in which sits a small observer who rolls and pats a small piece of dough almost as well as mama. An older child delights in making a genuine small cake when her mother bakes a large one, following the recipe but using spoonfuls where her mother uses larger quantities.

MOTHERS' CLUBS.—Most of the prominent Kindergarten training classes now offer a course of study to mothers. At the Teacher's College, New York City, the course is a short one of eight weeks, including with each lesson a lecture on Froebel's theory, the learning of songs and the practice of games selected for home use.

At Pratt Institute, Brooklyn, the course extends over two years. The class meets once a week for forty weeks, each session being of two hours' duration. The gifts and occupations suitable for home use are studied and lessons are given in each. Songs and games are practised and applied to occupation and gift. The *Mother-play* and *Education of Man* are studied with the view of making their lessons applicable to such subjects as obedience, truthfulness and punishments. Experiences are exchanged and discussions take place on hygiene, food, clothing and other allied topics. The art of story-telling is studied, and lists of the best books and playthings for children are made. Mothers may also have the advantage of the many lectures offered there on educational subjects and topics of the day.

At the Chicago Kindergarten College the course is extended over a period of three years. Its catalogue has this to say regarding the "Mothers' Classes:"

The first year's work includes practical work with such gifts and occupations as can best be used in the nursery; study of Froebel's *Mutter und Koselieder*, which will enable the mother to grasp the principles of the system and to re-apply them on the innumerable occasions which arise in the home life; also discussions and the answering of questions concerning the study and experiences of the week previous.

The second year includes work with gifts and occupations, science work for little children, the study of Froebel's *Mutter und Koselieder*, discussions and the answering of questions.

The third year the lessons include advanced work with all the gifts and occupations, games and stories of the Kindergarten, the study of Froebel's *Mutter und Koselieder* and *Education of Man*. All mothers belonging to this department, who request it, are furnished with courses of collateral reading and are assisted in other ways to enlarge their knowledge and insight in this direction.

The lessons in all three of the institutions mentioned are open to any woman interested in Kindergarten work, but, of course, there are no certificates or diplomas given for these courses of study.

The Chicago Kindergarten College also offers to assist classes or clubs formed in towns and villages at a distance from Chicago. These clubs are called "Local Unions" and, as far as possible, are given the same course of study as that carried on at the College. For this purpose the College has a special Secretary of the Mother's Department, who will organize classes, arrange and superintend their work, conduct the correspondence with the classes, and give information to all interested in this department of work. Further information, constitutions and plans of organization will be furnished any one upon application to the College authorities.

I have given the above for the information of mothers, including those to whom I have written personally explaining, as fully as possible in a letter, the advantages offered them by three prominent Kindergarten training-schools. Better satisfaction is obtained by following such a plan and seeking aid from such a source, where the work is systematic and is in charge of specialists. However, if it is not possible to follow this plan, a home club may be formed among a group of friends somewhat as follows: Decide to meet at the house of each member in turn once a week, or once every other week, for from one to two hours. Take up each time one of the *Mother-play* songs to read and talk about. Try to recall familiar songs, stories and experiences with children that bring out the same thought, studying with the *Mother-play* and the Baroness Marenholtz-Bülow's book, *Child and Child-nature*. Let each mother make notes during the week of perplexities and happy experiences with her children to relate for discussion and mutual helpfulness. Let a record be kept of these discussions for additional light upon future child study. Learn songs, games and stories, mothers also giving the ones they have used. Select subjects and decide what use can be made of the gifts, occupations, songs, games and stories to illustrate those subjects. Programmes of work for the week or month would thus be formed. These could be tested with the children and afterwards discussed and criticised from the standpoint of actual practice. If found unsuccessful, learn why. Family excursions or familiar stories may be worked out in this way. Froebel's "Farmyard Gate" would be an interesting subject for a country child's actual Winter observation, or for the city child recalling his Summer visit in the country, and might include learning the names of the animals in the farmyard, cutting out and mounting their pictures, building houses like the ones they are kept in, finding out the food and care they need, what they do for people, etc., etc. There may be found plenty of material for stories, songs, games, gift lessons, sewing, weaving, paper-folding and cutting and drawing.

HOUSEHOLD WORK.—Household experiences may also be used to good advantage. For instance, in the paper on the fourth gift, some illustrations were given of how the subject of baking and the baker could be developed. Commence with the germination of seeds as there directed. Select finger plays and songs such as, "This is the Way the Rain Comes Down," "Shower and Flower," "Wake, Says the Sunshine," "The Farmer," "The Mill Wheels are Turning" and others. The "Baker Sequence" in the paper referred to shows how to use a gift in illustrating a subject. Decide what other gifts and what occupations could be used. Make lists of the tools used. Collect as many pictures as possible that will show any phase of the subject from the first preparation of the field for sowing to the completed loaf of bread. To carry out Froebel's law of unity, show first the grain, then the loaf of bread and connect them by the steps between. Take only the main points; too much detail is tiresome to the child and renders the subject confusing. Show all the grains used for bread-making and let the children learn to know and be able to sort them.

The general rule, for either the mother or the professional Kindergartner, is to first get full information herself concerning the subject and processes. Select the main points that are instructive, helpful and interesting, keeping in mind the age and characteristics of the child. As the subject is presented, encourage the child to invent new uses of the gift and occupation illustrating the subject, to turn every-day materials to account, to look for pictures and suggest songs. This will show the child's line of associations and classifications, indicate his individuality and aid in correcting wrong ideas.

The children might be allowed to accompany the mothers to meetings of the mothers' club. Devote the first half of the allotted time to them and then send them out of doors to play while the *Mother-play* is read, experiences exchanged and other meetings planned. The programme for the children would admit of great variety. At one time they could learn songs and finger plays and at another, games, marches or dances (see "A Day in the Kindergarten," for an illustration of the Kindergarten ring); the work could be divided among the mothers present, one telling a story, another showing pictures illustrating a gift, and a third giving an occupation lesson. After many songs, games and finger plays had been learned, a certain number of children might be asked to bring pictures, and one at a time rise in the ring, show these pictures, tell what they were and give some explanation or a short description of them. Then another child might be asked to name a song, game or finger play suggested by the picture in which all could join.

There are many games for testing the senses that might be used with profit at such meetings. For sight there are: First, the naming of the various visible objects; second, the sending of several children each to a different window for a short time to tell upon their return what has been seen; third, sending a child into another room to name upon return the furniture, etc., seen; fourth, having a child walk past a table with a variety of objects upon it and recall as many as possible; fifth, distinguishing between fresh and dried fruits. Insist upon good language being used. When a child learns to write, the result may be written instead of being given orally. If the child has been accustomed to recount his experiences, he will take great delight in putting his little stories upon paper. Be careful to have him omit personal details. The color top will be useful in this connection.

Similar exercises may be applied to smell, taste, touch and hearing. With hearing the child may be taught to name the object by sound and also to locate the direction from which the sound comes, trying different parts of the room and also sounds in other rooms. With these sound exercises the musical scale may be practiced, first as "do, re, mi, fa, sol, la, te, do," then sing to "la" or "ah," and finally give ear tests on different notes, singing them to "la" or "ah." The Tonic Sol-Fa music system accomplishes much in this direction, its adherents claiming that most children can learn to sing, if training for the ear and vocal organs is commenced early. This system also has a series of simple hand signs to aid in the teaching. Books of first steps and directions for this system can be obtained from most music dealers.

BOOKS FOR MOTHERS.—For a mothers' club the following books may be recommended as comprehensive and not too technical:

Mottoes and Commentaries on Froebel's Mother-play, Susan E. Blow.......D. Appleton & Co. $1.50
  New free translation; more readable than old editions.
Froebel's Mother Songs and Games, Susan E. Blow......................D. Appleton & Co. 1.50
Froebel's Poems and Pictures for Songs and Games, Susan E. Blow........D. Appleton & Co. 2.00
  For the children.
Kindergarten Papers, Sara M. Kirby...............................Butterick Publishing Co. 1.00
  Explaining gifts, etc.
Child and Child Nature, Baroness Marenholtz-Bülow....................E. Steiger & Co. 1.00
  Exposition of Froebel's theory.
Reminiscences of Froebel, Baroness Marenholtz-Bülow..................E. Steiger & Co. 1.50
  Froebel's life and times.
Contents of Children's Minds, Dr. G. Stanley Hall..................E. L. Kellogg & Co. .25
  Explains development of child's mind.
In the Child's World, Emilie Poulsson............................Milton Bradley Co. 2.00
  Stories and morning talks for all the year round. References for collateral reading.

KINDERGARTEN PAPERS.

Finger Plays for Nursery and Kindergarten, Emilie Poulsson.......Lothrop Publishing Co. 1.25
    Songs and finger games.
Merry Songs and Games, Mrs. Clara Beeson Hubbard..................Balmer & Weber 2.00
Songs and Games for Little Ones, Misses Walker and Jenks.............Oliver Ditson Co. 2.00
Paradise of Childhood, Ed. Wiebe..................................Milton Bradley Co. 2.00
    Practical work with gifts and occupations.
Kindergarten Magazine.....................................166 S. Clinton St., Chicago 2.00
Kindergarten News, Editor, Henry W. Blake..........................Milton Bradley Co. .50
    Devoted to stories, programmes, specimen lessons, news concerning Kindergarten work.
Seven Little Sisters Who Live on the Round Ball that Floats in the Air, Jane Andrews....... .50

    The following list of supplementary readers for children will also be found useful to Kindergartners and mothers for story telling :

Child's Christ Tales, Andrea Hofer........................Kindergarten Literature Co. $1.00
Fairy Tales, Hans Christian Andersen......................................Ginn & Co. .50
Leaves and Flowers or Plant Studies for Young Readers, Mary N. Spear................... .30
Seaside and Wayside, Julia McNair Wright.
    In three parts.
Skyward and Back, Lucy M. Robinson............................School Education Co. .30

    These books may be purchased through almost any dealer. If purchased for a club, a liberal discount should be obtained.

    MATERIALS FOR THE HOME KINDERGARTEN.—In preparing for a home or other small Kindergarten, first secure a catalogue from some firm dealing in Kindergarten supplies. As there is such a variety of materials offered for some of the gifts and most of the occupations, it is difficult for the inexperienced to decide just what to purchase. The following list includes only what is most practical. For a large class of children divided into groups, one group having an occupation while another has a gift lesson, supposing there are two or more teachers, it is usually sufficient if only one-half or at most two-thirds as many gifts of each number are bought as there are children. For example, if there are thirty children, buy from fifteen to twenty gifts of each number, unless there is only one teacher, when it would be necessary to keep the children in one group. Here is the list :

FIRST GIFT.—Six soft balls, standards of the six colors, to be made at home by directions given on page 33.
SECOND GIFT.—If for several children, obtain in bulk.
THIRD GIFT.
FOURTH GIFT.
FIFTH AND SIXTH GIFTS.—Omit unless there are children six years old. Do not give until most positions possible for the third and fourths gifts as mentioned in these papers on those gifts have been given.
SEVENTH GIFT.—Use all forms for the older children, but only circles and squares for the younger ones. Use the circles with the first and second gifts, the squares with the third and fourth and half squares with the fifth gift.
PARQUETRY PAPERS.—These are used to repeat the work of the seventh gift by pasting the designs upon paper. Select Ungummed Coated Assortment No. 6-a in each of the forms. For later use get what is known as Ungummed Coated Assortment No. 6-b in each form. For small quantities buy Ungummed Coated Parquetry Papers in small envelopes. These contain 100, 200 and 500 pieces, as desired.
MOUNTING SHEETS FOR PARQUETRY.—Style No. 2, 12 leaves 7 x 9 white Bristol.

EIGHTH GIFT.—Paper box with 1000 sticks assorted from 1 inch to 5 inches. This is sufficient for a good-sized class. Colored sticks may be purchased if desired, but they are not necessary.

NINTH GIFT.—Soldered rings. A double order is required for any but small classes.

TENTH GIFT.—Lentils, a German bean, to be obtained at grocer's or seed store.

DRAWING PAPER.—Dotted sheets 7 x 9.

PAPER CUTTING.—Papers 4 x 4, ruled and coated, beginning with "Assortment A." Blunt pointed scissors.

SEWING.—Use at first the simplest patterns in "Design Cards" 4 x 5½ inches, or square white Bristol, and draw and prick them at home. Miss Arnold's "Natural History Sewing Card" may be used for older children. Sew in the natural colors. Moderately fine embroidery silks are preferred, and may be bought at home stores. Cultivate a nice taste in color. Scenery, buildings and animals may be done in fine black silk and will then resemble pen-and-ink sketches. Use worsted needles having long eyes and blunt points. If it be necessary to use worsted, buy "split zephyr." The wrong side of the card must be neat.

WEAVING.—Mats 4¾ x 4¾ inches, stripes either ¼ or 1-6 inch wide. It is best to order several packages of different color combinations and not to waste mats or have crude combinations. Mrs. Hailmann's mats are used for the babies.

FOLDING PAPERS.—Squares 4 x 4 engine color, assorted.

PEAS WORK.—Dried marafats from the grocery or seed store will answer. Soak and use them with wires or sticks.

CLAY.—Buy at a pottery or use fire-brick clay from the stove store.

BEADS FOR STRINGING.—Buy 1000 of Mrs. Hailmann's ½ inch beads, spheres, cubes and cylinders.

PEG BOARD.—Make at home, either using a wooden board or paper box lid, perforating the holes and using shoe pegs colored with Diamond Dyes. See illustration No. 342 on page 108.

COLOR TOPS.—Valuable and inexpensive.

TABLES.—These are not necessary for home use. If desired, buy 4 feet long, 16 inches wide. Squared enameled cloth or ruled unbleached muslin tied over any low table is sufficient. For schools, use a table 6 feet long and 16 inches wide.

Made-up boxes of Kindergarten materials advertised "for home use" are generally unsatisfactory.

SIXTEENTH PAPER.

TRAINING AND TRAINING SCHOOLS.

BEFORE undertaking to become a Kindergarten teacher, a young woman should consider very seriously, first, whether she possesses the natural qualifications for this work, and, secondly, whether she can spend the time and money for thorough general and special training without which she will find herself at a distinct disadvantage. She should question herself, and consider the work from the child's standpoint, making a conscientious self-examination as to whether she is the right person to assume such a responsibility. It was once thought that anyone could teach little children, but long ago school boards found it most important to engage skilled teachers for the primary grades, since the work at the beginning makes itself felt through every succeeding grade. If the foundation is insecure, how can the superstructure be firm and symmetrical?

In preceding papers we have shown the need of the best care and training for the child from birth to school age. This should include, first, a better preparation for their duties on the part of the mothers, and then a careful selection of nurse and Kindergarten.

No person can really decide for another in any important matter, since no one can enter exactly into the thoughts, feelings and circumstances of another. What might be a great undertaking to a timid person would prove only an exhilarating excitement to one of greater nerve and self-reliance. All the outsider can do, no matter how friendly and sympathetic, is to present reasons for and against any given cause. In all the great questions of life every individual stands alone and must decide for himself. Let him gather all the information he can, weigh it carefully, and, after he has decided, press on. It is not the purpose of this paper to discourage any woman from becoming a Kindergartner who has the natural qualifications and feels that she has it in her to do that work, but as we all want to choose what we are best fitted for, we should first ascertain what the work includes, and what are the chances of success.

LOVE FOR CHILDREN.—"More important," says Froebel, "than age and school education, is the girlish love of childhood and an ability to occupy herself with children, as well as the serene and joyful view taken of life in general. There ought also to be a love of play and playful occupations, and a love and a capacity for singing. It goes without saying that purity of intentions and a lovely, womanly disposition are essential requisites. The fuller the educational accomplishments of a lady, all the more rapid and satisfactory will be her progress in the science."

The first requirements of a Kindergartner are good health, a happy, wholesome disposition, plenty of tact, and a real love for and pleasure in the companionship of children. No person who is sickly or morbid should ever undertake the care of little children. As to good health, although the Kindergarten hours are short, there is very little of the time that the teacher can set for her charges a definite task and leave them to it. She must be the guiding, controlling, impressing spirit; she must keep out friction and insure interest and good-fellowship. If she is listless or uninteresting, nervous or irritable, her audience will quickly reflect her state of mind and be vastly more harmed than benefitted. If it requires vitality and energy on the part of a public speaker to hold an audience of grown people capable of forcing interest and self-control for an hour and a half, it is reasonable to suppose that to give out one's-self for three continuous hours in the service of restless, active little folks requires a physical and mental self-poise not easily disturbed.

The Kindergartner, of all others, needs to forget herself, to enter the child's life, to adapt herself to changing conditions, to have true sympathy and tact (which last, by-the-way, is nine parts sympathy and one part common sense), to be a child with the children and at the same time to possess the dignity, wisdom and firmnesss of maturity. If physical pain is always present with her, or she is disturbed by distressing mental anxieties, she cannot forget herself, and the passive education of the children is not what it would be if she had health and buoyancy of spirits. A friend in speaking of two sisters, both Kindergartners, said: "One is nearer the ideal Kindergartner than the other because she has such an illumined countenance which attracts and holds children."

A Kindergartner should be a religious person, filling the childish mind with the beauty of truth and goodness, teaching the child to instinctively seek the right and shun the wrong, and that life is what he makes it by his own work and the part he plays in it. This should be the result of the personal example of the Kindergartner, the atmosphere which emanates from her rather than the effect of direct religious instruction. Says one of Boston's prominent workers in regard to Christian character: "It is not unfair to say to the young women who are crowding the ranks of the Kindergarten to-day, that there can be no yawning chasm between the public and private life of a Kindergartner. The fountain as well as the stream, the hidden pools and rainbow-hued spray, of their lives must be forever the same, whether in the noonday of publicity or the twilight of home." In one of my note-books I find an important place given to these words: "To lead others we must advance; to govern others we must first govern ourselves; to develop harmoniously the character of little children we must perfect our own characters in every possible way."

Music.—A pleasant voice in speaking and the ability to sing well are distinct advantages to a Kindergartner. The inability to sing may not debar a girl from undertaking Kindergarten work, although many of the best training-schools do not accept a candidate unless she possesses at least a spark of ability in this direction. If she cannot under any circumstances sing, she must be especially proficient in other directions—that is, be able to write or translate Kindergarten literature, go upon the lecture platform or possess great executive ability. Two of the most prominent promoters of the Kindergarten movement in this country cannot carry a tune, but one has done valuable work by changing Froebel's obscure German into clear English, while the other, also an accomplished writer, possesses a personal magnetism and keen sense of humor which carry all before them, whether her audience be a group of little children or a large body of cultured men and women. If one can be a leader, it does not so much matter about the singing or playing, as these can be supplied, but even then a knowledge of music is an added power. In the Kindergarten, leadership is only held by experienced and cultured women who can educate the public and show the people who give their money to such causes why it is a better investment to add the Kindergarten to the public schools than to build more prisons and reformatories. Again, those who have worked their way up to prominent positions have generally passed through the apprenticeship of assistant, principal, supervisor and training teachers.

If the Kindergarten is too small to afford more than one teacher, she must necessarily sing and play or pay another to do this work for her, and this is apt to be less effective than if she could do it herself. If a teacher can neither sing nor play, she must seek for a Kindergarten with some one who can do both, and thus be obliged to take a subordinate position. Even in a large Kindergarten with several other teachers, her group work, without the simple melodies that often render the gift lesson so effective, will be below that of her more fortunate sisters. This fact would be especially noticeable if she had charge of the youngest children.

Another effective accomplishment is simple blackboard sketching. There are so many helps now in this line of work that patient, painstaking effort, with a good eye, backed by even a little skill, will suffice. The simplest outlines, if true to nature, are more pleasing and comprehensible to a child than elaborate drawings.

GENERAL PREPARATION.—As to general preparation, a thorough high school education is the very least that one ought to possess before presenting herself at the doors of the Kindergarten training-schools. If the young woman has a college diploma, so much the better, for then she is more likely to have deliberately chosen the Kindergarten with a full knowledge of her own powers and of the work required. Do not consider any preparation too much or any accomplishment wasted. One can never tell when the thing thought unnecessary will bring us the very object we are striving for. Choose the occupation, if possible, when a young girl, get as broad an education as possible and make the most and best of yourself in every way.

We do not wish to lay down any set rules, but on all these points we endeavor to give the concurrent opinion of Kindergartners, in connection with individual experience.

There are many Kindergartners now in the field who began late in life, but most of them did so to supplement or complete work undertaken long before. Many primary teachers, feeling the need of a knowledge of the Kindergarten because of its intimate connection with their own work, while studying have found themselves more drawn to it than to their regular occupation. Others have first studied it to teach their own children. It is said of the Baroness Marenholtz-Bülow, that she first became interested in the problems of education from superintending the studies of her husband's children. Prominent philanthropists and educators have been led back to the Kindergarten in an endeavor to get at first principles and the beginnings of reforms and in this way have become advocates of its cause. Froebel himself went back step by step from the higher grades ("higher" in the accepted sense) of teaching until he stood beside the infant in its mother's arms.

PRIVATE, PUBLIC AND MISSION SCHOOLS.—The subdivisions of the work cover private, public, mission and training schools. As private schools are classified, those owned by the Kindergartner herself, by other individuals and by societies (boarding or day schools). By public schools are meant those under the usual public school boards. Both these classes of schools allow the Kindergartner more leisure outside of the regular school hours than do the mission schools, because in them she does not so often visit her pupils at their homes. Of course, every Kindergartner must plan all orders of exercises and have all materials ready and at hand before the day's work begins, and also allow for circumstances necessitating a sudden change of programme. She must study and belong to clubs and teachers' associations.

In the mission schools, those supported by the charity of an individual or society or connected with churches or College Settlements, the actual teaching, though the most important, is yet only one part of the work. Here the Kindergartner becomes the visitor, friend, confidante and counselor of the parents, the instrument for relieving distress, finding work, arousing to better lives, teaching the mothers how to care intelligently for their babies, stimulating an interest in sewing, cooking and the sanitary laws. The Kindergartner's work here is incalculable because she first interests and wins the child and through him the parents. She has her mothers' club, where she cultivates a better social life and simplifies Froebel's teachings to the mothers. She must also be prepared to give reports of her work to the public and arouse its interest by writing and lecturing. All this demands a Christian, cultured and *practical* woman. We emphasize "practical" because a sentimental love for children or for the Kindergarten work is the last thing needed. Anyone who establishes a mission Kindergarten and places the right woman at its head is surely following Christ's injunction: "Inasmuch as ye have done it unto the least of these, my brethren, ye have done it unto me."

THE TRAINING TEACHER.—The greatest work of the training teacher lies not in teaching the technicalities of the Kindergarten system, but in broadening the lives and enriching the characters of those who are expecting to become Kindergartners. She must inculcate "the true spirit of Froebel's educational theories, as well as an enthusiasm for humanity and a clear conception of the application of these theories, to render these young women not only conscientious but intelligent Kindergartners." In most training schools the actual Kindergarten work is divided among several teachers, one, perhaps, supervising the programmes, another the gift lessons, and so on, at the head of all being one who gives the theory and mother-play, a woman whose daily example should carry inspiration to everything elevating, one who can really give her pupils that which will never become old but will go on deepening and enriching them forever.

The life of the training teacher does not allow of much leisure, for, outside of her regular lecture periods, she directs the work of both the children's class and that for the older students, sees inquiring visitors, represents her school in the various educational associations and clubs, attends public functions, writes for the press, organizes mothers' clubs, goes on lecturing tours, attends to a large correspondence and keeps in touch with all the vital questions of the day. All this requires a strong personality, vigorous health, great powers of endurance and continued study. If it were not for the complete relaxation and change of place during the Summer months, few women could endure the nervous strain of such an undertaking.

SALARIES.—As to salaries, those for private school Kindergartens and for assistants in public and mission schools, range from $300 to $600 per year; for principals, where visiting mothers' clubs and other outside work is included, from $600 to $800, in a few cases $900 and $1,000, per year. For superintendents, whose work it is to visit and report on all the public and mission Kindergartens

of a city or district and lecture before the teachers, the salaries are $1,000 and
$1,200. Training teachers earn from $1,000 to $3,000. They generally have
their traveling expenses defrayed when lecturing and receive additional fees
for lectures. All teachers must at their own expense buy necessary books and
magazines to keep up with the work and the times, must pay their own membership fees for associations and clubs and traveling expenses to and from such
gatherings. They do not profit by being too economical in these outlays. Contact with others engaged in the same work arouses enthusiasm and smoothes
many a discouragement.

The Kindergartner, to keep up to her best, needs pleasant recreations,
good clothes, nourishing food and a pleasant home and surroundings. Her
artistic and practical training ought to aid her in any home work she may
undertake, but the requirements of her profession are too exacting to permit
her, in justice to her health, to do much sewing or take an active part in household affairs. She needs her free hours for outdoor exercise, recreation and a
pleasant social life. Nor should any woman think that she can be both a Kindergartner and a society devotee. Late hours and morning languor are not
conducive to the fresh and wholesome spirit she must needs bring to her work.
But there are hosts of simpler pleasures that will be both enjoyable and profitable and prevent her from falling too much into mental grooves. The Kindergartner, both for her own sake and for her children, needs a large life, change
of faces, scenes and thoughts. More, perhaps, than any other teacher she may
have, if she chooses, the society and friendship of cultured people.

We cannot speak more strongly for adequate training than in the words of
Mrs. J. N. Crouse, of Chicago: "The Kindergarten is as much a technical
department of education as chemistry or biology ; as much a profession as law,
theology or medicine. A young woman might as well expect to be a Patent
Office lawyer or the counsel for a railroad corporation after studying six
months in the office of a county justice of the peace, as to expect to be a Kindergartner when she has mastered the three R's and studied Kindergartning
'by herself.' Better be a surgeon without preparation and maim the body, than
to experiment with a child's soul. What we need and must have is better prepared students to begin with and longer courses of study." *

Finally, the study of the Kindergarten develops "love and intelligence,
infinite patience, perseverance and tact, while it demands the very highest
endeavor and the greatest culture."

TRAINING-SCHOOLS.—Most of the prominent Kindergarten training-schools
require an entrance examination. The Chauncy-Hall School, 593 Boylston
Street, Boston, Mass., of which Miss Lucy Wheelock has charge, has the following requirements for entrance : Ability to sing, good health, a love for children, a high school education or its equivalent and broad general culture.
Applicants must furnish testimonials as to scholarship and moral character
from the principal of the school last attended, or from some clergyman of their

---

* Essay : *The Kindergarten and its Opportunities for Women.*

town, and must be at least eighteen years of age. Ability to play the piano is desirable. The course covers two years, a certificate being given at the end of the first year for satisfactory work, and a diploma for the full course. There is also a special course of one year for those who have had experience in teaching, embracing work in both classes. The course of study includes: Psychology, Froebel's *Pedagogics*, *Mother-play* and *Education of Man*, theory, gift work, occupations, songs of games, physical culture, science lessons, music, history of pedagogy, observation and practice in Kindergarten, collections of stories, original programmes, work for connecting the class and primary room. The expenses for the first year are: Tuition, $100; books and materials, $15. For the second year: Tuition, $75; books and materials, $5.

The Chicago Kindergarten College, 10 Van Buren Street, Chicago, Miss Elizabeth Harrison, Principal, makes about the same entrance requirements as the Chauncy-Hall School. It has three courses, Freshman, Junior and Senior. The Freshman course is for one year, a certificate being given for satisfactory work. The Junior course admits those who have taken the Freshman course and also graduates from other Kindergarten training schools where the work has covered the Freshman course. These two years cover about the same course of study as the Chauncy-Hall School offers; a Junior certificate is given for the completion of this course. The Senior course follows the Junior, and includes "Advanced field work in science," "*Die Mutter und Koselieder*," pedagogy, philosophy of history, programme work, and psychological study of games, and special work with assistants. Students who complete the full course receive the college diploma. There is also a normal course for experienced teachers and graduates of the College, designed to prepare them as directors of training-schools. This course has a special diploma. Branch classes are sometimes established in other cities to fit students who cannot leave home for the second year of College, and misses' classes are carried in the College each year from January to May. The yearly expenses for the teachers' department are: Tuition, $125; materials, $15; books, $10.

The Teachers' College, Morningside Heights, New York City, has but one Kindergarten course, that of two years, for which the regular College diploma is conferred. The entrance requirements demand a well-trained voice, free-hand drawing, modeling and color, natural science, physical training, English, (based on the requirements of the Eastern Association of Colleges), algebra, geometry, arithmetic, geography, American and English history, and history of European civilization, physics and chemistry. The expenses are $150 per year for tuition, materials and books. The course covers about the same ground as that of the two other schools mentioned and is very broad and thorough. The students share the advantages of the many other departments of the College through lectures, etc., and those qualified have opportunities offered in the alliance between the Teachers' College and Columbia College, now situated near it. Its entrance examinations are more rigid than those of the other colleges named.

Pratt Institute, Brooklyn, has about the same entrance requirements as the

Teachers' College and has an excellent course of Kindergarten training, covering two years.

Armour Institute, Chicago, gives Kindergarten training free.

These schools, although by no means the only ones of national reputation, are given as illustrations of the work. The prestige of their diplomas is unquestioned. There are excellent schools throughout the far West, on the Pacific coast, at Jacksonville, Fla., and, in fact, in nearly every city of the Union, as well as at Toronto, Canada.

In preparing for this, as for any other profession, it is always wisest and most economical in the end to get the very best instruction, whatever the expense. In going to the large cities there are distinct advantages in the way of a wider field of observation and general culture. The student can thereby get a practical insight into all phases of the work.

As to expenses, $500 will usually cover board and tuition for the school year. If one can live at home or with friends, the expense will be materially lessened. Occasionally this sum might be made to also cover clothing, but that is doubtful. The Kindergarten student especially needs light, free, comfortable clothing, good food and pleasant surroundings; otherwise she can hardly endure the exactions and close application of the course. She should not find herself a nervous invalid at the end of her course of study. It is wise to live near the training-school. Long journeys to and fro are wearing and consume time that could be more profitably spent. A change of occupation and surroundings for Saturday afternoon and Sunday promotes good spirits and health.

The Teachers' College, New York, has a boarding hall near the College. Comfortable places are often found in College Settlement or Y. W. C. A. homes, which, to the stranger in a large city, are likely to prove more homelike, refined, secure and wholesome in every way than the regulation boarding-house.

The Kindergarten diploma will not exempt the public school teacher from the usual city or county examination. When changing from one state to another, another examination must be passed before the candidate is allowed to teach in the public schools. There is no certificate good for the whole Union, though there should be.

There are Summer Kindergarten schools at Bay View, Mich., Glens Falls, N. Y., Martha's Vineyard, and Mountain Lake Park, Garrett County, Md.

SEVENTEENTH PAPER.

TOPICS OUTLINED.

THERE should be a general outline, though not a cast-iron plan, for the year's work in the Kindergarten. It should be made out, if possible, before the school year begins after the Kindergartner has informed herself as to the main points of each subject, collected materials and learned the songs and games to be used. It is an excellent plan for the mother or Kindergartner to keep a note book, jotting down subjects as they come to her from outside reading or as they arise from the children's conversations and questionings. The season of the year and the climate, with their characteristics, products and occupations, must necessarily be considered when making plans. The age, condition and needs of the children must also be carefully taken into account. Do not forget that the Kindergarten is for the child and not the child for the Kindergarten. It is sometimes wise for the Kindergartner to drop her own preconceived plan for the time being and take up the subject suggested by the child. The same general plan may be used for several grades of children, giving the youngest less of detail than the older ones. Much of the Kindergarten work could also be carried on to advantage in the primary school, affording an interesting way of presenting geography and science lessons, while the reading lessons could be illustrated and their interests enhanced by the gifts and occupations of the Kindergarten. The programme here given according to seasons may be simplified or enlarged to suit any Kindergarten grades, and may be adapted to the first three primary school grades.

FOR AUTUMN.—Preparations for the cold.

Fall fruits and nuts. Summer fruits, how preserved.

Exercises with the senses in this connection.

Jack Frost and his work.

Preparations on the part of people, indoors and out of doors.

Farmer, miner, miller, baker.

Preparation by animals, as squirrel, etc. Migration of birds.

Preparation of plants, buds formed for following year, falling leaves, etc.

Idea of the world as a ball.

Ideas of place, direction, distance, time: record of the weather commenced.

Ideas of weight, form and color commenced.

Develop ideas of animal, mineral and vegetable substances.

Thanksgiving. Patriotism. Loving and giving.

Mother-play songs of birds' nest and flower basket.

FOR WINTER.—Christmas.

Winter clothing. Vegetable substances used for clothing, as, straw, cotton, hemp, flax, India-rubber. Animal substances used for clothing, as, silk, fur, wool, leather, hair.

Animal and vegetable substances used in manufacturing.

Food: Plants, fruits, etc., used for food; animal substances used for food. Substances used for fuel.

Occupations: Carpenter, shoemaker, weaver, tailor.

Transportation: Sledges, wheelbarrows, wagons, street-cars, railroads, ships. There are several lines of work in this subject of transportation. The Kindergartner could take up some one of them and follow it through different countries, gather pictures to illustrate it, etc. It would afford excellent work for Winter evenings, and would prove interesting to both young and old. Things transported. Condiments and fruits brought from other countries.

Exercises for the senses as to these eatables.

Moon and stars.

Other countries compared with the home country; difference in living, clothing, occupation and climate.

Jane Andrews' "*Seven Little Sisters Who Live on the Round Ball that Floats in the Air*," would prove excellent for this work.

Water: Its forms in Winter, snow, ice, hail, etc., with occupations connected therewith.

Animals in Winter, their covering, care and food.

Wood and its uses, logging, etc.

St. Valentine's day. Courtesy. Postman and other government messengers. Interdependence.

Washington's Birthday. Ideas and love of country.

Stories of Columbus and other brave men; lives and childhood illustrated.

Early American history.

Benefits of good government in harbors, light-houses, buoys on reefs, armies, shoals, churches.

Deeds of heroism, obedience, peace and order.

FOR SPRING.—Wind and its work, for plants. Commence the germination of seeds. Bursting of buds, sap flowing, manufacture of maple sugar.

Egg and chicken, cocoon and butterfly.

Sunshine and its work (heat and light).

Coming of birds, building of nests. Young animals. New life. Easter.

Occupations: Farmer, blacksmith, gardener, house-cleaning.

Color, by spectrum and color top.

FOR SUMMER.—Flowers, bees, pigeons.

In the forest, at the sea-shore, on the farm, in the city.

Forms of water: Rain, dew, vapor, steam, clouds, fog, rainbow.

Fishes.

Grains and seed-bearing plants. Pod-bearing plants. Roots and bulbs.

Occupations: Farmer, sailor. Making of butter and cheese.

Different races, brotherhood of man.

It would be permissible to change many of the subjects above classified to other seasons. For instance, wool may be introduced in connection with Winter clothing or with the farmer's Summer work of sheep-shearing. The wind and its work could be made to apply to the Autumn distribution of seeds, as well as to Mother Earth's Spring.

PLANT LESSONS.—Edward G. Howe* in the *Kindergarten Magazine* for June, 1891, gives the following outline for plant lessons. There is much of the work that is too advanced for very young children, and most Kindergartners prefer to introduce the germination of seeds with the Easter work.

SEPTEMBER: Germination of the root.

OCTOBER: Root action and the stem and leaves.

---

* Professor Howe's book, *Systematic Science Teaching* is published by D. Appleton & Co., and costs $1.50.

NOVEMBER: Preparation of plants for Winter. How Jack Frost helped.
DECEMBER: What we get from plants.
JANUARY: How to tell our native trees.
FEBRUARY: Study of twigs and buds.
MARCH: Starch, etc., become sugar, and buds open into flowers and leaves.
APRIL: Parts of flower and their uses. Mayflower and her friends.
MAY: What happens after the flower fades.
JUNE: Fruits and their uses.

Know the common animals by their names, habits, young, where they live, food, covering, and what they do for us.

Know the common plants by their seeds, fruits, flowers, leaves and stems.

Know the common metals by their color, sound and use.

By all means collect pictures, songs, games, myths and stories, and, if possible, tools to illustrate all this work.

EASTER.—Awakening. Poems, songs, games and stories.

> Little white snowdrop just waking up,
> Violet, daisy and sweet buttercup,
> Think of the flowers that are under the snow
> Waiting to grow! *

Preparations for Easter follow Washington's Birthday and begin with the first indications of Spring. The new and changed life which is being wrought from the old should be pointed out. Show the first pictures of Fall and Winter, bare trees, snow-covered ground, frozen streams, quiet forests. All are resting and sleeping, but are soon to awaken to renewed life. Then gather twigs and place them in water to show the first bursting of the buds. After that there are the frogs' eggs to show the tadpoles change to frogs, the cray-fish, the egg and chicken, the planting of seeds and bulbs, the early Spring flowers and pussy willows, the birds, the young lambs, the cocoon and butterfly. For all of these there are innumerable songs, stories and games. The list given in the note below is only a beginning of what may be used. The teacher should collect as many real objects and pictures as possible to illustrate the work.

As to the gift and occupation work, we may represent: Trees by sticks, lentils or drawings; the pussy willow and alder by sewing; a stream by lentils or half-rings; a frog by paper foldings; the hen and chickens by a yard of sticks and Hailmann bead cubes; a chicken by half and quarter rings and sticks; a barn and chicken coop with the fourth gift; a feed pail with a cylinder

---

* From *New Franklin Third Reader*. See also:
"Spring Procession and Apple Buds," from the *Kindergarten Magazine* for April, 1891.
"Pussy Willow," from *In the Child's World*.
"In My Little Garden Bed" and "The Hen and Chickens," from *Nursery Finger Plays*.
"The Maple Tree's Surprise," "Spring and her Helpers," "A Surprise," and "The Nest of Many Colors," from *In the Child's World*.
"The Story of the Dragon Fly," from Kingsley's *Water Babies*.
"A Lesson of Faith," from *Parables from Nature*.
"At Easter Time," "The Song of the Rain," "The Alder by the River," "The Bluebird," "Pussy Willow" and "In the Branches of a Tree," from *Songs and Games for Little Ones*.
"Garden Bed" and "Little Worm," from *Merry Songs and Games*.
"This is the Meadow" and "Fussy Little Caterpillar," from *Nursery Finger Plays*.
"Snowdrops, Lift Your Timid Heads!" from *Little Pilgrim Songs*.

of the second gift; birds' nests, eggs, fishes or boxes may be made of clay; green grass with the peg board and one-inch green sticks; balls may be used for many-colored butterflies; the lambs and meadow, by the fourth gift sequence already pictured in a former paper (see page 57); the third gift is used to illustrate "A little bird once built a nest," and "Fly, little birds, fly East and West"; the garden bed, by sticks or rings to lay it out, using clay for seed, pans and watering pot, making the tools from paper folding, sorting the seeds, using sticks for rain, a ring for the sun; Fall seed pods by tablets of half-circles, half-rings and sticks. The sand-table may be used to represent the garden, the meadow, the fish pond, and the forest with all its trees budding out. Use the color top to match the colors of the early Spring flowers and leaves.

Show how the old is everywhere changing into the new and beautiful. Thus, without dwelling on the sad part of death, the child learns from the bud, the seed, the bulb, the cocoon and the egg, about the after life. Through the workings of Nature he sees his own life symbolized. That is why Froebel enjoins us to study Nature and to early bring our children into right relations with her. We may tell them that our bodies, like the bud, the cocoon and the egg, are the houses we are living in for the present, but that some day we shall not want these houses any longer and then we shall go away to a home in Heaven where we shall have a new life and a new and more beautiful body. They should be brought to realize that all the world is beautiful and God is good.

> Joy comes, grief goes, we know not how;
> Everything is happy now,
> Everything is upward striving;
> 'Tis as easy now for the heart to be true
> As for grass to be green, or skies to be blue;
> 'Tis the natural way of living.—JAMES RUSSELL LOWELL.

GRASS-MOWING.—Coming on to Summer, we study that wonderful food, milk, from Froebel's *Mother-play* song "Grass-mowing." To fulfil the law of unity we show, first, a bunch of grass, milk, butter and a child's picture. Collect pictures of meadows, farmhouses and haying and dairying utensils with songs and games relating to them. Represent, first by gift and occupation, the meadow with the grass growing, the farmer cutting and curing hay, the children playing near by at making daisy chains. Next, show the farmyard with barn, hay-mow, cow stable and water trough; then, milking, the milking pail, the milk-pan, the cooler and skimming; then, the child drinking milk last, churning and preparing the butter. With rolls from the baker we now have bread, butter and milk for the child's supper.

The songs are: "All's Gone," "Grass-mowing," "The Farmyard Gate," and "Alice's Supper."

Stories may be told about the cow from Miss Wiltsie's *Kindergarten Stories and Morning Talks*; also from Miss Poullson's *In the Child's World* and *Nursery Finger Plays*.

THE CARPENTER.—Contrast pictures of the heavy timber forest and a complete house. Show the different seeds that these trees grow from, as the maple, acorn, chestnut, and tell of the long time required for them to grow to be large enough to use in building a house. Show trees or pictures of trees in different stages of growth. Speak of how the sun and rain helped. Tell how men go in Winter to the woods where these large trees grow; they take along sledges, axes and other needed tools. Then they build themselves a rude house, called a camp, in the woods, get their tools ready and when the first snow comes they begin to chop down the trees. Some chop, others cut off branches, and others haul the logs on sledges or send them down logging chutes to some river near by. When the ice breaks up in the Spring the men leave the camp and, with long poles, float the logs down the river to the first sawmill. At the sawmill whirling saws cut the logs into boards and then they are ready to go to the lumber-yard to dry or season, as it is called. From there the carpenter buys them to build a house.

Represent with gift and occupation the logging camp, logging chute, logs, axes, sledges, sawmill, circular and cross-cut saws and planes.

These songs and games may be used:

"Zish, Zish," "Oh! See the Carpenter," "A Brook is Flowing," and "The Nailor" from *Merry Songs and Games*.
"Sawing Game" from *Songs and Games for Little Ones*.
"The Cheerful Carpenter" from *Kindergarten Chimes*.
"The Flower Basket," "The Family" and "Happy Brothers and Sisters" from *Mother-play*.

Some of the carpenter's tools are: Axe, chisel, saw, auger, hammer, mallet, square, rule, plane, file, nails, saw-horse and work-bench. What does he use each of these for? To older children show more tools. Represent these by gift and occupation. Build a house from sticks or the building gifts. Make the doors and windows. A square paper folded once in half illustrates a window with two panes of glass, or an upper and lower sash; folded twice in halves it shows a window with four lights. Some of the most important pieces of furniture may be made, and thus from the seed and the tree in the forest we have the happy home for father and mother, brothers and sisters.

> This is the *Family*, all are here.
> Father and mother and children dear,
> Who live in the *House* with windows and doors,
> With timbers and rafters and roofs and floors,
> Which was built by the *Carpenter*, skilful and strong,
> Who planed all the *Boards* so straight and long,
> Cut by the *Saws* which, with buzzing sound,
> Were moved by the *Wheel* that went whirring round,
> Turned by the *River* whose flowing tide,
> Carried the *Log* that was rolled to its side,
> Rolled by the *Woodman*, who, every one knows,
> Wielded the *Axe* whose steady blows
> Cut down the *Tree* of the forest. *

---
* "An Old-Fashioned Rhyme," from *In the Child's World*.

ADDENDUM.

THE CENTURY BUSY WORK.

In the Kindergarten gifts, games and materials generally the child is readily taught to symbolize and typify the objects and relationships of Nature. With his lively imagination he does not find it difficult to see a house in three blocks or a flock of geese in a few shoe pegs.

But there comes a period in the child's development when he grows measurably critical as to the points of resemblance between the objects of the material world and the pictures and symbols used to represent them. When this time arrives it is important that the objects and pictures provided for his instruction shall be the very best obtainable. He has also to learn that beyond and supplementing the pictorial methods of representation there is another, far briefer and more conventional than either, whereby written and printed words are made to stand for all things, material and spiritual. It is highly desirable that the child's transition from the simpler early methods of representation to this puzzling and arbitrary plan of written words be made as gradual and natural as possible.

Supplementing Kindergarten instruction by a method allied both in the principles involved and the materials used is the pictorial "busy work" for primary schools published by the New Century Educational Company, of New York and Boston. Let us examine a little in detail what it is. We will take, for example, the box of domestic animals. It contains eight neat, white cards about 3 x 4 inches in size, upon each of which is a picture of some domestic animal, with its name plainly printed below in both script and Roman characters. These pictures are black-and-white reproductions of *chefs-d'œuvres* by famous animal painters. Here is one of Landseer's dogs, great, velvety eyes shining from a face full of nobility and courteous wistfulness, painted with this great artist's loving insight into canine character. It is an ideal dog, and as such worthy to be associated in the fresh and uncontaminated mind of the child with the little word "dog" printed below it. Is it not a fine thing, when one considers the vividness and persistence of first impressions, that a child may thus all his life long carry in mind as his typical and first-recurring notion of "dog" this sweet and serene concept? Can it do otherwise than materially affect all his thoughts about and treatment of the real dogs he meets?

The picture illustrating "camel" is a reproduction of Horace Vernet's study of one of these patient "ships of the desert," heavily burdened and standing with pathetic resignation upon three legs, the fourth hobbled by a rope attached to his head gear, while his master, with slippers cast aside, kneels on the prayer-rug spread upon the sands of the desert, and with his face to the rising sun, offers his morning orisons. The history, religion, topography and tradi-

ADDENDUM.

tion-hallowed customs of Arabia are compressed into that picture, and even the dull child can not but gain from it a just impression of an important phase of life in the Orient and a better knowledge of the uses and nature of the picturesque animal which figures so largely in its economy than he would probably acquire by a dozen trips to the menagerie. The donkey and sheep are borrowed

from famous canvases by Rosa Bonheur, the goats are from the brush of Auguste Bonheur, the cows are by Van Marcke, the cats by Adam and the horse by Landseer.

The box also contains twenty-four other cards, which, when properly arranged, reproduce the eight above described, each of the original cards being cut into three sections, one bearing the picture, one the script title and the third the title in Roman letters. After the child has thoroughly familiarized himself with the set upon which the titles are printed below the pictures, he may first use it as a copy from which to rearrange the dissected set and finally, rejecting it altogether, he may depend entirely upon his memory in placing the titles under the pictures to which they belong. He will find that the process has a charm of its own from the manipulation required and the suggestion it affords of working out a puzzle. When the hand and mind work together neither so soon wearies of its task.

The same admirable plan of association is carried out with like thoroughness in all of the other sixteen sets. The first of the series for beginners is a box of the numbers from one to five, showing five ways of indicating each number, viz.: by spots in domino fashion, by the Arabic figures, by the Roman numerals, by words in plain Roman type and by the same words in script. The pupil is required to arrange the twenty-five bits of orange cardboard so the numbers will read in order across from left to right, first the dominoes, below them the figures, next the letters, then the words in plain type and finally the script, thus:

•	• •	• •	•
•	•	•	• •
•	•	•	• • •
1	2	3	4	5
I	II	III	IV	V
one	two	three	four	five
one	*two*	*three*	*four*	*five*

The cards while varying in height are of uniform width, so that when thus arranged all the methods of expressing any given number form a perfect column, reading up and down. By arranging and rearranging these the child fixes in mind all the customary ways of indicating the numbers under consideration, and is not puzzled when he finds "IV" where he might otherwise expect "4."

Next in the series for beginners comes a box for "word building," in which four sets of simple base-words, such as "ill, ear, ate, ark," are placed upon cardboard strips under which a variety of small cards, each containing a word rhyming with one of the base words, are arranged, by copy on a printed sheet, according to rhyme. Thus, under "ill" come "fill, hill, kill, will, pill." Bright pupils would after a few trials, be able to "build" by sound alone, rejecting the copy. Thus do we pave the way for the poets of the Twentieth Century!

A box of script and print contains several six-word sentences—for instance, "Little by little one goes far," reading down a slip from top to bottom. If the sentence is printed in plain type the chopped-up identical words composing it, which the child is asked to place alongside their fellows on the strip, are in script, and vice versa.

A box of inch cardboard squares containing ten each of the primary colors, red, orange, yellow, green, blue and purple, also a like number each of black and white, provides material for the child to assort after they have been thoroughly mixed—an admirable color drill almost identical with that used in the Kindergarten.

ADDENDUM.

The set of domestic animals first described and a similar one of wild animals complete the series for beginners.

A second series for the latter part of the first year and for second year pupils begins with a box of numbers running from six to ten, supplementing that for the numbers one to five. The other nine boxes are as follows: Color, intermediate hues, with and without names in script and print; color, intermediate hues, for assorting; common birds, excellent half-tone reproductions from photographs of the blue jay, screech owl, northern shrike, downy woodpecker, king-bird, cedar wax-wing, flicker and kingfisher; oak and maple leaves, being reproductions in green from careful pen-and-ink drawings from nature, with and without the names in script and print; birch and poplar leaves, do.; flags of great nations in colors, with and without the names of the countries; weather signals in colors, with and without their interpretations; a *Hiawatha* catechism on the fifteen lines beginning,

> Then the little Hiawatha
> Learned of every bird its language,

with pictures of the animals alluded to; and finally, an envelope containing reproductions of twenty noted works of art for language work.

It will thus be seen that a variety of practical and useful information may be derived from the material contained in these neat little boxes—information it would puzzle many a well-educated adult to furnish impromptu.

Suitable for use after the above material has been pretty well digested, is a dainty first reader, *Fairy Tale and Fable*, compiled by two practical educators, John G. Thompson and Thomas E. Thompson, and published also by the New Century Company. It differs from the usual first reader both in the material chosen—world-famous fables, myths, fairy tales and simple rhymes—and in the illustrations and printing. Thus, Rosa Bonheur's "Lion Family" is used to illustrate the fable of the donkey in the lion's skin. In the front of the book are printed in alphabetical form the two hundred simple words, nearly all mono-syllables, with which the pupil is expected to be familiar before beginning to read, and at the top of each selection appear the three or four new words which it adds to the child's vocabulary. The list is an interesting one, but two letters must suffice to indicate its character. Under "a" are classified: "a, an, and, about, afraid, again, all, always, am, are, as, at, ask," and under "c" the list simmers down to "cat."

Hitherto between the Kindergarten and the laboratory work of the technical schools and higher universities there has been a wide and dreary hiatus wherein the learning of abstractions has replaced the study of the things themselves. Such enterprises as that of the New Century Educational Company show that we are coming into a more intelligent appreciation of the value of Nature's own methods of imparting instruction, and are lending understanding ears to Froebel's beneficent invitation, "Come, let us live with our children!"

www.ingramcontent.com/pod-product-compliance
Lightning Source LLC
Chambersburg PA
CBHW020259170426
43202CB00008B/432